THE TRAITORS' CLUB

CLUB

A memoir

Marina Christofides

To young people everywhere.

CONTENTS

ACKNOWLEDGMENTS

I would like to thank my editor, Bill Roorbach, for his encouraging words and invaluable insights. My daughter, Selena, produced this wonderful cover by not listening to me and insisting that, as a design student, she knew better, while my son, Leo, spotted mistakes that no one else picked up. I'm ever grateful to my sister, Celia Macpherson, for her perspicacity and her invaluable ability to kill my 'darlings' with sensitivity. Paul Hadland gave me the 'foreign' point of view and a lot of encouragement and last but not least, a big thank you to my husband, Stelios, for being my long-suffering sounding board and for his endless support.

.

1 IT'S A MESS

July 2004

We're in a hurry. Andreas and I are driving towards the checkpoint where we have arranged to meet up with Hasip and Hasan before going to see the British High Commissioner. He has promised us half an hour between meetings before he dashes abroad and we're about to miss our slot.

It isn't every day that High Commissioners agree to meet with civilian nobodies like us. And we don't want to wait for him to come back. We want to reunite our country, Cyprus. Now, today. Time for us, unlike for our politicians, is precious. We've been waiting since the war that split the island in 1974 and were almost there earlier this year with a plan to establish a federation. But Turkish Cypriots voted YES and Greek Cypriots voted NO in the referendum and so we missed yet another in a long line of opportunities to solve what is known as 'the Cyprus problem'.

Unfortunately, the High Commissioner didn't specify exactly where our meeting would be held. The traffic moves at a snail's pace as we make our way through town.

"It must be in the south," Andreas argues over the phone to Hasip, one hand on the driving wheel. "That's where the British High Commission has always been."

He's right. After all, how can the British have an official representation in an unrecognised state?

"No, it's in the north," I hear Hasip insisting on speakerphone. "I've had four meetings with the High Commissioner and they were always in the north. And since I was the one who sent the email to him requesting the meeting, I believe it's in the north." He pauses while we digest this information. "It's in Shakespeare Street," he adds firmly, as if the name of the street lends weight to his argument.

1

"Maybe the two offices are connected?" Andreas says, staring into the distance as if trying to visualise it, as we head north in the direction of the grey blue Kyrenia mountains just visible above the red rooftops.

For a moment I wonder if this is possible. It's true the two buildings are close together huddled on either side of the Green Line, the ceasefire line that has become the border between our two sides. But what about the UN buffer zone, the checkpoints, the Turkish army? Could the British have a secret entrance so the High Commissioner can nip from one office to another depending on whom he has to see? Could they have an underground tunnel?

Andreas decides to give Hasip the benefit of the doubt. A row of handsome neo-classical houses, some of which are half derelict, are a sign that we are approaching the cease-fire line and the checkpoint. He parks his car in a field and we quickly walk past the two-metre high barricades covered in faded posters commemorating dead heroes killed by "Turkish Law and Order" which make up the Greek Cypriot checkpoint in the south. Our walk takes us into no-man's land, or the buffer zone, and past the Ledra Palace hotel. Once considered one of the most glamorous hotels of the Levant, where high society gathered for afternoon tea dances, it is now pocked with bullet holes, run down and derelict, serving as UN army barracks and occasionally hosting conflict resolution workshops between peace-builders looking for neutral ground. At the Turkish Cypriot checkpoint, four different posters within a few metres of each other welcome us to the Turkish Republic of Northern Cyprus, declare that this is Turkish Republic of Northern Cyprus, and assure us that the Turkish Republic of Northern Cyprus is FOREVER. We subject ourselves to the border formalities, showing our ID cards and filling in the necessary visa form in order to go from one part of our own country to the other.

On the other side we spot burly Hasip standing next to his car waiting to pick us up. Hasan is in the passenger seat. Andreas and I jump in the back and Hasip speeds us

off to Shakespeare Street.

"See? There it is," Hasip beams when we arrive at the imposing wall that surrounds Her Majesty's premises, proof to us doubters that the High Commission does indeed have a branch in the unrecognised state in the north. He exchanges a few words in Turkish with the guard at the gate who disappears, leaving us to wait in the hot sun. When he reappears, he speaks at length with Hasip before disappearing again.

Hasip turns to us looking sheepish. "Unfortunately it seems our meeting was in the south after all," he says. "They are sending a car to take us there straight away."

Andreas gives him a wry half smile. "It's because you want equality, Hasip," he teases. "You think you have it, but you don't really." He is referring to the Turkish Cypriot minority's desire for recognition as equal partners in a Cypriot state.

Hasip shrugs. His portly shoulders sag as he slumps on one of the benches. As we all sit down to wait under the shady pergola, he apologises profusely for the mix-up.

I try to reassure him. "It's not your fault, Hasip. It's everyone who voted NO and chose to keep this stupid border in place."

"Yes," he sighs. "And you know it gets more and more complicated every day. Do you know that our taxis cannot cross, but Greek taxis can? It's a small thing. But it makes us angry. We are turning against the Greek Cypriots more and more. Even I have to remind myself that it's not the fault of ordinary people."

"And the phones," Hasan adds. "To call your side we have to go via Turkey. We all have to carry two mobiles all the time, a Greek one and a Turkish one."

"At least we can dial direct now Turkey has recognised the Cyprus numbers." Hasip says. "That's one bit of progress."

"Not enough," Hasan says.

Hasip looks at his watch. Still no sign of the guard. Around us on the benches under the jasmine, a number of Turkish Cypriots are waiting to apply for a visa to the UK. One of them is eyeing us curiously. He leans over and says something to Andreas in Turkish.

"I'm sorry, I don't understand," Andreas replies.

"Kıbrıslı Rum," Hasip tells the man by way of explanation. I still can't get used to the fact that even though this is my homeland, I cannot understand what is being said.

"Ah," the man says and looks us over with even greater interest. We Rum, or Greek Cypriots, are a rare species on this side.

The guard announces that our car is here. We quickly follow him round the back through the High Commission's beautiful gardens to a Land Rover waiting in the driveway. The driver opens the doors for us to get in. Hasip takes the front passenger seat because of his size, the rest of us squeeze into the back. We speed off through the automatic gates.

"You realise, Hasip," Andreas says leaning forward, "that I've left my car keys in your car, which means that after our meeting in the south, I'm going to have to come back to the north again to pick them up so that I can then return to the south to get my car."

"It's all such a mess," Hasip sighs, as we arrive back at the checkpoint.

Our driver slows down as he approaches the border guard, who steps forward as if to stop us. Another car has just gone through ahead of us and the barrier is still open. The minutes tick by. Our meeting looks less and less likely.

"Will we have to fill in the visa forms, or can we just go through, since we're in a diplomatic car?" I wonder out loud.

"Push through, push through," Andreas urges our driver. He accelerates, saluting the border guard as we go past, leaving him no time to ask for papers.

"Get ready, Hasip, to spend the night in jail," Hasan laughs. "On the way back they will arrest us."

"Yes, now our lot will not have us in their computers. They will not know how we got out." He makes the north sound like it's a jail.

The traffic in the south is heavy, much heavier than in the north. I daren't look at the time. We are held up at a couple of traffic lights, but soon we are zipping through a less frequented residential neighbourhood of large houses shaded by tall trees and surrounded by beautiful gardens, then copses and fields opening out onto a view of the north and the Kyrenia mountains. I get the feeling that we are virtually on the other side of the demarcation line from where we had set off.

The official High Commission practically straddles the border. We jump out of the car and race inside only to be stopped for a security check and to deposit all our mobile phones. As we stand on the entrance steps under the royal coat of arms waiting for the glass doors to be buzzed open, I notice Hasip and Hasan staring across the fields to the north.

"It must be very close," says Hasan, trying to figure out where in relation to Shakespeare Street this High Commission is.

I say, "Isn't it near the golf course?"

"What golf course?" Andreas says.

"Don't you remember? The Nicosia Club," I remind him. "It had a golf course." Vague memories well up from the fifties, when our country was whole, of my father proudly showing me his new golf clubs and my mother dressing up for fancy tea parties. "In any case they can't be connected. There are fields between here and there. Come on let's go in."

The doors open and we are ushered into the High Commissioner's office. The room is dark and spacious with a huge sitting area filled with numerous comfortable armchairs where I imagine many an important meeting must have been held. The High Commissioner is friendly and knowledgeable. We tell him why we're here, that not everyone was against the peace plan, that there are people on this island who want reunification and those people are us. We wonder if there is anything we can do to help change the situation.

He is sympathetic but he doesn't think anything much will happen soon. At least not with our current rejectionist president, he seems to imply. He says that much has been achieved through quiet diplomacy and that considerable effort is being put into persuading Turkey that it is to its own advantage to solve the Cyprus problem, which, he says, was like "a thorn in its side". It was to Turkey's credit, he adds, that they'd seen that. They had also seen how they could seize the initiative.

"Hopefully, since they've done it before, they can do it again," he says, giving us a slight ray of hope.

In the car on the way back, Hasip, Hasan, Andreas and I are silent. The road takes us past a point along the thick sandstone Venetian walls which skirt the dividing line. Hasip looks up and catches a glimpse of a Turkish soldier standing on the ramparts.

"Before the borders opened I was standing up there looking down at my compatriots the Greek Cypriots." He pauses a moment and rubs his chin. "I remember thinking, why can't I go there? After all, this whole island is my country, why can't I walk along that road, visit those shops, go anywhere I want. Well, now I can. But I'm still not satisfied. I want more."

MARINA CHRISTOFIDES

2 SATURDAYS AT THE BÜYÜK HAN

We all wanted more. But in the six years since that meeting, little has changed. I still have to pass a Greek Cypriot checkpoint, where the policeman on duty eyes me suspiciously as I head over to 'the other side' and into a state that doesn't officially exist and is recognised by only one country in the world: Turkey. I still have to walk along the short stretch of land that forms the buffer zone, supposedly the demilitarised zone, but which is one of the most militarised areas of the island.

Today I'm standing in line at another checkpoint in the centre of the old town along with a crowd of tourists and a smattering of Greek Cypriots. Around me I hear all kinds of languages and only occasionally some Greek. I take a form from a pile at the portakabin window and start to fill it in with my name, identity card number and nationality. This form, which the Turkish Cypriot authorities probably insist on because it gives them a semblance of statehood, is the reason why many Greek Cypriots refuse to cross into what they call the pseudostate or occupied areas. Only one in ten Greek Cypriots will do what I am about to do. Crossing this line that has split Cyprus into Greek and Turkish sides, makes me a traitor in the eyes of most of my compatriots. To them it's as if I'm recognising the fact that forty years ago, Turkey invaded and occupied the northern part of the island, kicking us out of our ancestral lands. It's tantamount to accepting an unfairness, an illegality. It makes that illegal entity real. As far as I'm concerned, this is my way of saying that I won't let this border change my view of the whole of the island as my country. While I'd rather this border wasn't here, I won't let silly formalities stop me from having coffee with my friends in the northern part of my home town, Nicosia.

When my turn comes I hand the form and my identity card to the official through the cubicle window and wait as he looks me up on his computer. He stamps and signs the form and hands it back to me.

"*Teşekkür ederim*," I say thanking him in the little Turkish I know.

He grunts in reply and turns to the next person in line. I take my papers and enter 'the other side'.

The other side is much like the side I've just left, with the same Mediterranean houses and gardens, same jumble of narrow streets. But take a wrong turn and you might come to a sudden dead end at the border, with sandbags and sentry posts, a physical reminder we Nicosians all live in half a city, each a semi-circular maze of roads that lead

nowhere, with one way out.

The dividing line dissects not just the whole island, but the capital city, with its old medieval centre encircled by the massive fortress walls the Venetians built to keep the marauding Ottomans out. Unsuccessfully, as it turned out. Their descendants are still here. I zigzag amongst them as they idly examine the shop displays of sparkling trinkets, cloying sweets and gaudy clothes.

I'm heading for the Büyük Han, or Great Inn. A large square Ottoman structure, it squats in the heart of the old town like a stout indolent pasha, looking down on his subjects through narrow slits for windows with an air of lofty superciliousness. Thick sandstone walls add to the impression of aloofness and impenetrability, though its attempted gravitas is spoiled by a row of small octagonal chimney pots incongruously perched on the roof, like party hats on a suited businessman.

I enter through the massive wooden doors on the west side and into the enormous cobbled courtyard, filled with people wandering around under the open sky, sitting at coffee shops and restaurants, or shopping for souvenirs. In the centre is a domed mosque with a fountain once used for pre-prayer ablutions. The largest caravanserai on the island, this building was commissioned by the first Ottoman governor of Cyprus, Muzaffer Pasha, a year after the Ottomans seized Cyprus from the Venetians in 1571. Later, when the British ruled Cyprus, it was used as a prison; later still, a builders' yard. I pass under the surrounding archway, past ground floor rooms used at different times as stables, shops, storage rooms, and offices. A stairway leads to the upper floor where the old lodgings used to be, each fitted with a fireplace.

Our group gathers round a long table under the arches by the east entrance, a row of typical Mediterranean faces, olive skins, dark eyes, and now mostly greying hair. They are predominantly men, with a few women joining from time to time. You cannot tell who is a Greek Cypriot and who is a Turkish Cypriot. There are about ten of us today. Andreas, Hasip and Hasan are here, of course. So is Suleyman, a veteran journalist with his Panama hat and camera at the ready to photograph whoever is in attendance. Mikis is engrossed in his newspaper, half listening to the conversation. Halil, who always has a smile on his face, is accompanied by

Sami, who never says a word. At the far end of the table, dapper Sarper, a physics teacher with twinkling blue eyes, is deep in conversation with Litsa, another school teacher, her long hair and large orange sunglasses making her look like a sixties flower child.

We come here every Saturday, rain or shine, heatwave or cold snap. For a few hours each week, we hang out together, as if nothing has happened to our country, as if the divide doesn't exist. We come to chat, to have coffee, to find friends. We come because we have nothing better to do and because this is the best thing to do. We come to talk politics and to get away from politics. We come to get the truth, to find out what is really happening on the other side, how the other side really thinks, away from the lies and propaganda we are fed daily by the media. We come to learn each other's language, like magpies picking up words from the day's conversation to add to our collection. And we come to affirm silently to the others that we haven't given up, that reunification is possible, and we are what it looks like. By our mere presence we are telling each other, we are still here for you, we're in it together. But most of all we come here to laugh. We laugh at our politicians, we laugh at the absurdity of the situation. And we laugh at ourselves.

They're all laughing now as I approach the table. I pull up one of the rickety wooden coffee shop chairs and find a place to squeeze in.

Andreas, who always sits at the head of the table near the entrance, where he can keep an eye on all the comings and goings, is unwrapping a turquoise shirt he has just purchased, proudly displaying it for all to see.

"I just bought this from one of those shops," he announces. "They gave me a very good price. It's a nice colour, don't you think?"

Hasan peers over the rims of his glasses, the long tufts of his eyebrows wiggling mischievously.

"Do you think all these bright colours will help you with your comeback?" he asks, his shoulders heaving in silent laughter.

"Oh, yes, with these bright colours the girls will not mistake me for an old man like you," Andreas replies. Recently divorced, he strives to maintain a youthful appearance, wearing his greying hair with a boyish side parting in almost the same way he has done since we were at the English School together.

"What's wrong with me?" Hasan says taken aback, his eyebrows jumping up and down indignantly as he looks down at his grey jumper. In contrast to Andreas' peacock colours, Hasan looks like a dowdy pigeon.

"What's wrong with you? I'll tell you what's wrong with you," Andreas says. "You are a *kocakari*."

"*Kocakari*, is that a Turkish word or a Greek word?" Mikis says, looking up from his newspaper. A biology teacher, he is always interested in broadening his general knowledge. "Because in Greek it means old woman.

Is it the same in Turkish?" He leans back in his chair, pondering the linguistic interweavings of our respective languages.

"Yes, it means the same. The word *koca* means husband and *karı* means wife or woman," Hasip explains. "But what are we having for lunch?" he adds, more interested in affairs of the stomach than etymology.

"And don't think you are any better," says Andreas turning on him. "You are just as much a *kocakari* with your clothes."

Hasip, who wears his portliness with pride, straightens the blue and white striped T-shirt covering his bulging belly.

"Actually, I'm wearing this to fool everyone into thinking that I'm not as fat as they think I am."

Andreas looks at him mystified. "And how is that exactly?"

"People will think that if I really was that fat I would, of course, be wearing a vertically striped shirt to make me seem less fat, so since I'm wearing a horizontally striped one, that means that I'm not as fat as I seem, and that it's only the shirt which is making me look fat, whereas in actual fact I'm not fat at all," he explains with indisputable logic. Everyone laughs.

"What sort of a hermaphrodite thing is this husbandwife word?" Mikis wants to know. "It doesn't make sense." He runs his hands through his curly grey locks and looks around expectantly.

With further prodding Hasip deigns to explain that *koca or kocaman*, apart from meaning husband, also means huge, big, great, enormous, gigantic. "So in this case it would mean a woman of a great age," he says.

"Oh, I see!" says Mikis. "We use that word too! We say *kocam*, although a little ironically, as in 'you have a *kocam* car and you still can't drive'. Or he's a '*kocam* man' and yet he still can't do up his shoelaces."

"Or he's a *kocam* president and he still can't solve the Cyprus problem!" Andreas cries.

Everyone laughs at the thought of our incompetent leaders.

"Are we going to have any proper food?" Hasip asks again. A loaf of olive bread that someone has brought from the *peynirli* seller down the road is passed down the table. Hasip contemplates it with disdain, but daintily grabs a piece anyway.

"Ahmet *dayı*," Andreas calls to the coffee shop owner.

With the countenance of a sleepy walrus, Ahmet, the *kahveci*, creeps from table to table almost imperceptibly, age having slowed him down. Originally a shoemaker, he was given the opportunity to run the coffee shop because his son worked for Evkaf, the religious organisation that now owns the building.

"You might not like the supporters of Galatasaray but at least ask them what they would like to drink," Andreas tells him when he eventually shuffles up. He turns to the table. "Ahmet *dayı* is worried because his team, Fenerbahçe, is not doing very well."

"You are wrong, *kyrie*," Ahmet protests in the Greek Cypriot dialect. He belongs to the dying generation of Cypriots fluent in both languages.

"I'm wrong? Everyone is saying this is the team that's going to go down," Andreas continues, trying to wind him up.

"They're not going down at all," Ahmet says crossly, taking the bait. "If Fenerbahçe goes down, everyone goes down."

"This morning," Hasan says, following Andreas' lead, "Ahmet *dayı* came into my grocery shop and saw me making a discount for someone. He said, you made a discount for them, why don't you make a discount for me? I said, because you're with Fenerbahçe!"

More laughter ensues round the table. It gives me a warm feeling to think how well we get on despite the prejudices we've grown up with and face daily in our media on both sides.

"So what do you think about the UN Secretary-General's latest statement?" asks Mikis, not in the least bit interested in football. "Do you think our leaders will finally agree to a solution?"

"Definitely," I say. "There's no other way."

"Not a chance," Andreas says. "They haven't managed in fifty years, they will manage now?"

It's true, just this current phase of talks has been going on for four years now, but I'm convinced they will eventually realise it's the only logical thing to do.

"Both our leaders are idiots," Hasan sighs. "The one in the south is a coward. He's afraid of his rejectionist partners. And the one in the north doesn't count. He does what Turkey tells him."

"They both lack the political will," Mikis says, nodding sadly in agreement.

"Can you ask all those negative thinkers what they will do when there is a solution?" Hasip says defiantly.

"Bravo, Hasip," I say, glad to have an ally. Hasip promptly rushes over to my side of the table and we shake hands enthusiastically, congratulating each other on our positive thinking.

Andreas gives us a sidelong look. "Can someone ask Hasip what happened to the dinner he was going to treat us all to when the Cyprus problem is solved? Every year he makes this declaration that the Cyprus problem is going to be solved by the end of the year."

"By the summer," I say even more optimistically, thinking that they *must* finally reach an agreement.

"No, no, not by summer," corrects Hasip, as if the extra time will make the outcome more certain. "That's too soon. By the summer they will set up the principles. But before the end of the year it will be finished. I'm telling you, but you don't listen to me. You will regret it."

"Yes, yes, and this handshake between Hasip and Marina, who are the two super optimists among us, also happens once a year," Andreas continues, rolling his eyes at us. "In fact, we should set up a Cyprus Optimists Society. It will only have two members."

"Don't worry my dear, we will get ten dinners," Hasip says licking his lips in anticipation.

"We might get a solution," Hasan concedes gloomily, "but what kind of solution?"

"You know what?" Hasip declares glowering down the table, daring anyone to disagree. "I don't care! I've had enough of the Cyprus problem!"

At this, Suleyman, who has been leaning back against the wall quietly listening to us argue, has also had enough. He jumps up, lifts his hands in the air, snaps his fingers and starts to sing.

"HEY MAMBO! MAMBO ITALIANO! HEY MAMBO!"

We all sit back deflated.

"Alright, alright," Andreas says. "We'll shut up."

Suleyman sits down pleased with himself.

"You stupid Cypriots," he says in his slow deliberate way, like a teacher enunciating every word so as to drum the lesson in. "Haven't you had enough? Week after week, all we ever talk about is the bloody Cyprus problem … nothing else…. We can never talk and enjoy ourselves. We said we would allow only one minute for political discussion, and then… Mambo".

I know, we all know, that he's right. I try to turn my mind to something other than politics. The wailing song of the hodja from a nearby minaret wafts over us signifying that it is noon. A large group of elderly European tourists enters the Han accompanied by a guide. They gather behind Andreas' chair and take in all the activity in the courtyard, some posing for a photograph.

"Excuse me, where are you from?" Andreas enquires, leaning backwards in his chair towards them.

"Germany," replies one of them, eager to interact with the locals.

"Ah, it's the Youth Club of Bavaria," Andreas whispers in an aside to the table.

"And what about you?" asks the German.

Andreas rises to the occasion, delighted at having been given the opportunity to promote the coffee club.

"We are all Cypriots here," he announces.

"But you are speaking in English?" the German asks puzzled.

"Yes, well, you see, unfortunately sometimes we cannot communicate, so we have to speak in English. Some of us are Greek-speaking Cypriots, and some of us are Turkish-speaking Cypriots, but we are all Cypriots."

"Ah," says the German, looking even more confused.

Andreas stands up to make the introductions. "I am Andreas, I am a

Greek-speaking Cypriot. Marina too." I nod approvingly at his having chosen language rather than ethnicity as our distinguishing characteristics. "Over there Hasan, he's a *bakal, bakallis*." He deliberately uses both the Greek and Turkish word stressing their common etymology. "Hasan is a Turkish speaking Cypriot and has the best grocery shop in Lefkosha with the best *loukoum*, Turkish delight." He goes round the table introducing everyone, ending with Ahmet. "Ahmet, our *kahvecis*, is Turkish Cypriot but speaks both Greek and Turkish. He comes from the village of Vatily. His surname is Vatiliotis. You see we are not very imaginative with our nomenclature in this country."

The Germans stand there nodding hello at the sea of names and faces. A short plump lady catches my eye and smiles politely. Does she understand what it feels like to live in a divided country, or is she bewildered at this country whose citizens don't even speak the same language? I cannot tell.

"My name is... Solomonides," Suleyman says, tipping his Panama hat.

"That's what the Turkish Cypriot nationalists used to call him during the referendum," Andreas explains more to the table than the Germans. "They turned it into a Greek name because his views were too much like those of the Greek Cypriots."

"Actually, I am not a Cypriot at all," Suleyman says sniffing haughtily, as the Germans move on. "I... am a Venetian."

Hasip will have none of this. "You think that because you are slightly more fair than the rest of us, you can claim you have Venetian origin?" he says. "You are just as much of a *köylü*, as the rest of us."

"A peasant! I prefer instead of saying *köylü*, or *horkatiko* to say... *villageois*", Suleyman says.

"Actually, it's because you're a *giavur*," Andreas says. The table bursts into laughter, at Andreas' ironic use of the word for infidel that the Ottomans reserved for the Greeks.

Suleyman laughs too. "It's true, they used to call me a *giavur* during the referendum. I was very proud of it actually. Because I was working for a YES, the nationalists got annoyed with me, so they looked for something to attack me with. They tried to find out if I had received any money from the government, if I hadn't paid my taxes, but they couldn't find anything. The only thing they could do was to call me a *gâvur*. He's a traitor, he's with the Greeks, they said." He laughs again gleefully, while at the same time, nodding a greeting to a passing acquaintance. Suleyman is a well-known figure in the north.

"We're all traitors here," Andreas says matter-of-factly, as another group enters the building. He watches them but this time does not try to engage them in conversation.

"Americans," mutters Hasip disapprovingly.

"Americans?" I ask perplexed. They don't look at all like Americans. The men are dressed in dark suits and the women are all wearing headscarves.

"It's our codename for Turks from the mainland," Andreas whispers, turning his back to them.

Hasip observes them indifferently, nonchalantly cutting off another piece of olive bread. "Yes, they are like the first settlers of America who came and threw out the natives. We, Turkish Cypriots, are the Red Indians! We are being exterminated."

"Exterminated? What do you mean, exterminated?" Andreas looks at him shocked.

"I mean like the animals whose species die."

"You mean become extinct."

"Yes, that's the word."

"You Turkish Cypriots were always the black sheep of the Islamic family," Andreas says, flicking his hair back away from his face.

"That's why they kicked us out of Turkey and sent us here in the first place," Hasip says. "We were an embarrassment. Not good Muslims."

Sarper joins in from the far end of the table. "The Roman and Byzantine Emperors used to banish undesirables to Cyprus and so did the Turks." Sarper is a mine of knowledge about our history, which he freely imparts at every opportunity. He has a gentle demeanour, but there's a certain sadness in his blue eyes. Tragically, a year after the checkpoints opened, he lost his older son in a car crash in the tourist resort of Ayia Napa. He's an active member of the Cyprus Friendship Program, a successful and popular peace-building programme which places pairs of Greek and Turkish Cypriot teenagers with an American host family for a month in the summer in the US.

"Some Turkish Cypriots are of Alevi origin," he continues. "That was one reason they were exiled to Cyprus after the Ottoman conquest of the island in 1571. These were the *yürüks, youroukkis* as the Greek Cypriots called them, a nomadic group of people from Anatolia. *Yürümek* means 'to walk', so the *yürük* were 'the walkers'."

"Nowadays they are walking in the opposite direction," Hasan says ruefully. "We are getting fewer and fewer as the young are choosing to look for work in Europe. It's easier for them now since Cyprus joined the European Union. And since the borders opened they have been able to come across and claim their Cypriot identity cards and Cypriot, therefore EU, passports."

"Most Turkish Cypriots have about four passports," Hasip says. "A Cyprus passport, a Turkish Cypriot passport that will only let us into Turkey, a Turkish passport, and some people also have a British passport from when Cyprus was a British colony. When we travel we have a special wallet to carry them all in."

"I remember we used to hide our Cyprus passport whenever we travelled to Turkey," Suleyman says. "We would take it with us, but we would hide it. Now we show it to the officials. Just to annoy them." He laughs at the thought.

"Yes, they get angry," Hasip says. "'Why are you using the Cyprus passport instead of the Turkish one,' they ask. 'Didn't we save you? Aren't you proud of being part of our great country?'"

"I wish they hadn't saved us," Hasan grumbles.

"Unfortunately it's not as simple as that," Hasip says. "The Greek Cypriots didn't do their share. And now we are stuck. Both the Greek Cypriots and us, we are both stuck. We are paying for our stupidity."

"So many mistakes," Andreas sighs.

"We make mistakes and we pay for our mistakes," Hasip says. "Sometimes we make fatal mistakes."

"Anyway they hate us in Turkey," Hasan says.

"The feeling is mutual," Hasip says.

The 'Americans' move on casting cursory glances towards our table. We watch them warily.

"Soon they will put us Turkish Cypriots in glass cages and tourists will come to look at us," Hasip says.

A lottery seller emerges out of the crowd of people going by and comes up to the table waving his tickets under our noses. Hasan takes out his wallet and chooses one and Andreas leans over to examine it.

"What does this word mean? It says *Piyangosi?*"

"Lottery," Hasan says.

"And *Devlet?*"

"State."

"Ah yes, State Lottery." Andreas turns the ticket over looking for more words to add to his vocabulary. "But it doesn't say 'pseudo' anywhere!"

Hasan peers at it closely. "Yes, I think it does say that somewhere!"

"That reminds me," Suleyman says, "I'm off to … Europe to buy a lottery ticket."

"Oh, so you prefer European lottery tickets? But why don't you tell us to bring you one when we come over, instead of insisting on going to Europe every Saturday?" Andreas asks.

Suleyman laughs. "I want to make them curious at the border. They must wonder what does this guy do every Saturday? Why does he cross the border for fifteen minutes and then cross back?"

Hasan rummages around in his wallet and carefully unfolds an old lottery ticket. "Since you're going to the other side…" He grins sheepishly. "I won five euros."

"Did we ask for the bill?" asks Andreas signalling that our session has come to an end. He catches Ahmet's eye and signs in the air, "how much?"

"*Kırk euro*," Ahmet says when he comes over.

"Forty euro? How much is that in pseudomoney, in Turkish lira?" Andreas says. While the south joined the eurozone a few years ago, in the north the Turkish lira is legal tender.

He and Hasan collect the various bills and coins that everyone has contributed in both monies, separating the euros from the Turkish lira, calculating the exchange rate and handing the pile to Ahmet. As we stand up to leave, another tour group enters and looks around.

"This table is like Skarinou station, " Andreas says referring to a village in the south, half way between Nicosia and Limassol. "There used to be a big inn there just like this one, where people changed horses and rested. Well, this table is like that station. People come, say hello, chat for five minutes and then go. It's like this every Saturday."

3 A GREEK SIDE AND A TURKISH SIDE

During my childhood in the '60s the Turkish sector of Nicosia was out of bounds for us Greek Cypriots. Unfortunately the out of bounds area expanded with the Turkish invasion in 1974, as the line that had previously split Nicosia now cut off the whole northern third of the island. So, when free movement was allowed with the opening of a few checkpoints, I discovered places, like the Büyük Han, I had not known existed, even though they were part of my country.

I also discovered new people, who became lasting friends, simply by virtue of the fact that we shared a common vision for our country. The core group of regulars at the Han often brought someone new, a relative, a friend or an acquaintance. Nowadays you never know who you'll meet here on a Saturday.

One Saturday I arrive at the Han to find Suleyman's beautiful eighteen-year-old daughter, Hazar, sitting with the group. It's rare that the younger generation joins us, mostly because they have better things to do than sit with us oldies. Hazar is studying acting in Istanbul and already has a couple of movies under her belt, one of which, *Shadows and Faces*, dramatises how the troubles on our island began. She has recently landed a part in a popular television soap opera in Turkey, which has made her a household name. Every now and then someone goes past who recognises her and asks to be photographed with her. She graciously complies, posing in front of the central fountain with her arms around her admirers.

"She's more famous than you, Suleyman, " Andreas says, watching Hazar flick back her long dark hair and offering her dazzling smile to the camera. "Soon they will be asking who is that with Hazar, and it will be you."

"Indeed," Suleyman says putting on a sour look, though the corners of his mouth and eyes betray his parental pride.

"Right, what is everyone having to drink?" Andreas asks returning to business.

He asks everyone round the table one by one, memorising the different degrees of coffee sweetness people want, then turns to Ahmet, who has appeared beside him.

"*Iki orta, dört sade.*" Two medium sweet coffees and four without any sugar, he says, combining everything so that Ahmet can more easily remember the order.

"*Ena lemonada,*" Hasip adds.

"*Mia lemonada,*" Andreas corrects. "Lemonade is female."

Hasip makes a gesture of exasperation as if brushing away an imaginary fly. "Female? Why on earth should lemonade be female?"

"It doesn't seem to matter for Hasip if things are male or female," Andreas tells the table. "It must be because of his age. Now, do you want *büyük bardak or küçük?*" Large glass or small.

"*Megali,*" Hasip says, using the female declension of the word 'large'.

"Actually it's *megalo,* because here the word refers to the glass, *potiri,* which is neutral not the lemonade, which is feminine," Andreas says patiently.

Hasip throws his arms up in exasperation. "Turkish is so much simpler!" He turns to Ahmet. "*Muhallebi lütfen,*" he says, ordering the traditional Cypriot cornflour custard in rosewater syrup.

"Do you remember that taxi driver in Istanbul?" says Andreas.

Hasan laughs. "Hasip and I were talking to each other in the Turkish Cypriot dialect, and Andreas and his then wife were talking in the Greek Cypriot dialect, and together we were all speaking in English!"

"We even used some French words," Andreas adds. "Like *villageois.*"

"The taxi driver got so confused," Hasip remembers. "I was sitting in the front and he turned to me and asked, '*Arkadaş,* brother, where are you from?' 'I am from Cyprus,' I said speaking in proper Turkish. He looked at me astonished. 'And you speak Turkish, as well?' "

"We do the same when we go to Greece," Mikis says. "We switch to proper Greek so they can understand."

"Then the taxi driver points to Andreas and Hasan sitting in the back and asks, 'But what about them? Where are they from?' I said, 'they are from Cyprus too—one is a *Kıbrıslı Turk* and the other is a *Kıbrıslı Rum.*' He was shocked! '*Rum?*' he said. 'Why are you travelling with *Rum*? Are they not our enemy?' I said, 'they might be *your* enemy but they're not *my* enemy.' 'But didn't we kill them all in '74?' he asked. The guy was so confused!" Hasip leans back in his chair his chubby cheeks glowing as everyone laughs.

"What did you reply?" I ask after a while as the question has been left hanging in the air.

"I told him, 'some got away.'" The burst of laughter from our table sends the pigeons flying off from under the arches in alarm.

In the distance I notice two women approaching across the sunny courtyard. It's Litsa with someone new.

"This is my friend Eleni," Litsa says when she reaches the table.

I know Eleni. She is a human rights lawyer and the first wife of the British writer and polemicist Christopher Hitchens. They met when he came to Cyprus on his first assignment. Hitchens used to describe her as 'his little terrorist' and, with her mass of wild curly hair and camouflage pants, I can see why.

"*Hoşgeldin*. Welcome," Andreas says. "Join us." He gets up and looks around for a chair for the new guests. His eyes fall on Hasan who, has taken over five chairs - one for his bottom and one each for his arms and legs.

"*Re!*" he tells him crossly, using the typical Cypriot expression that often accompanies or substitutes people's names. "You are sitting like a true *köylu* Cypriot! Get up and let the ladies sit."

Hasan reluctantly gathers himself and offers up one of his chairs. Eleni smiles pleasantly at everyone and sits down as if she belongs.

"What would you like to drink?" Andreas asks the new arrivals.

"Can I … is it OK to have a Turkish coffee?" Eleni ventures, twisting a strand of curls, not quite sure of etiquette on this side of the divide. Her accent is that of a Cypriot who has lived many years in the UK.

"Yes, yes, here you can order Turkish coffee without fear," Andreas reassures her, raising his hand for Ahmet to come and take an order.

"You know, at first we didn't know that you guys had stopped calling it Turkish coffee," Hasip says, remembering how coffee was also one of the victims of the island's politics. After the invasion, Greeks everywhere stopped calling the small cups of rich coffee brew, Turkish coffee, although they still continued to drink it. Practically overnight it became Greek coffee, Cyprus coffee, or even Byzantine coffee, as if they could not bear to imbibe a substance that bore the name of their mortal enemy.

"When I was going to university in Manchester just after the war in '74," Hasip continues, folding his hands over his belly and settling into the telling of a story, "we decided to drive through Europe via Turkey. When we arrived at the Greek border, the official there wouldn't let me in because I had a Cypriot passport. I insisted this was a legal document and refused to turn back. I asked to see his superior. While we were waiting in his office he offered me something to drink. I said I would like a Turkish coffee. I was a little puzzled when he gave me a strange look and said he would be having a *Greek* coffee, with the emphasis on Greek. I didn't know what Greek coffee was, but I didn't think anything of it. When the coffee arrived, the cups on the tray all looked exactly the same. So I said 'Which is the Greek coffee, and which is the Turkish coffee?'"

We all burst into laughter and Hasip beams with pleasure as he digs into his *muhallebi*.

In the courtyard Hazar is posing for another photograph with two young girls. "Say halloumi!" Andreas calls to them and they laugh obligingly.

"So how long have you been meeting here?" Eleni enquires.

"It's all Andreas' fault," says Hasan, pointing an accusing finger at him.

"Yes, I'm the guilty one," Andreas says looking more pleased with himself than guilty. "When the borders were opened I decided to look up an old classmate of mine from the English School." Our old high school was the only school where both Greek and Turkish Cypriots could attend together. "So I thought of asking the Turkish Cypriot officials at the checkpoint if they knew where I could find someone called Hasan Ahmet. Since everyone knows everyone else on our island and the Turkish Cypriots are even fewer than we are, I figured they would be sure to know. They looked at me and said '*Peeeh*', and waved me away." *Peeh*, is a versatile Cypriot expression that could mean any number of things from 'a lot' or 'Jesus', to 'you're mad'.

Andreas continues, "I said, 'What do you mean, *peeeh*?' Apparently Hasan Ahmet is the equivalent of John Smith or Andreas Georgiou. It could be anyone, you see. They said, 'Don't you know the new name?' I said 'What do you mean, new name?' 'His new surname,' they said, 'do you know it?'"

"You see in the past people didn't have surnames," Hasip explains.

"Yes, it was the same on our side," Mikis says. "We were known as the son or daughter of our father. So Andreas Georgiou was the son of George. Hasan Ahmet was the son of Ahmet."

"On our side," Sarper says, "they passed a law whereby we had to declare once and for all our new surname and stick to it from then on."

"On the Greek side this custom died out naturally," says Mikis.

"Anyway," Andreas continues. "I didn't know the guy's new name, so I asked them if they knew anyone who had been to the English School. They thought a moment and then remembered that there was a Hasan in the old part of Nicosia who used to go to the English School. He's a *bakal* they said. So I went and found the shop, which is just round the corner from the Büyük Han." He points towards the entrance. "I found Hasan inside the shop and asked him, 'Are you Hasan, my classmate, who went to the English School?' Hasan looked at me, thought for a minute, and said 'No'." Andreas pauses for effect while everyone laughs. "I insisted, 'Are you sure you are not the Hasan who went to the English School?' Hasan said, 'I went to the English School, but I am not your classmate.' We discovered Hasan was a couple of years above me. But, since that day I saw Hasan thousands of times." He contemplates their friendship briefly. "In fact I wish I had seen less of him."

Hasan jumps up to defend himself. "On the contrary! Since the day *kargaşalık,* the chatterbox, walked into my shop —"

"Your life changed for the better!" Andreas says.

"For the worse!" Hasan exclaims. "I can't get rid of him!"

"He walked into your shop and you made him walk into our lives," Suleyman says gloomily.

"I tried to pass him on to the rest of you but failed," Hasan says. "Every weekend, every holiday he comes and sits in my shop."

"Yes, it makes you wonder what he used to do before the checkpoints opened," Hasip says.

The shock decision to open the checkpoints in April 2003, a year before the referendum was due to be held to reunite the country, was a landmark event for all of us. Before that there had been virtually no contact between our two communities for almost thirty years. Only UN staff, journalists, diplomats and a few peace-activists had been able to cross to the other side. For the rest of us, the only way across the physical obstacle of the border was visually, letting our eyes roam across the wide open central plain, towards the Kyrenia mountain range, standing like an enormous wall in the distance, obscuring one's view of the beautiful seaside town of Kyrenia and the villages that lay on the other side, just a fifteen minute drive away, so close, yet totally out of reach. For me the north was like dreaming of a silent land that only existed in my memory, materialising only at night when twinkling clusters of lights appeared, making me realise that life went on there, too, in the towns and villages on the other side. The truth is that I rarely looked north, either because I was too busy getting on with my life in the south to look up, or because I wanted to avoid seeing the gigantic Turkish flag that had been painted on the mountainside. At night it lit up like a Las Vegas light show, disappearing like the smile of the Cheshire cat, only to reappear again a few seconds later to flash at us tauntingly, a permanent reminder of the loss of a part of our island, as if the Turks were giving us the finger, rubbing salt in the wound.

"So how did you guys find out that the Ledra Palace checkpoint was to open?" I ask Hasip wanting to know what that day was like on their side.

"It was around eight or nine in the morning when the order came," he tells me taking another spoonful of *muhallebi.* "It came directly from Turkey."

"Really?" I say. "On our side they were always telling us it was Denktash who opened the border. We thought it was a trick."

At the time we were all suspicious of the move and thought it was an attempt by Rauf Denktash, the Turkish Cypriot president, to gain recognition for the state in the north, because it was his son, Serdar, who had made the announcement.

"No, it was Turkey," Hasip says firmly. "Nobody knew about it beforehand. Not even the Turkish ambassador knew. We were in a meeting with him at the Saray hotel, as Hasan and I were members of the board of the Turkish Cypriot Chamber of Commerce at the time, when it was announced. He was just as surprised as we were."

Hasan nods meaningfully, "Yes, even Turkey's representative was in the dark. A messenger interrupted the meeting to inform the ambassador of the news." He looks around at us to make sure we had taken in the importance of his statement. On this island of rumours, as a former British Governor of Cyprus once called it, where nothing ever remains a secret for long, this was quite a feat.

He stops while Yusuf, the young waiter Ahmet has recently hired, comes to take away dirty coffee cups and bring fresh ones, which he distributes round the table along with plastic water cups.

Hasip continues: "We all got up straight away and headed to the Ledra Palace checkpoint. I stopped only to take a bottle of water with me. There were already hundreds of people gathered there, Greeks crossing over to our side, Turks to the Greek side. I saw an elderly Greek woman in her car waiting in line. She looked very hot and stressed. I knocked on her window and offered her my bottle of water. 'Welcome to your country,' I told her. She burst into tears."

Indeed, those were memorable days. Shortly after the announcement, crowds started to gather in expectation on both sides of the Ledra Palace checkpoint. When the gates were finally opened people surged across, like prisoners whose guards had suddenly unlocked the gates and abandoned the place. There was a party atmosphere at the checkpoint with Greek and Turkish Cypriots, who didn't even know each other, embracing each other like long lost brothers, before going off to revisit their respective memories. For a brief joyful moment, people followed their hearts and ignored the politicians and the media, who through fear-mongering tried to prevent people from crossing for supposedly patriotic reasons. I sat riveted to the television set watching moving interviews of people describing their visits to their lost homes and villages. I heard Greek Cypriots describe how overwhelmed they were at the way the Turkish Cypriots had greeted them, waving as they came out of their shops, shouting "welcome" in Greek, clapping and cheering and calling to them as they drove by like visiting royalty. I watched in disbelief as a Turkish Cypriot couple went into a back room and brought out an old family album which they then returned to its Greek Cypriot owner. They had kept it all those years in expectation of this day. And they weren't the only ones. All over the north this scene was repeated time and again. It was as if they were making reparations for having taken over someone else's house. Since they couldn't give the bricks and mortar back, at least they could give them their mementos back.

"Everyone was very excited," Hasan tells me, as he remembers how all around the neighbourhoods of the north, Greek Cypriots began arriving. "Have your Greeks come yet?" they would ask each other, and when 'their' Greeks did come, it was with joy, not guilt, that the Turkish Cypriots welcomed them, partaking in the bitter-sweet pleasure of their guests who had at last, albeit temporarily, come home, inviting them to dine with them, in typical Cypriot hospitality. Those who accepted became quasi-friends, bound together by virtue of having lived in the same house, while those whose Greeks did not come—because they refused to cross, or perhaps had emigrated, or sadly died—sat waiting forlorn and rejected as the days went by and no one showed up.

Yet underneath the smiles and cheers there was also great sadness. Many Greek Cypriots described their disappointment. Everything had changed. Things were not as they remembered. After their initial visit, many people never returned. As they realised that reality did not match their memories and that the places they remembered with such fondness were no longer the same and, worse, belonged to someone else now, they too resolved never to go back again. They had no reason to. It wasn't the same and they felt they were like tourists in their own country.   One friend of mine told me that he had cried his heart out when he went to see his former home and decided then and there he would never cross again. "Why should I?" he said. "To get used to it?" His question still haunts me to this day.

At first I too was unsure about what it all meant. I had no qualms about crossing and rushed across to see the beautiful horseshoe harbour of Kyrenia as soon as I could, but other things bothered me. What did crossing mean? Is it true that in doing so I was in effect recognising the state in the north? Did it mean I was a traitor, undermining the national cause? Was it dangerous? Although there were no physical signs of the Turkish army, I did feel uneasy on the other side. What if something happened and the borders were suddenly closed? I would be trapped. This was a place where I didn't speak the language, whose customs I was not familiar with. I was even reluctant to spend money there. They stole our houses and we're going to pay them on top of it and help them prosper? The propaganda still held me in its sway.

"Yes, it was a very confusing time," Andreas says. "I remember going to a restaurant and being served by a waiter who was a settler from Anatolia. I thought, oh no, a settler from Turkey! But he was just a twenty year old kid earning his living."

"We had been brainwashed for years against the Turkish settlers," Mikis says. "One of our slogans was that all the settlers should go back where they came from if there was ever to be a solution, because we believed that Turkey had sent them over in a deliberate attempt to change the demography of the island. We forget they are just people, who came here from Turkey looking for work, settled down, got married and had children.

Many of them have been here for over thirty years."

I say, "The more I went across, the more I found myself changing. I realised it was silly not to spend money there, or even mind about helping the economy of people who were really our compatriots. Far from feeling like a tourist, I felt as if my country had expanded."

"It was confusing for us as well," Hasip says. "Before '74 anyone who crossed to the other side—'rapprochement' they called it—was labelled a traitor. After the borders opened it became much easier because now everyone was talking to the enemy!"

I think about how lack of trust can make one suspicious and prejudiced against fellow human beings. "That's the trouble with walls," I say. "As long as they exist, they allow us to demonise those on the other side. It's easy when you can't see them or get to know them. Nor can they answer back, tell us off and give us their point of view."

"If history is anything to go by, walls don't last," Mikis says.

Hasan laughs and says, "The most important thing that happened in Cyprus when the checkpoints opened is that Turkish Cypriots could take their girlfriends to the south and not be found out!"

"And vice versa!" Andreas says and everyone laughs.

At the other end of the table Sarper is teaching Mikis a new word and Mikis is practising how to pronounce it. "*Oyallanmak*. It means to while away the time, *poskolioume*," he tells me when I ask. "Like we're doing here!"

Sarper laughs because he has mispronounced it and corrects him.

Mikis laughs too. "All those years ago whenever someone made a mistake in Greek we would laugh at them and say 'you speak Greek like a Turk'. Now it's our turn to make mistakes and make you laugh at us!"

Meanwhile Hazar gets up to go. She puts her bag over her shoulder, kisses everyone around the table goodbye and goes off with her friends.

"Where is she going?" Andreas asks. As *muhtar*, he needs to know everyone's comings and goings.

"Shopping," Suleyman says. "She is going to the Rum *tarafı*."

"The what?" I ask.

"You know how in Greek we say this is my *tarafı*?" Andreas explains. "Well, it turns out it's a Turkish word."

"Does it mean the same thing?" I ask.

"Yes, it means area, territory, side."

"*Ben* Apoel *tarafı*," Suleyman declares. "I am on the side of the Apoel football team. Unfortunately Hasan is on the Galatasaray *tarafı*".

"So *Rum tarafı* means the Greek side and *Türk tarafı* the Turkish side?" I ask making sure.

"Yes, you see we Cypriots are strange," Andreas muses. "We live in a country smaller than Connecticut and we have decided that there should be two *tarafs*."

"Only three quarters of a million people and we managed to screw everything up," adds Mikis shaking his head.

Just then there's a commotion from across the courtyard. Some members of the group jump up from their seats to greet a passer-by who they've recognised. First to get up is Andreas. "Mr Downer, Mr Downer, come and join us, Mr Downer," he calls.

Alexander Downer, an Australian diplomat, is the latest in a long line of appointees by the UN Secretary-General as his Special Representative in Cyprus. He has the unenviable task of being the middleman between the two sides and trying to find common ground. Most of the time he gets a lot of flak, mostly from the Greek Cypriot side. Whenever he puts forward something that sounds even remotely close to the Turkish Cypriot point of view, they conclude that he must be biased. He looks younger than he does on television, but I hope his boyish appearance belies his ability to knock heads together. With so many hands waving at him, he approaches the table, albeit reluctantly.

"Can't stay, can't stay," he says, his round cheeks glowing. "I've got my wife and mother-in-law here to show around." Behind him two ladies smile pleasantly.

But Andreas won't let him go without a bit of fun. "Mr Downer, this table consists of both Greek and Turkish speaking Cypriots. Can you tell who is who?"

Amused, Downer looks up and down the table and takes up the challenge. We all sit there beaming up at him, eager for him to get it wrong.

"Let's see, you're … Greek, and you're Turkish, Greek, Greek, Turkish, Turkish," he points at us one by one going round the table. Although he does make a few mistakes, he is mostly right, but that doesn't stop Andreas from drawing his preordained conclusion.

"You see? We are all the same. *Una fatsa una ratsa*, as they say. This is where the Cyprus problem gets solved, Mr. Downer. Come and have coffee with us."

"Thank you, I will," Downer says amiably. "Whenever I feel depressed that the talks are going nowhere, I'll come here."

He never does. And that's not to say that the talks went anywhere.

That evening at home, my husband, Stelios, and I are in the kitchen preparing dinner. The television is on in the background showing the evening news. The Cyprus problem is, as usual, the main topic, even though nothing newsworthy is happening at all. The latest media talking point is a surreal argument over whether any new partnership state would derive from the 'evolution' of the Republic of Cyprus or whether it would be a 'virgin birth'. A politician is being interviewed who believes the latter would be a catastrophe for the Greek Cypriots.

I say, "What's the big deal if it's a continuation or not?"

Stelios places two pieces of pitta bread in the toaster. "What they're worried about," he says, "is what would happen if the new state collapses, as it did in 1960. Because then it would be an easy step for the Turkish Cypriots to seek recognition, and where would it leave us Greek Cypriots? Now at least we have an internationally recognised state."

Behind him on the television set the news has ended and a football match has begun. I watch the game absent-mindedly out of the corner of my eye, while I chop up a cabbage, briefly contemplating human behaviour. We separate ourselves into groups, bag little patches of land to call our own, which we then defend at all costs, creating differences out of thin air that turn us into mortal enemies on our little pitch. The ball goes backwards and forwards, now heading down one way, now the other, as each team tries to achieve its goal. Every now and then a nonsensical battle chant goes up from the fans of one side or the other and the camera shows close-ups of someone pumping the air aggressively with his fists, immediately copied by the others around him, in a form of social bonding whereby 'I' becomes 'we' in a fight against 'them'.

I take the tray of halloumi out from under the grill and place it on the kitchen table. "Instead of each of us ruling our little patch of the island separately, isn't it better for both of us to rule the whole island together? Shouldn't we at least try and make it work?"

On the pitch one player is being called off and replaced by another fresher player, who runs on energetically. The team will never die but fights on to achieve its objective. It's a longterm struggle.

Stelios takes a bite of his sandwich. "Our patriots are quite happy for the situation to remain as it is, as long as they can continue to feel they're in the right …"

He breaks off, his attention caught by what's happening on the pitch where play has been halted. The referee is holding up a yellow card, eyeball to eyeball with one of the players, who is vehemently arguing his case. Stelios joins in the collective outrage on behalf of his team, letting forth a flow of invectives, blaming the referee for being biased, the linesman for not having eyes with which to notice a clear rule violation and punishing the culprit. We think things are clear, but sometimes they are not as black and white as we believe they are.

"… as long as they can go to the UN asking for the international rules as expressed in the UN resolutions on Cyprus to be implemented, they can stay like this for ever," he continues, munching.

On TV play resumes and suddenly the commentator's voice reaches a crescendo. The orange team has scored. The orange fans go wild, jumping up and down triumphantly and cheering in unison. Stelios too has jumped up hands held high shouting "goooooaaaal" as loudly as if he were actually there on the stands, taking a victory lap round the kitchen table as if he were one of the players, an extension of the fans, almost tripping over his bathrobe in the process. The camera briefly pans over the opposite stands where everyone is standing still in deathly silence, a black mood having fallen over them. Collective triumph on the one team is met with collective grief on the other. I watch half-amused at the behaviour of football supporters the world over and in my kitchen in particular. At least sports don't leave people dead and displaced.

4 OUR HOUSE IN KYRENIA

Some time after the checkpoints opened, Stelios, my sister, Celia, and I are seven hundred metres above sea level, perched on the top of the Kyrenia mountain range, looking down at the coastline from the ruins of the medieval castle of St Hilarion. Like the other great castles along this mountain range, Buffavento and Kantara, St Hilarion was built by the descendants of Guy de Lusignan, the deposed King of Jerusalem, who took Cyprus over from Richard the Lionheart in the 12th century. He and his Frankish family ruled over what became the Kingdom of Cyprus. For three hundred years the ruling class of our island all spoke French. This was one of their summer retreats, a bit like our house in Kyrenia was to us. The view from the Queen's Room is legendary. From up here you can see for miles along the coast and out to sea. In the distance I can just make out the shadow of Turkey's Taurus mountains hanging over the horizon, like a dark cloud or the threat of bad weather. The castles also served as lookout points, as well as dungeons, as the Lusignans lived in fear of attack from marauding Arab hordes. I shield my eyes from the bright light and scan the horizon. Today, I think, the enemy is already here. He is in our house.

We have come up here to see if we can catch a glimpse of our house before driving into Kyrenia town to see if we can get a closer view. The sea shimmers in the viewfinder of my binoculars as I try to locate it. I focus on a large square brown structure amongst the jumble of smaller whitewashed boxes, which I recognise as Kyrenia castle standing guard at the harbour entrance as it has for centuries, amongst the jumble of whitewashed houses of old Kyrenia town. From there I follow the coast about three miles to the west until I locate Snake Island, an uninhabited islet lying a quarter of a mile or so from the shore. Our house is just across from it.

"There it is," I say. "I can see the tree mummy planted." The tree has made it, even without her care. Throughout my childhood, she used to cover it in a plastic tent to protect it from the strong westerlies that constantly blow in these parts. "It's taller than the house now."

"Let me see," Celia says impatiently. I hand her the binoculars. "Kyrenia sure has been built up," she observes after a while.

"What did you expect? It's been thirty years," Stelios says.

"Yet, look, the area around the house has remained almost exactly as it was."

She is right. For a square mile or so around the house, it is still scrubland as it used to be; no new buildings have been built whatsoever.

"Must be because it's a military zone," I recall. "All they had to do was move into the old army camp across from the house and simply block the rest of the area off. Look over there, near Snake Island beach—that looks like a helicopter-landing pad."

"And what's that on the island? It looks like some kind of fuel depot," Stelios says taking his turn to look through the binoculars.

I lean back against the grey stone walls of the castle and take in this precious view. Up here, where a tenth century monk chose to create a hermitage years before the Franks, peace reigns. High towers hug the vertiginous drops of rock, while wisps of cloud drift slowly by, seductively weaving in and out of the branches of the cypress trees, like a cat rubbing itself against a pair of legs. Only the timeless sound of the wind whispering through the branches and the occasional bird twittering breaks the silence. In the distance the ancient magenta blue sea twinkles in the sunlight as it always has. The struggle and strife of yesteryear are over now. It's as if they never happened. How pointless it all seems now. From up here, all the bloody and brutal dramas that have played out on this land in the course of our ten thousand years of history, as one conquering nation after another swept over the island, all the petty scheming of the politicians, that have led to so much human misery, people losing their lives, their loved ones, their property, their livelihoods, through the generations, just so they, rather than anyone else, can be rulers of a little patch of land on a rock hurtling through space in the vastness of the universe, all seem so meaningless.

It feels so good to be seeing the house again, even at such a distance, that my heart skips a beat. It's like catching sight of an old lover, for whom one is still carrying a torch. I need to get closer.

We make our way back down through the castle, imagining knights in shining armour milling along well worn flagstone pathways, meeting fair damsels beneath arches and domes that frame the spectacular views. Tumbledown walls blend in with the craggy bare rock so that it's hard to tell where the building ends and nature begins. Just below the castle, on land that used to be the knights' jousting arena, Turkish soldiers are exercising.

We get back into the car and drive off down to Kyrenia. Here and there remnants of the old road from our childhood can still be seen along the side of the new four-lane highway. As we round the bend through the mountain pass, "the road falls like a swallow towards Kyrenia," as Lawrence Durrell so aptly put it in *Bitter Lemons*, his classic memoir of his time in 1950s Cyprus. The view takes my breath away, just as it always has. Today, however, the pleasure of seeing this beautiful coast is tempered by the ugly urban spread that has taken place in the intervening years. Kyrenia used to be so picturesque.

A gigantic statue of a soldier looms over us from a hilltop. Monuments to the great Turkish army abound and busts of Kemal Ataturk are everywhere. Red and white Turkish flags festoon the roundabouts and main crossroads or flutter on top of minarets that didn't exist before.

"It's a sign of insecurity," Celia says, crossing her arms with indignation. "The more guilty they feel at having usurped this land, the louder they need to proclaim ownership."

As we enter Kyrenia, the buildings along the main street become more and more familiar. Heraklis, the ice cream store we used to stop at every day after our water ski; Maroulla's souvenir shop selling Lefkara lace to tourists; the pharmacy where my girlfriends and I used to while away the time on lazy afternoons trying on different shades of nail varnish before walking down to the harbour for a drink and to hang out with our friends. But the placards, the signs, the ads, the names over the shops, the words are all in Turkish now. And we can't read them.

The town is much bigger. Previously it came to an end at the bottom of the main street. Now I cannot tell where that was any more. Shops and new buildings follow one after the other. Where there were once fields, dotted with olive and carob trees, there are now ugly apartment blocks. A few remnants of the past still remain, serving as landmarks. I recognise what used to be the Dudley Court hotel, a bungalow we used to visit, the low wall and iron railings of the army camp near our house, the spot where I used to stand to hitch a lift into town. We're getting closer. The bus stop at the turning of the dirt road that leads to our house. It still leads to our house, but the dirt road is now asphalted. A barricade blocks our way and a sentry stands guard at the gate. We stop the car a little distance away contemplating what to do. The sentry guard eyes us suspiciously. As we don't seem to be making any move, he finally approaches the car.

"We want to go to our house," I say opening the window and pointing in the general direction of the house.

He shakes his head. "No entry."

"But it's our house, we just want to see it."

"No entry," he repeats, probably the only English words he knows.

We're not surprised. We knew that we wouldn't be able to visit the house. Cyprus is a small place, little remains secret; not even hermetically sealed borders can keep information from getting out. We've known for years that apart from being in a military zone, the house has been taken over by Mr. Denktash, himself. Occasionally over the years I would read about foreign dignitaries who had visited him at "his" summer house, where they were charmed by his sense of humour and his smart and witty repartee, belying the personality he presented in our media of a wily, arrogant and belligerent hardliner with dictatorial tendencies, who blocked all attempts at reunification making sure the island stayed divided. I would often imagine him, short, bald and stocky, showing off the aviary that he had built in our back garden, or the photographs he took of scenes of Cyprus, as he prided himself of being an amateur photographer, before offering his guests tea on our veranda, and embarking on a passionate rant against us Greek Cypriots, who had afflicted such suffering on his people, even as he sat in a Greek Cypriot's house. He told an interviewer once that he knew he would be known as "Mr. No-No", the one who is always intransigent, but he insisted he had no choice. "We are like little candles in a sea of Greeks," he said. "One storm and we are all snuffed out."

We turn away disappointed and drive a few metres down the main road until we're out of sight of the guard, parking by a row of half-finished shops next to a Chinese restaurant. This seems like a good spot to catch a glimpse of the house. We get out of the car and enter one of them. Through the window at the back, we can make out some military vehicles across the scraggy undergrowth, and in the far distance sure enough we catch sight of the unmistakable grey stone wall of a corner of our house, the sea twinkling behind it.

Our house came about as a result of an argument between my mother and father in the early years of their marriage. They had just bought some land in an up-and-coming northern suburb of Nicosia, called Ortaköy, or Kermia, and were debating what architect to hire to design their home, when they went on holiday to Florida. Enchanted by the beautiful houses of Miami Beach, my mother, who came from a wealthy Limassol family and was used to a privileged life, promptly decided that she had to have an American architect design her home. No amount of reasoning on the part of my father, a refugee from Asia Minor and a self-made man, would change her mind.

"Do you know how much American architects charge?" he had pleaded. "Do you have any idea how much it would cost just to bring him half way across the world to Cyprus just to build you a house?"

My mother was adamant, so my father decided to go ahead on his own. He bought a piece of land he liked by the sea, browsed Italian architectural magazines and, with his engineering background, designed the house himself and hired a contractor to build it. All the while it was being built, my mother pointedly refused to even have a look at it. Only after it was finished did she reluctantly agree to go. As he proudly showed her what he had done, she relented, instantly falling in love with the place and devoting herself to making it as chic and stylish as she was.

Our house stood in an acre of terraced garden overlooking the shining sea with an air of benign contentment. With the nearest neighbour a mile or so away and approached along a perilously steep and bumpy dirt road, it basked in an atmosphere of splendid isolation. Surrounded by unkempt bushes and scrub, it was like an elegant socialite who'd accidentally strayed into the wrong part of town.

The garden my mother created was to be looked at and admired, but not touched. An army of canna lillies with massive red and yellow blooms stood guard at the entrance, their leaves like unsheathed swords at the ready. Past them, up a few steps, a purple bougainvillea sprawled over a railing like a drunk at a party, its thorny branches mischievously grabbing onto your hair or pinching your bikini bottom as you went by. Round the corner a magnificent veranda swept across the front of the house offering a breathtaking view of the sea, with Kyrenia to the east and Snake Island to the west. On a clear day you could see Turkey on the horizon. Neat geometric terraces flowed downwards, guiding the eye to the pool and the sea beyond. Below the veranda a rock garden with sharp edged volcanic stones interspersed with prickly cacti contrasted with soft carpets of lush emerald green Bermuda grass that begged to be walked on barefoot, although we did so on pain of death at our own mother's hands. A row of white-leaved bushes framed the lawn's edges like a hairband from which perfect tresses of mesymbrianthemum, or Aphrodite's hair, tumbled over the terrace walls with an air of wild abandon, adorned here and there with bright purple flowers. To one side, multicoloured zinnias lifted their faces in adoration to the sun, while on the other, powder blue plumbago flowers perfectly picked up the colour of the pool, sea and sky.

Seeming to float just above the sea, the swimming pool took up the whole of the lower terrace. In the shape of an irregular polygon, the result of the inebriated scribbling on a paper napkin by a famous architect, who my father ambushed at a cocktail party ("design me a pool"), the pool had character. It also had a voice, a cacophony of gurgling, sucking, and choking noises emanated from its primitive filter system, purring contentedly when we were in its liquid embrace, grumbling loudly for us to come back in when we were up at the house. We children practically lived in this pool, staying in it so long our skin would be wrinkled and our eyes bloodshot. We would spend hours floating on the surface mesmerised by the patterns of the sun on the tiles, or diving down to touch the bottom holding our breath to stay as long as we could immersed in this liquid turquoise world. The pool's strange shape created corners which we avoided where dead insects, twigs and leaves collected, as well as other areas we loved, like the shallow part, where we soaked in the warm bath-like water, crawling back and forth on all fours like prowling animals. Sometimes you'd think there was no one in the pool, only to find us in the shade under the diving board, hanging off it like monkeys.

But it was the azure Mediterranean sea that dominated the house and our life. We felt its presence everywhere, the blue expanse visible from every corner. Its mood affected ours. When it was calm and mellow, so were we. When it was rough and angry, we would be irritable. I always wanted to be in its company, and even when curled up with a book, I would choose a spot where I could watch the sun's reflection on the waves, like a million flashbulbs greeting the arrival of a film star.

Each morning when I woke, the first thing I would do was check to see what state it was in. Usually this involved nothing more complicated than going to the window and peering out, but occasionally it did not even require getting out of bed. Depending on how much light filtered through the cracks in the shutters, our bedroom became a *camera obscura*, as an inverted and blurry image of the scene outside would be magically projected onto the ceiling. A wash of emerald green from the garden spilled into a splash of turquoise from the pool, which in turn blended into an expanse of cobalt from the sea, all forming a moving picture in glorious technicolour, complete with speedboats to-ing and fro-ing and my mother watering the garden, her swimming cap perched like a chef's hat on top of her head.

I could tell, as precisely as any clock, how late I had woken up simply by the number of boats going by in the sea in front of the house or anchored in the sheltered waters by Snake Island. If I recognised uncle George's white speedboat, I would know that I had overslept. I would quickly jump up, pull on my swimsuit hanging on a hook behind the door and run downstairs, past my mother, by now sunbathing on the veranda, a cigarette in her fingers, a cup of Turkish coffee on the floor next to her sunbed and the BBC World Service on the radio. I would fly down the three flights of steps along the side of the garden two by two, until I reached the sea, where I would carefully make my way across the slippery rock pools to stand and wait on the water's edge, gripping onto the rough furry undergrowth with my toes as the movement of the waves tried to unbalance me. When the boat approached to pick me up, I would hesitate a moment before plunging into the ice cool morning waters, swimming up to the boat and greeting whoever happened to be on it. Skis would be thrown to me, the boat would circle round me, the rope would tauten, a sudden surge of power and I would be skimming over the smooth blue sea.

The mornings were the best time for skiing when just the faintest breath ruffled the water. Uncle George always followed the same clockwise circular trajectory around the front of the house. In the lee of the island the sea would be flat like a mirror, allowing us to venture out of the wake before the boat entered an area of rougher water where white horses rode the waves and millions of suns radiated from deep midnight blue depths. As it approached the promontory on which sat the church of Glykiotissa and next to it the army camp that lay across the bay, the boat would turn towards shore again before straightening out in front of our house, allowing us to show off our clever tricks to whoever happened to be watching from the veranda.

Every now and then there would be a heat wave when nothing stirred and the entire sea became like a mirror. On days like these there was no point in hanging around by the island as everywhere was calm, so we would head out towards the horizon in the general direction of Turkey, our skis smoothly hissing through the waves, accompanied by schools of flying fish soaring out of the silvery waters alongside us, their iridescent fins making rainbows in the light.

After everyone in the boat had had a ski we would anchor by the island for a swim, watching the other boats go by, exploring the rocks, or just diving into the deliciously cool clear waters. At the end of the morning we would be dropped off back home where we would soak in the pool until we were called up to lunch.

Lunch was an extended family affair round the dining room table, the beautiful sea invitingly framed in the window. Somehow food seemed to taste better in those days; the beef tomatoes were more aromatic, the cucumbers were smaller and sweeter, and even the watermelons had giant pips, which we used to break with our teeth in order to get at the sweet nut inside, passing the time before being allowed to leave the table. As our father wouldn't come back from the office in Nicosia until late afternoon, our mother would sit at the head of the table dauntingly serious, saying little. Her silence was more than made up for by the chatter of our paternal grandmother, Calliroe, and her two older sisters, our great aunts Ourana and Niove, who would all stay with us in the summer. Aunt Ourana especially had a tendency to talk non-stop, much to the annoyance of her sisters, who would often try to hush her, to no avail. The three old ladies were originally from Smyrna, now Izmir, in Asia Minor. My grandmother had lost her husband when the Turks burned down the city; Aunt Ourana had never married after a love affair that went wrong, while Aunt Niove, the oldest, had married a German and lived in Düsseldorf for many years. Now a widow, she'd come to Cyprus to live out the rest of her days. Almost doubled over from scoliosis, she still kept herself well groomed in her wigs and brightly printed silk pant suits, remnants of the couture business she once ran with her late husband until *prêt-à-porter* forced her to retire. All three of them adhered to values of beauty of a long gone time. For them a pale complexion was the ideal and they avoided the sun at all cost. My grandmother loved to swim but would only venture into the pool in the late afternoon or early morning when the sun was weakest, a scary sight silently doing the breast-stroke with her entire head covered with a white muslin cloth draped over a broad-brimmed hat and tied under her chin.

Much as we begged, we were never allowed back into the pool straight after lunch. We were told to "go and rest", but as a siesta was not something we wanted to do, we would invariably spend the time in our room reading Archie comics, Tin Tin books, Peanuts cartoons, as well as more literary tomes, in fact anything we could get our hands on.

Late afternoon would find us down by the sea looking for something different to do. At that time the tide would have gone out, stranding sundry creatures in the rock pools that had been transformed into furry baths heated by the sun. We would immerse ourselves in the least populated ones wallowing in the warmth until the nips from tiny transparent shrimps became too annoying to bear. Sometimes we would don mask and flippers and explore the underwater countryside, following schools of silver fish as they weaved their way along the gaps between the rocks, like roads in a thickly populated city, until we knew the lay of the land as intimately as if it were the fields behind our house. Later we would make our way along the rocky shore, carefully stepping across the volcanic rock that had formed the island in ancient times, sharp in places, slippery where it was in contact with the sea. Along the way we would look for multicoloured shells hiding in the recesses, the most prized being the cowry shells, 'little piggies', we called them, which we would later use to play families with, grouping them according to the patterns on their backs and creating little houses for them by drawing floor-plans on sheets of paper. Back up at the house, if we passed our mother watering the plants, we would goad her to hose our salt-crusted skin down, shrieking and howling with pleasure as the blast of icy cold water hit us, though more often than not, she would happily leave us be with the day's salt on us. "It's good for you," she would say.

Some afternoons my mother's friends would drop by and they would sit together on the veranda, discussing the news of the day. This was rarely calm and civilised. My mother loved a good argument. And, like all Cypriots, she especially loved to argue about politics, often relishing the more controversial point of view.

Mostly she liked to argue international politics with my father when he got back from work and was sitting enjoying a glass of ouzo and cucumbers on the veranda. Here she did not fare so well and yet she always managed to have the last word, or at the very least, reach a standoff. Often when she felt she couldn't prevail, she would resort to a higher authority: "But I heard it on the BBC", knowing there could be no comeback. When Palestinians hijacked a plane at Entebbe airport, she wagged her finger at him and said,

"Just you wait and see, the Israelis will go in and rescue them." No amount of his explaining the impossibility of such an operation, the distance they would have to cover, and the difficulty of getting there undetected, would dissuade her. "Wanna bet?" she said. When her predictions came true, a crestfallen father told us: "Your mother is unbearable today." And she was, whooping and taking victory laps at every opportunity, as well as making rude gotcha gestures whenever they crossed paths. He was delighted one year when she fell for the BBC's April Fool's Day joke that a bridge would be built linking Australia and New Zealand. "Do you realise the distance involved? The depth of the ocean? It's a physical impossibility!" he told her. But she remained unabashed, even in defeat; how clever of the BBC for managing to fool her!

In the island's first elections after independence from the British, she had supported Archbishop Makarios, much to the dismay of my father, who didn't like the idea of a priest as head of state. The only way he had of winning that argument was by wishing she would go into labour with my sister on election day so she wouldn't be able to go and vote. To her annoyance, his wish came true. In later years, though, she saw the error of her ways and just as fanatically changed allegiances, so much so that she would be inclined to support the 'other side' when discussing the Cyprus problem, to the shock of her friends who would accuse her of "speaking like a Turk".

In the evenings I would listen to the latest pop hits on *The International Programme*, sitting on the stairs near the bougainvillea at the entrance of the house where you got the best reception on the radio, or perched on the wall next to the concrete army bunker that had been built at the end of the drive to our house. Such bunkers, though never manned, dotted the whole of the Kyrenia coastline, supposedly to act as lookout points in case of a Turkish attack, recalling the castle lookout points in the Middle Ages built on the mountain range. At sunset the lugubrious sounds of a bugle call would drift over from the army camp across the bay, after which I would watch the soldiers obediently line up and march to their barracks.

As evening fell the sound of the night cricket filled the air, while the cloying smell of the night-blooming jasmine overpowered us, even though my mother had made sure to plant it some distance from the house. We would wait for the programme on the solitary state television station to begin at 6pm so that we could watch our favourite American serials, in black and white, of course—*Bonanza, Bewitched, Lassie, Flipper, Thunderbirds, Stingray*. Sometimes my grandmother would want me to sit with her to watch a Greek comedy, which I would do, just for the pleasure of hearing her laugh, or the regular weekly Turkish melodrama that everyone loved, during which she would surreptitiously sniff into her hankie and wipe her eyes.

Occasionally a summer storm would break out when the wind would howl around the house, rattling windows, slamming doors and sending us all indoors for the duration. The white horses would suddenly multiply and migrate from their usual galloping presence beyond the island's lee to cover the whole of the sea, as the island no longer offered any protection. As the storm progressed, the sea would gradually change from its usual friendly blue into an angry grey, then into a vast three-coloured flag of yellow, green and blue. Fortunately these storms didn't last long. Our imploring questions to any adult as to when the wind would stop were met with the mysterious "when the moon changes", which sure enough it would, calming down gradually and allowing us to get back into the gentle sea again and explore whatever interesting flotsam and jetsam had been thrown out onto the shore.

Weekends felt distinctly festive, as the sea would fill up with boatloads of Nicosians escaping the heat of the city. Sounds of fun and laughter would drift up to the house from the island anchorage. Boats pulling skiers or just going for a ride would churn up the water, so that even on calm days it became almost too rough to ski. On alternate Sundays our parents would throw all-day pool parties in return for the many invitations they had received over the course of the year in Nicosia, part of the active social life that their generation and social class enjoyed. On those occasions, all the living room windows would be open wide providing a total panorama of the sea and allowing the cool breeze to stir the heavy curtains. My grandmother and Aunt Ourana, who, in the tradition of Asia Minor, were great cooks, would start preparing a lavish buffet days in advance, with the help of Koulla, our live-in housekeeper. They would roll out the homemade pasta dough, fill it with little spoonfuls of halloumi mixture, while we would gleefully help cut the ravioli shapes using a Turkish coffee cup as a cutter. Aunt Ourana would make her famous cheese pie, reluctantly allowing us to brush each sheet of phyllo pastry with butter, anxiously hovering over us and taking over at the first opportunity in case we made a mess. They would order a suckling pig and someone would have to drive into town to fetch it. There would be *gelatina*, pork in aspic, which is rarely served today, and my grandmother's *imam bayeldi*, the traditional dish of roasted aubergines that the proverbial priest supposedly fainted over because it was so delicious. The whole meal would be topped off with meringues drenched in fresh cream and drizzled with molten chocolate and praline. We children would spend most of the time in the pool, jumping off the diving board, pushing each other in, floating on the lilos or just soaking, while the adults would congregate on the veranda getting more and more inebriated as the day progressed and having heated political discussions usually featuring Makarios' latest escapade. Towards late afternoon, when only our parents' closest friends remained, they would bring out a deck of cards and play poker or black jack on the veranda.

The house was once used as a film set, with a scene in a movie called *Doctors Wear Scarlet* starring Patrick McKnee being filmed around the pool. American actress Raquel Welch also visited, wanting to rent the house while she was filming on the island. Shortly before the invasion, a wealthy Arab offered my father a million pounds for the house, a deal that my sister and I emphatically vetoed, a decision we would often come to think about in later years.

Now the house has become the spoils of war. Two years after the war, Mr. Denktash chose our house as his summer residence, part of the reallocation of property to rehouse the Turkish Cypriots who moved to the north in the weeks and months after the ceasefire. They were given the empty houses the Greek Cypriots had abandoned on a points system based on the value of property they had left behind in the south. Denktash got ours in exchange for just a field with a couple of olive trees in his home town of Paphos, as the press reported, an inequity that irked many Turkish Cypriots who would often bring it up whenever elections loomed.

After the war my parents moved to Athens where, twelve years later, my mother died. My father was heartbroken. He remembered a brightly coloured portrait of her that had been hanging over the fireplace, painted by John Corbidge, a popular British artist, who had made the island his home, and decided to write a letter to Mr. Denktash asking for it back. When he heard that Denktash was going to give a lecture in London, he got a friend of his to attend and deliver it to him. But Denktash replied that he had found nothing in the house. This is quite likely, as we heard the house had been used as an army officers' mess before he moved in. I sometimes wonder whose living room my mother's face now graces, or even whether the painting will one day show up for sale on the international art market, like some long lost masterpiece of unknown provenance.

Just a year before the checkpoints opened, my father died too. Mr. Denktash continues on, however, having lived in our house for more than thirty years. Almost twice as long as I ever did, which sometimes makes me wonder, who does the house belong to now? Or rather, do I still belong in this house? In the event of a solution what will prevail—the right of ownership, or the right of tenancy?

"Let's go and have a drink in the harbour," Celia says, bringing me back to the present with words that bubble up from the past.

We turn away from the house and head back towards Kyrenia. The drive takes us through the new town that has sprung up without us. Ugly, vulgar, characterless buildings, painted in kitsch colours of lilac, or pistachio green, or pink. Turkish colours, the Greeks call them derisively. Yet are the buildings on our side any less ugly and characterless? It occurs to me that what makes these buildings feel so alien is that we haven't been witnesses of the town's growth. Watching each building go up in the course of time is how we become attached to them, how a city becomes our own, warts and all. I wonder what it might have been like had it not been for the war. I remember how whenever new buildings appeared, like the Ambelia Village up in the hillside village of Bellapais, a holiday village with a restaurant round a pool, or a new house built by a friend, we would all go to check it out. We lived through none of this growth here, so cannot own it. This place isn't what it used to be. We are strangers here. We no longer belong. This makes me sad, but strangely enough, also glad. It makes it that much easier to let go.

Back in the old town we find a place to park and eagerly make our way to the little horseshoe harbour, down the uneven flight of ancient cobbled steps by the side of the old square castle. When we reach the bottom, the harbour opens up before us just like it used to in a burst of shimmering light, sparkling water and bustling activity. It takes my breath away and I have to pause a moment to believe that I am seeing it again. We slowly walk along the promenade, taking it all in. It is almost exactly as I remember it, restaurants on one side, tables and chairs on the water's edge. Scenes from my life well up from the past as we walk. Here is the spot where I slept in the car while my parents dined at the Corner restaurant with friends, my mother tall and elegant like Jackie Kennedy, in psychedelic prints and false eyelashes, my father a cross between Fred Flintstone and Jack Lemon. Sixties music from the restaurants adds to the feeling of having slipped through a time warp. The biggest change is the type of boats in the harbour; gone is the fleet of speed boats we used to rent to go skiing; the luxury pleasure yachts have been replaced by rows of chunky Turkish ketches and converted trawlers that take groups on day trips along the coast. Gone are the harbour characters I used to know—Costis and Costis, who drove the boats with their long hippy hair, tanned bodies and gold medallions; their deaf and mute brother, Andros, with his curly golden locks mending his fishing nets; Ismailis, who entertained us with his sense of humour at the Harbour pub where we used to gather as teenagers.

We walk from one end of the harbour to the other where the old stone Customs House sits and continue on as far as the Dome Hotel. This was the place to be in the fifties and sixties, with its stately banqueting halls and large terraces overlooking the sea, where the older generation drank their afternoon tea. Its main attraction was a natural swimming pool in the rock at the edge of the promontory, with an underwater passage through which most days you could swim straight into the sea. The hotel is now a casino for rich Turks from the mainland, the liveried doormen standing guard at the entrance, making it too daunting for us to enter and explore. We pause a while by the stone embankment, watching young men fishing on the rocks down below, breathing in the fresh Kyrenia sea air with its familiar fishy smell, caressed by the cool breeze, briefly hypnotised by the incessant orderly march of waves in their familiar journey from the west. In the south, waves have a different flow, they seem more haphazard, their direction not so pronounced. The light is different here too. In the south the sun dazzles and blinds, here darker colours prevail. The blue of the sea is more magenta than silver, the green on the land more cypress than dusty olive, the wheat fields ochre not straw. We look longingly across the rugged coastline to the east towards Snake Island and our house. It seems closer than I remember it, just a short walk away. We turn back and walk the other way, just as we used to do, past the Customs House and back towards the castle again, this time going round its massive walls along the water's edge to the other side. Here, in the narrow passage leading into the harbour, was where our two torpedo boats used to be anchored, the ones on which, Phivos, a friend, was serving his army service, the ones which went out to greet the Turkish navy that fateful day, never to come back. Memories flicker, like the reflections of the harbour waters playing on the castle walls. Some memories are so distant that I'm surprised I can still access them, for here, in the shadow of the back of the castle, looking out onto a broad sweep of bay, is the Slab where I learned how to swim. More a slab of concrete than a beach, it was where everyone came to swim in the fifties. The iron railings of the stairs we used for getting in and out of the water are still here, though the wooden changing huts are long gone. Today it's empty and desolate, with broken bottles and litter lying here and there. Across the bay, the Kyrenia Country Club looks down at us from the cliff above. Two versions of me superimpose themselves as I look up at it—one of me as a little girl of seven posing for a photograph on the club's veranda, wearing fashionable capri pants and matching cut off tops that my mother had brought back from a trip to Paris, the other of me as a teenager at a party there, bored and out of place.

We turn back to the harbour and sit down at one of the restaurants to order a drink. Lanterns with cut-out patterns of stars and half moons, Turkish symbols, light up the tables as twilight approaches. Eighteen-year-old me sits down with present day me, along with my ghostly gang of teenage friends, watching the people walking up and down the harbour, greeting our many acquaintances passing by, listening to the boys talking endlessly about cars and the girls gossiping, thinking about the evening ahead, the disco we will all be going to, probably at the Mare Monte hotel a few miles outside Kyrenia, or debating whether to drive to Famagusta, where a whole different scene was taking place along a long golden beach.

Now, as I look around at the boats bobbing up and down in the water, at all those unfamiliar faces milling about in the street, speaking a language I don't understand, my sense of loss increases, as does my awareness that this place is no longer mine, that I am indeed just a visitor, a tourist, who came, saw and left by nightfall. I'm just clinging to a hazy past, a past that is, of course, gone. I realise that it will be impossible to reclaim anything. This place is lost to me forever, something I'm finding very hard to accept.

For old times sake, we leave the harbour through 'the hole in the wall', a narrow corridor between two of the buildings just wide enough to fit one person, emerging onto the backstreets of old Kyrenia with its picturesque whitewashed houses and flagstone streets, the only town on the island reminiscent of Greek island architecture. Yet it is Turkish words that we hear mothers yell at their kids with, making me painfully aware that the clock cannot be turned back. This place once predominantly Greek, is now entirely Turkish.

How did it all go so wrong?

5 A PATTERN OF BEHAVIOUR

It's hard to pinpoint a time in history when one can say with absolute certainty that this was the day things started to go awry. Settle on one day, and a hundred other possibilities leading up to that day come to mind, receding further and further into the past. But how did we get to the point we are today where the island is divided and its people segregated? Is it the result of the century-old murderous feud between Greeks and Turks? Did it arise out of the breakdown of the Ottoman Empire which enabled the Greek populations elsewhere to demand their freedoms, but was delayed in Cyprus because of colonialism? Or was it the outcome of the struggle to implement the vision of a greater Greece by bringing together all the territory that was culturally Greek? If you ask a Cypriot when the Cyprus problem began, he or she will probably give you a different date depending on which side of the divide they come from. Greek Cypriots, especially the younger generation, will tell you it started in 1974 with the Turkish invasion and occupation of the island. Turkish Cypriots will say it started in 1963 with the intercommunal troubles. A few might say it started towards the end of British rule of the island.

Britain was the last (or almost the last) in a long line of conquerors of our island. Throughout history, whoever happened to be the regional alpha male at the time, took their turn on Cyprus. The whore of the Mediterranean, is how some plain-speaking politician, I forget who, once described our island. Julius Caesar had his way with us, before giving us to his best mate Mark Anthony, who in turn gave us to Cleopatra as a token of his love. Alexander the Great, of course, had us too. The Franks, the Byzantines, the Genoese, the Venetians, the Ottomans, all had their turn. So it went down the centuries.

You'd think there would've come a time when we would have said enough, let's go it alone. We didn't. Instead of opting for the single life, instead of relishing having the whole bed to ourselves, what did we do? We hankered after another master. We wanted union with Greece—*enosis*, we called it.

Perhaps a natural aspiration given that the vast majority of us spoke and felt Greek, but did we stop to think about it for a moment? Greece! That economically destitute, no good down and out who kept on getting into fights with his neighbour, and getting his arse kicked at that. And untrustworthy; wouldn't think twice about double-crossing you. Not to mention dictatorial. And it's not as if we didn't know what he was like—*kalamaras* (pen pusher), we called him disparagingly. But we had stars in our eyes, and didn't want to see reality, deluding ourselves that he still had what he had in his youth—the gift of the gab, the healthy body and brilliant mind. From astronomy, to politics, from philosophy to mathematics, he could hold forth on everything!

Truth be told, even Britain was somewhat smitten. So when we flirted with Greece, they tolerated our nonsense. A sentimental, irrational infatuation, they thought. It'll pass. Surely we would see that Greece's best days were so far in the past they were practically non-existent. But we insisted. We had to go. Britain was hurt. After all we've done for you, they said. We built you roads, brought water and electricity to your main towns, planted forests to stop soil erosion, built iron piers at your ports, set up a fair justice system, got rid of locusts and malaria. Tell us, what other country in the Mediterranean is better off than you?

We didn't care. We were in love! Britain didn't understand that that's what comes from not paying us enough attention. They had patronised us, treated us like a stubborn child, or worse, a dumb airhead totally incapable of looking after ourselves. We'll show them, we thought. They're just a fuddy duddy, preferring slippers and sitting in front of the fireplace, to partying all night long. Hot headed as we were, we didn't think twice about kicking out a staid and trustworthy, albeit stodgy master, who valued fair play and justice, in favour of a mad romantic adventure.

It all started civilly enough. From the moment the British set foot on the island we made our intentions perfectly clear. Whenever there was a ceremony, we subjected them to a long boring speech and petition for *enosis*. The British were so fed up of it they almost let it happen in 1915 in return for Greece joining the war. But Greece didn't want us and the offer was withdrawn. We should've got the message then.

Instead we were forced to watch jealously as Greece linked up with other floozies it had split from during its history. Crete was allowed to unite in holy matrimony in 1913, despite having a larger Turkish minority than Cyprus did, although a few did get massacred in the process. After Crete joined, we pined for years to follow suit. In 1931 we got so frustrated, we burned down Government House.

Like a concerned parent telling a disobedient child what the consequences of certain behaviour would be, Britain warned us that the Turks would not be happy if there were a change of sovereignty. What did they want to open their big fat mouth for? Up to that point, the Turkish Cypriots, the outcome of a previous liaison, had been quiet and docile. You hardly even noticed they were there. If the British hadn't said anything, they might never have been any the wiser. Cyprus could quite easily have been transferred to Greece, sleeping Turks and all, without any conflict. The British woke them up!

But the Turks hadn't been asleep at all. They were watching. They didn't want the same thing that had happened to their kin in Crete to happen to them. They started muttering crazy things along the lines of Cyprus has never belonged to Greece, historically its people were not Greek, and geographically it was an extension of Anatolia. They said they would not accept any change in the status of the island without Turkey's consent. In fact, they said, the island should be partitioned. And when thoughts like that are put into words, they can suddenly take off in unexpected ways.

When the British said that Cyprus can 'never' expect to be fully independent, Archbishop Makarios, who had taken on the role of our ethnarch and leader, gave the go-ahead to Colonel George Grivas, a staunch anti-communist, who believed that only violence would get rid of the British from Cyprus, to start a campaign of sabotage using an underground organisation called EOKA. While ostensibly set up to end British rule, it was a nationalist organisation with *enosis* as its ultimate aim.

On 1 April 1955 the transmitters of the Cyprus Broadcasting Service were blown up and a series of simultaneous explosions took place across the island. So began a four year guerrilla war against the British, on a morning that, as Durrell wrote, "like some perfect deception, dawned fine", but which changed the peaceful life on the island forever.

As the fighting got worse and casualties on both sides mounted, the British tried to get out of the hole of 'never' they had dug themselves into. They suggested that the situation might change if we could show that we could govern ourselves in such a way as to safeguard "the interests of all sections of the community".

Archbishop Makarios for the first time agreed to negotiate and in 1956 he and the British Governor of Cyprus, Field Marshall Harding, reached a transitional agreement towards self-rule. The Secretary of State for the Colonies, Alan Lennox-Boyd, arrived on the island to sign the deal, but little did he know how devious Makarios was. The night the meeting was due to take place, nineteen bombs exploded in Nicosia. Makarios and Grivas immediately pointed fingers at each other, but Lennox-Boyd was having none of this. He abruptly ended the meeting telling Makarios, "May God have mercy upon your people". Makarios tried to backtrack, but it was too late. That was probably his biggest mistake and a turning point for Cyprus, one not for the better.

Years later, Makarios admitted in an interview with Italian journalist Oriana Fallaci that he had a penchant for brinkmanship. Boasting about his negotiating tactics, he told Fallaci, "I always enjoyed driving myself to the brink of the abyss, and then stopping just in time not to fall." He overdid it with Lennox-Boyd, and on several occasions after that, and we paid for his arrogance. In this instance he lost Cyprus the opportunity for self rule without the power sharing privileges for Turkish Cypriots, only to end up having to sign a 70:30 power sharing deal with independence five years and many lost lives later.

The British exiled Archbishop Makarios to the Seychelles and brought in an eminent jurist, Lord Radcliffe, to draft a new plan for self-government. But, even though he came up with a plan giving only minority rights to the Turkish Cypriots, in a pattern of behaviour that was to be repeated many times in the future, the Greek Cypriot side rejected it immediately because they didn't get everything they wanted, in this case, *enosis*. As usual, going for something better, we ended up with something worse.

But perhaps the worst thing that happened during this time and which set the scene for all the subsequent events, was that Greek and Turkish Cypriots fell out. In response to the increasing violence, the British relied more and more for support on the Turkish Cypriots, using them to build up the police, filling the gap left by intimidated Greek Cypriots and to form a mobile reserve. Not surprisingly, this drove a wedge between us.

The Turkish Cypriots on their part set up a Turkish paramilitary organisation, the TMT (*Turk Mudya Teskilat*—Turkish Defence Organisation). Rauf Denktash was one of its founders. More significantly, it was directed by the Turkish government. *Taksim*, partition, became its slogan to counter the Greek cry of *enosis*, union. It was at this point that the Cyprus problem turned into an intercommunal struggle.

Grivas started preparing for reprisals against expected Turkish attacks. Whereas he had previously banned the killing of Turks, now he allowed it. November 1957 saw the start of nine months of intercommunal violence. Hundreds of Cypriots were killed. The brutal murders of eight Greek Cypriots in Gionyeli and five Turkish Cypriots outside Kontea by EOKA still loom large in the collective memory of our two communities to this day.

As the island lurched towards civil war, it all started getting a bit too much for the British. They had tried every possible permutation for governing the island and each had been rejected by one or all of the parties involved. Prime Minister Harold Macmillan started believing that Britain didn't really need the whole of the island. "An airfield on long lease or in sovereignty would be enough," he wrote. "Then the Turks and the Greeks could divide the rest of the island between them."

Finally, convinced that partition was not just an idle threat, Makarios agreed to accept independence for Cyprus rather than "*enosis* and only *enosis*" with Greece. The Greek and Turkish foreign ministers met together in Switzerland where they drafted the Zurich Agreement and the Treaties of Guarantee and Alliance. These were then presented to the British and Makarios as a fait accompli. Makarios flew to London accompanied by a forty-one-man delegation from Cyprus to take part in the special conference called to discuss Cyprus, but in the end he had no choice but to sign the deal, one that had been drafted without his participation.

6 WHO ARE WE?

One gorgeous spring Saturday, I'm sitting at the Han basking in the sunshine as it streams in under the arches. It's early and only a few of us are here. Mikis has brought Kokos, a relatively new recruit, who rivals Hasip in rotundness. Even though he struggles with English, he has become a regular, priding himself on being very knowledgeable about the Cyprus problem.

Halil, a permanently joyful fixture at the table, is also here, as always accompanied by Sami, his brother-in-law, who sits quietly, never uttering a word, just happily listening to the conversations around him, and grinning broadly. I smile to acknowledge him, and he smiles back. At first I thought Sami was shy, but then I was told that several years ago, a stroke and subsequent brain operation left him with his memory impaired and unable or unwilling to speak. Nothing his family did could make him utter a single word, until one day he started speaking what they thought at first was gibberish, but which they later realised to their amazement was Greek, which he had learned in his youth working for a Greek Cypriot businessman. Since then Halil has brought Sami regularly to the coffee club, in the belief that coming here, listening to us chat in Greek, would be therapy for him.

I sip my coffee in the bright sunshine and watch the comings and goings in the courtyard through one eye. A couple are browsing through the stands at the nearby craftshop, while a small group sits down at one of the tables nearby. At the far end, Ahmet is standing in the doorway of his kitchen waiting for an order.

Mikis is quietly reading his paper when a Turkish Cypriot man from a nearby table leans over and asks in Greek if he can have a look at it when he's finished.

"Of course," Mikis says. He stops reading immediately and hands it

49

over.

"But does he read Greek?" I ask surprised. It's one thing to speak the other's language as a result of daily use, but to read and write I thought would have required formal tuition.

"Under the British the kids could learn both the Turkish and the Greek," says Halil. His answer confuses me. As far as I knew, both languages were never taught together at school. But Kokos clarifies things for me.

"When the British took over Cyprus in 1878, they kept the existing structures of education in Cyprus. Christian and Moslem schools were kept separate from one another, allowing Greek to be used in the former, and by extension Turkish in the latter," he said. "Unlike in other British colonies, in Cyprus they didn't insist on English being the compulsory language of instruction in the island's schools.

"The British thought Classical Greek was the basis of all Western civilisation," Mikis says, taking a sip of water. "They couldn't very well ban it in Cyprus. So they made an exception." He grins at the dilemma the colonists must have faced.

"Unfortunately this meant that schoolchildren were taught from textbooks produced in Athens which promoted a strong sense of patriotism," Kokos says, a half-smile playing on his lips. "No wonder *enosis*, or union with Greece, became a passionate cause."

"The English School was the only school that had both Greek and Turkish Cypriot pupils by law," says Hasan, who has just sat down together with Hasip and Andreas. "There, classes were taught in English."

"Canon Frank Newham, who founded our school envisioned a multicultural school where there would be mutual respect and brotherhood," Andreas says, raising his hand to call Ahmet. "The original motto he chose for the school was 'Respect Each Other's Feelings'. He would often enter a classroom holding a Greek Cypriot student in one hand and a Turkish Cypriot student in the other. That's why he obliged his fourth year students to learn the language of the other community. And that's why the school adhered to the main religious festivals of both communities. In those days there was no nationalistic parents' association interfering in the daily affairs of the school as there is now."

Hasip makes himself comfortable on a chair next to him, crossing his hands over his belly. "Not teaching both languages in schools was our downfall," he says.

"*Kalimera*," Mikis says in Greek to a man entering the inn. He is carrying a newspaper called *Afrika* tucked under his arm. *Afrika* used to be called *Avrupa* (Europe) but it was critical of the Denktash regime—until one day Denktash closed the paper down and had the owner and editor, Sener Levent, arrested and imprisoned. When he got out of jail he republished his paper renaming it *Afrika* to reflect his view of the state of affairs in the north.

"What does your newspaper say?" Mikis says. "Any good news?"

"*Ta idia*," the man says. Same old same old.

"We're fed up," Mikis says. "How many years?"

The man shrugs, "What can we do?" and continues on his way.

"Do you know who that is?" Mikis says turning back to the table. "It's that Turkish Cypriot who used to get arrested for flying the Cyprus flag alongside the Greek and the Turkish flags on the anniversary of Cyprus' independence."

"They've stopped arresting him now," Halil says.

"But why did they arrest him?" I ask.

"Because for a while it was illegal to display the flag of the Cyprus Republic, instead of the TRNC," Sarper says, who has also just joined us. "Now they don't mind so much."

I say, "Flags may serve to bond groups together but they also increase conflict."

"The British weren't strict enough," Hasip says. "They should've banned the use of the flags of both motherlands."

"It's not the style of the British to be strict," Mikis says. "They tried to find a compromise for us. They came up with all sorts of ideas for self government in stages. But we rejected them all outright. In the end Harding—he was the British governor— accused us of 'refusing what was possible because we were not given what it would have been disastrous to grant'."

Just then Litsa arrives. The group is swelling to its normal size, so another table is added to make room for everyone. "How are you?" she asks, squeezing in next to Hasip. She takes off her sunglasses and smiles hello at everyone.

"*Mia hara*," Hasip replies quickly. "*Kala. Polla kala. Shishi. Bomba*," he continues in ever increasing superlatives of the word 'well'. Litsa throws her head back and laughs her loud raucous laugh.

"He's just learned this in his evening Greek lessons," Andreas explains. "Earlier this morning Hasip came to Hasan's shop and told him 'you look *halia*', dreadful! It's his new word."

"In my lesson the other day I had to write down a whole conversation," Hasip says proudly.

"Yes, the dialogue went like this," Andreas says. "*Gia sou Hasan, ti kanis? Ego ime kala. Esi ise halia.* 'Hello Hasan, how are you? I am well. You look dreadful.' And then he called me up to ask for the correct spelling. Just so he could beat Hasan."

"Is there a big competition between the two of them over who can learn better Greek?" Sarper asks.

"Yes, and Hasan has an advantage because he's a *bakal* and knows all the numbers in Greek," Andreas says. "He gets more of a chance to practise since many Greek speaking Cypriots come to his shop,"

"The other day our teacher suggested she give us a test," Hasan says. "Of course, being cleverer, I suggested she test us on numbers."

"Hasan is a cheat," Andreas says. "He calls me up half an hour before the class to ask for help with his homework. I say, 'but Hasip didn't ask for help.' He says, 'well let's not tell him then'."

"Oh, is that so?" Hasip says, shaking his head in mock disapproval.

"With friends like these you don't need enemies," Hasan says, glaring daggers at Andreas.

But Andreas is no longer listening, having spotted a friend coming towards us in the centre of the courtyard with his two young boys. "*Yia sou Nico!*" he calls.

Nicos waves back, one arm round his youngest.

"*Mashalla*, this Andreas, is worse than us!" Hasip says. "I thought we Turkish Cypriots know everyone, but not only does he know everyone on his side, he knows everyone on our side too!"

"Look at it this way," Andreas says, "it was twenty four per cent of Greek Cypriots who voted YES in the referendum and from those only a portion live in Nicosia, and from those in turn only a portion are willing to cross over to this side. We know them all."

"You mean *you* know them all," Hasan says.

"*Pos ise?*" Nicos says when he and his boys arrive at the table. He and his older son are wearing the uniform of their respective generations—Nicos, baggy jeans and his older son, a tracksuit; the younger boy is in fancy dress.

"*Mia hara*," Hasip replies lazily leaning back in his chair. "*Halia, halia.*" He's like a parrot repeating every word he has learned just for practice or to get a reaction. "Andrea, explain to them what we discovered about *halia.*"

"Yes, they know, Hasip," Andreas says, but obliges. "We found out that *hal* is a Turkish word. It means state, condition. We made it into *hali* in Greek and then gave it a plural and made it *halia.*" The way our two languages interconnect never ceases to fascinate us round this table.

Nicos sits down with his younger boy on his lap. The older one hovers behind him.

"Come *leventi*, let's have a look at you," Andreas tells the boy. "What are you wearing?" The boy looks away embarrassed. He is wearing the white *foustanella*, a pleated skirt worn by the *kleftes* who fought the Ottoman occupation of Greece in 1821.

"He is dressed as a *tsolias* for a school play," his father says grinning sheepishly. He has the typical Mediterranean face of men his age, olive complexion, fleshy jowls and greying hair.

"Ah, yes, the revolution against the Ottomans," Andreas says. He leans towards the boy and says in a low voice, as if sharing a secret. "Look, do you see these people?" He points at Hasan and Hasip. "*These* are the Ottomans. They are the enemy!" he teases. The boy smiles and squirms uncomfortably.

"No, *he* is the Ottoman," Hasan says pointing to Hasip majestically reclining in his chair, arms behind his head and belly protruding. "He is the Ottoman pasha."

Hasip smiles benignly. "Before '74 the Greek Cypriots didn't used to call us Turkish Cypriots, they called us *Othomanos*."

"Just like you used to call us *Christianos*," Andreas says.

"Or *Romios*," Nicos says. Romans.

"*Rum*," Hasan says.

"Actually, *Rum* means a Greek from Cyprus, as opposed to the *Yunanlı*, meaning a Greek from Greece, from Ionia," Sarper says. He goes on to explain that the generic term *Rum* was used at different times in Turkey and the Muslim world to refer to the Greeks living under the Ottomans. The name comes from the Byzantine Greeks who, as the continuation of the Roman Empire, called themselves Romans. They called ancient Greece by the name *Yunan* (Ionia) and ancient Greeks *Yunanlı*, Ionians. Nowadays *Yunanlı* is used for the mainland Greeks and *Rum* for Greek Cypriots, perhaps in an effort to reduce the validity of the Greek Cypriot ethnic alliance with modern Greece.

Andreas says, "I remember when the checkpoints opened I was driving in the area of Kythrea and stopped to ask directions from a lady. 'Do you speak English?' I asked her. She replied in Greek, 'No, I speak Roman!' I thought, Roman? What does she mean? Afterwards I realised she meant Greek."

Sarper reminds us that next week is a holiday on the Greek Cypriot side. "It's also April Fools' day," he points out, his blue eyes twinkling.

"What a coincidence," Hasip says sarcastically.

"Not a coincidence at all," Andreas says.

"The 1st of April was the beginning of EOKA," Sarper says matter-of-factly. He starts reciting in Greek:
"*Itan proti tou Aprili tis EOKA i arhi,*
pou akoustike stin Kipro,
I foni tou Digeni".

Andreas is impressed, and translates: "It was on the first of April, the start of EOKA/ When the voice of Digeni / Was heard in Cyprus. Even we don't remember that!"

"I'm sorry, but it makes my hair stand on end," Litsa says with a shiver. "The destruction of Cyprus, that's when it all started."

"EOKA killed more Greek Cypriots than British or Turkish Cypriots," Mikis says. "If you didn't support them you were considered a traitor, so they killed you. Especially people connected with the Left."

It's true that EOKA, the nationalist guerrilla organisation that fought to end British rule of Cyprus and whose ultimate though unstated aim was union with Greece, was not universally accepted especially as communal violence escalated.

"And what did we achieve?" Litsa says. "We lost half our country. And this mentality still exists today."

Litsa knows all about the brainwashing that goes on in schools. "Up until a few years ago, Greek Cypriot history books stressed that Cypriots were and are Christian Orthodox, excluding all other ethnic groups on the island. Turkish Cypriots are hardly mentioned."

I roll my eyes in exasperation. "No wonder the young are the single demographic group least favourably inclined to reconciliation."

Sarper says, "On our side new history books were introduced in 2004 that moved away from Turkish nationalism to a more Cypriot identity. The books had illustrations showing Greek and Turkish Cypriots looking exactly the same, like identical twins in fact, their arms around each other enjoying a meal together. Unfortunately now that Eroglu's right wing party has come to power, they changed the books again and replaced them with ethnocentric ones, like the ones we had before."

I ask Litsa something that has always puzzled me. How come our teenagers accept all this brainwashing? After all, aren't teenagers hardwired to question and rebel against adults?

"They're just not interested," she says with a wave of her hands. "They're bored with it all. And then there's this sick patriotism that they have… One day I shocked them by telling them 'Cyprus is not Greek'. They said 'what is it then?' I said it's Cypriot. Or European, I suppose. That should be our identity."

"You know what the problem with our country is?" says Hasip. "We never had a Cypriot identity. We've always been either Greek Cypriot or Turkish Cypriot. Never simply Cypriot."

"Actually a British Foreign Office directive exists from the 1930s instructing that the terms Greek Cypriot and Turkish Cypriot should be avoided and replaced by "Greek-speaking" and "Turkish-speaking" Cypriots instead," Mikis says. "That way the island's people would all see themselves as Cypriots but who happened to speak different languages."

"And very right, too!" Andreas says. "Frankly, I don't want people calling me Greek any more. I'm not a Greek. I'm a Cypriot. If you think about what we have in common with the Greeks and all that they've done to us…"

"In that case," Kokos says, "our policemen at the checkpoint are very progressive. They no longer ask if you're a Greek Cypriot, but if you're a Cypriot." He smiles at the irony of it. Everyone laughs.

"That's because they consider only the Greek Cypriots as Cypriots and the Turkish Cypriots as Turks," Andreas says. "In fact many Greek Cypriots do it, too, almost without realising it. It shows they don't think of the Turkish Cypriots as one of them, but something other. Personally I tell them off."

"Tests have shown that Greek and Turkish Cypriot DNA is closer to each other than to each of our motherlands," says Mikis. "The nationalists hated that idea. They tried to suppress it when it came out. Now they say that the Turkish Cypriots were actually Greek Cypriots who had converted to Islam during Ottoman times in order to avoid paying the exorbitant taxes that were imposed on the Greek population of the island by the Ottoman rulers."

Andreas says, "Yes, and apparently after Ottoman rule when the British took over and some of them wanted to convert back, the Archbishop wouldn't let them."

Hasip says, "The emphasis was always either on being Turkish or Greek, never Cypriot."

Kokos says, "For many years if you said you were a Cypriot, you got beaten up." He shakes his head sadly. "That's how they deprived us of our principal identity."

"At least one good thing happened as a result of '74—the Greek Cypriots started calling themselves Cypriots," Hasip says and laughs. "But up until ten years ago, Turkish Cypriots never did. We felt we had been chucked out, that you didn't want us." There's a sadness in his eyes as he says this.

Kokos says, "For Greek Cypriots the big blow was the coup and invasion. It put an end to dreams of *enosis*." He looks around the table to see the effect of his words. "It hasn't been spoken about since. We finally learned our geopolitical lesson."

"We should start educating our children about these things in primary school," Hasip says, scratching his head. "I wonder if it's not too late. And we should encourage our children to marry someone from the opposite community."

"That didn't stop animosities elsewhere in the world," I remark gloomily. "I'm thinking of Rwanda, where people even massacred members of their own family."

The table has no explanation for that.

The man from the next table, the one who borrowed Mikis' newspaper, leans over to return it. "You have many crazy people on your side," he says in Greek, miming circles above his head. His tone isn't confrontational, just stating what he thinks is a fact.

Kokos bristles. He then lets forth a quiet stream of passionate Greek even I have trouble following, let alone the man. "You're right, there are a lot of crazy people on our side. Probably a lot more than on yours. But you too have your share of crazies. Let me tell you, you're talking to a guy who as a kid watched one group of Turkish Cypriots beat his dad up leaving him for dead, lying on the ground with a dislocated jaw, and then watched another group of Turkish Cypriots come and carry him to safety into their homes, tie up his jaw and take him to hospital."

The man listens to him expressionless. Kokos turns to us to continue his story in more detail. "In the late fifties, my father was involved with the Left, so there was always someone from EOKA on the pavement outside our house watching him. We used to live in the old town, a few metres from the Ayios Kasianos roadblock. The first clashes between Greek Cypriots and Turkish Cypriots were in 1956. I don't remember those, but I do remember 1958. There had been trouble brewing and my father told us not to go to school, but we disobeyed him, as it was only a few hundred metres down the road. When my father heard that a bunch of Turkish Cypriot extremists were in the neighbourhood, he came to get us. Holding each of us by the hand, he had just managed to get about half-way home when the nationalists surrounded us. One of them ran at him and kneed him in the back. We let go of his hands and watched as he collapsed in the street. My brother was ten and I was eight. Three or four others started kicking him. After they left, our Turkish Cypriot neighbours ran over and carried him into one of their homes. They bandaged his broken jaw and called my mother, who arranged for him to be taken to hospital where he was guarded by the British." He turns back to the man at the next table again, who has been half-listening while sipping his coffee. "I ask you, who are the real Turkish Cypriots, the ones who beat him up or the ones who saved him?"

The man shrugs, in a way that says, that's life. Kokos turns back to us again. "Years later I decided to investigate that period. I read all the books and studies I could find. I became an expert on the Cyprus problem. I discovered that at that time about a hundred Cypriots were killed in one month—in Gionyeli, in Kontemenos. We were lucky we survived."

The hodja's wail starts up and somewhat drowns out the discussion. It's noon. Activity in the courtyard has picked up and appetising smells of food entice us from the restaurants across the way.

"*Na pame fae?*" Hasip says.

"*Na pame na fame,*" corrects Andreas. "I don't believe it, he's talking about food again! We are not talking about food! We're talking about serious things at this table."

Hasip sits up straight and says solemnly, "Food is a very serious thing."

"Actually, more important is that we should discuss the *lale*, the *tulipa cypria*, and our trip to the Karpas," Andreas says, suddenly remembering an excursion the coffee club is planning. The dark blood red Cyprus tulips, which are endemic to the island, are flowering and can be seen in only in a few select spots each spring. One of these is in the Karpas peninsula, a wild and beautiful part of the north, which is where we are going.

Andreas' face suddenly darkens. "Would you believe that the other day someone on Facebook criticised me for writing Karpaz, with a 'z' like the Turks do, instead of Karpas with an 's'? They accused me of being a Turk lover!"

Halil leans towards him from the opposite end of the table and laughs. "Don't worry, Andreas," he says. "On our side they are accusing us of being Greek lovers all the time."

Andreas gives him a half smile and turns to Sarper. "So, Sarper, did you find out if the tulips are in bloom?"

7 TULIPA CYPRIA

"Our mission," Mikis says, "is to find the origin of the name of the village we are going to."

We are heading for the village of Kaleburnu in Turkish, Galinoporni in Greek, in the Karpas peninsula. Suleyman, Andreas, Mikis, Kokos, Sarper, their wives and I, as well as a few others, have gathered at Mustafa's petrol station on the outskirts of northern Nicosia, mainly because there's room here for everyone to park, but also because Mustafa is a traitor like us, an honorary coffee club member, having worked hard during the referendum to change hearts and minds in the north. I am on my own, as Stelios suffers from hay fever so avoids going out into the fields in spring. It's a beautiful mild day, hazy but warm.

"Do we have a theory about its etymology?" I ask as we stand around waiting for everyone to arrive.

"As a matter of fact, we do," Andreas says shielding his eyes from the sun, which is bright despite the haze. "The story goes that a ship full of prostitutes arrived in the Karpas a long time ago. "

"That's why it's called the oldest profession," says Mikis. "It existed even then." He laughs at his own joke, his cheeks a shade redder than they normally are.

"That explains the 'porni' part of the name, now why the 'galino', I don't know," Andreas continues. He flicks his hair back and puts on his sunglasses. "Maybe they were French, or Gallic. Or perhaps they all had blue eyes. *Galazio* in Greek means sky blue."

"Maybe they were Venetians," Suleyman says.

"We are waiting for three more cars," Andreas says. "Ali, Hasip and Veli. Veli has seven people in his car. Does everyone know Veli? He is a Turkish Cypriot who lives in the south."

I don't, so Sarper fills me in. Veli's father was head of Barclays bank in

Famagusta and has been missing since 1964. When Veli was just four, his father was abducted from his office and never came home. The Committee of Missing Persons recently discovered his body along with five others down a dry well in what used to be orange groves in the southern part of the town. He had been shot three times—one bullet hole was clearly visible in his cranium, the others in his pelvis and torso.

"Have we booked the restaurant?" Andreas asks Sarper who has undertaken the responsibility of organising lunch.

"As soon as we know exactly how many we are, I will call the man at the restaurant so he can put extra pieces of meat on the barbecue," Sarper says. "He's making *kleftiko*. But there might not be enough." He seems slightly anxious about it.

"No problem," Andreas says to reassure him. "If there's not enough *kleftiko*, we will have *bulgur*."

I chat with Mustafa, who I don't get to see very often. He never attends on Saturdays, though he does on occasion join us on our excursions. I first met him at a workshop shortly after the referendum when we were brainstorming ideas on ways to proceed after the NO vote. He was the facilitator deftly fielding people's interjections in his gentle and accommodating way.

I'm curious about how the opening of the checkpoints affected prices between north and south. The price of petrol is a case in point. When the borders first opened it was a lot cheaper to fill up in the north, and it became a reason for Greek Cypriots to cross to the other side. Gradually, the authorities changed this, and nowadays the price is more or less the same. I wonder out loud how they do that.

"I believe a committee keeps prices the same," Mustafa tells me. "It's a secret committee. They don't want us to know about it. I don't mean a committee with Turkey, but with the south. Neither side wants to see cheaper prices on the other side."

"At least that's one thing they manage to agree about," I say. "Especially since most of it is tax."

"Money will always find a way round barriers," Mustafa says. "It's a basic law of economics."

Hasip pulls up in his four by four. His wife, Sevil, is sitting next to him and Hasan and his wife, Nurdan, are in the back. "Good morning, good morning!" Hasip says beaming, his elbow sticking out of the car window. "Nice to see you again!"

"Is this Cypriot time, or is it English time?" Andreas says, pointedly looking at his watch. We were supposed to meet at nine, but it's already ten o'clock.

"Since we are going to the Karpas, this is Karpasiti time," Suleyman says affably, his Panama hat casting a shadow over half of his face.

"*Ti kaneis?*" Hasip says enquiring about everyone's well-being. "Ise kala?"

"*Doksa to Theo*," Suleyman says, thanking God.

"*Halia, halia,*" everyone else choruses.

"*Halia mavra,*" Andreas says.

"Oh, I don't know that one," Hasip says.

"It's one stage worse than *halia.*"

"Andrea, which way are we going to go?" Hasip asks getting out of the car and joining us in the middle of the petrol station.

"Since we're small dictators, we have already decided that we are going to go along the new Kyrenia/Girne road to the east, we will stop for coffee at Davlos/Kaplica, and then we will go to find the Cyprus tulips. From there we will go to Kaleburnu/Galinoporni for this huge lunch that Sarper has ordered for us. We will come back via Bogaz along the Famagusta road."

"I like it," Hasip says. "Especially the huge lunch!"

"You see, dictators know what they're doing," Andreas says.

"I always said that good dictators are better than democracy."

"You mean benevolent despots," Mikis says.

"As my father used to say, *opou eshi pollous petinous arkei na ximerosei*— where there's too many cockerels, day break takes longer," Hasip says, reciting one of a few Cypriot sayings he knows off by heart. "You need someone to take decisions."

"It's decided then," Andreas says. "Hasip will lead us."

"But who will lead Hasip?" Mikis asks.

"Hasip doesn't need anybody to lead him," Hasan says. "He will smell the lunch from miles away and find his way!"

Before long everyone has arrived. The Bulgarian contingent, Maria and Electra, is also here. They're not really Bulgarians, we just call them that because they became friends while studying in Bulgaria. Electra was actually born in Greece and married a Greek Cypriot who has been missing since the war, leaving her to raise her young children all alone, while Maria, married a Turkish Cypriot. Hasip's brother, Ali, also arrives with his wife, Salise, and Veli pulls up in a four by four brimming with people.

Andreas starts organising who will go with whom so no one has to drive alone. He and I join Ali. There are seven cars in all, parked at the side of the main road waiting to set off. As we wait for everyone to gather, one car peels itself off the line of parked cars and tears off down the road.

"Is that Mustafa?" Andreas says doing a double take. "Where does he think he's going?"

"Didn't he see us?" Ali says. "How could he miss seven cars one behind the other like this?"

"He's driving fast because he thinks he's lost us and is trying to catch up!" Andreas says, laughing. "That's so typical of him. He's always getting lost. He'll turn back soon."

"He's probably taking the Famagusta road. Chances are we'll meet up with him at Kumyali," Ali says. He picks up his mobile and starts speaking in Turkish. When he hangs up, he laughs. "You were right, he thought we had all set off and he was driving fast to catch up with us! He's turning back now."

"Good, the Kyrenia road is a much nicer drive," Andreas says.

We set off through the suburbs of northern Nicosia, through what I think must be Gionyeli, the village we used to drive through with the convoy, but which now is a residential part of the town. We stop briefly at a junction which, even though it's a roundabout, also has traffic lights on which a timer lets you know in how many seconds the light will change. There's nothing like that in the south. We turn right, past the roundabout festooned with red and white Turkish and Turkish Cypriot flags and onto the new motorway leading up towards the Kyrenia pass. Ali slows down for the speed camera that he knows is hidden there. Bright spring annuals in specially created flower beds lend splashes of colour to the greyness of the road.

"Was that Neshe?" Andreas says as a car overtakes us. Suleyman's wife is in the driving seat, judging by the flash of red hair I catch sight of through the car window. "Looks like she is now leading the way. Does she know that Hasip wants us to stop for coffee along the way?" Yet another car overtakes us. "And now there goes Kokos!"

"Why is Kokos overtaking us?" Ali says.

"Probably because Neshe overtook us and he was following her. We're all changing positions," Andreas says. "I think it must be Suleyman trying to be clever." He waits to see if there are any more realignments, but it seems the group has finally settled down.

"So, Ali, try and think of a nice place where we can stop for coffee."

"We could stop in Kaplica," Ali says. "It's nice there, by the sea."

"Yes, Davlos is very nice," Andreas says. "How is Hasip's back? He's been having some trouble recently. Finding it difficult to walk."

"His legs are ok. But it's age."

"Ali, it's not his age," Andreas objects. "It's his weight. He keeps telling me, it's old age. But I know eighty year olds who go for walks all around Nicosia."

The phone rings. "It must be Mustafa again," Andreas says laughing.

Ali answers and we hear him say, "*Bogaz, iki kilometr.*"

"Tell him, NOT the Famagusta Bogaz!" Andreas says. "We might lose him again!"

Turning to me he explains that there is a place called Bogaz just here where the road turns up towards the pass through the Kyrenia range, not to be confused with the village of the same name on the east coast where we are heading.

"*Bogaz* means a passage, an opening," Ali says, "that's why there are many places called Bogaz in Cyprus."

"There is a military post up here," Ali says indicating a spot in the hills above us. We have now turned up into the mountain and are heading towards the pass.

"There always was as far back as I can remember," I say. In the '60s when the Turkish Cypriots controlled the Kyrenia road, Greek Cypriots could only travel along it by UN convoy unless you had permission if you were a foreigner, like my father had, because he was from Greece.

"On the left hand side is the village of Ayirda," Andreas recalls. "It was one of the biggest enclaves in the '60s, the Nicosia Ayirda enclave."

As we drive, my memories come flooding in as they always do in these parts. We used to travel along this road from Kyrenia very early in the morning in order to go to school in Nicosia. In those days it was a very windy road and my sister would invariably get car sick. I remember the authorities were trying to improve the road at the time and were in the process of dynamiting the mountainside so as to widen it.

"I think this is one of the most beautiful parts of Cyprus," Andreas says looking out of the window. To our left the craggy grey rock of the mountain soars above us, dotted with bushes and stunted pine trees. To the right, the whole of the Mesaoria plain, the vast flatland that links the two mountain ranges of the island, spreads out before us, with Nicosia like a huge sprawling metropolis just below us, the division invisible from up here.

"It's especially beautiful when you go through the pass," I say and minutes later, the whole coast of Kyrenia opens out in front of us, the sea today more opalescent than lapis lazuli, the urban sprawl as always a stab in the heart.

We hurtle down towards the town, making our way past a busy junction, then turning east to pick up the coastal road and less populated regions. In the green hills above us lies beautiful Bellapais, where Durrell used to live, with its majestic abbey surveying the land and the famous Tree of Idleness restaurant where we enjoyed many a family outing together with some family friends who also lived just above the village. I briefly wonder what our lives would be like if we all were to get our houses back again.

I raise the million-dollar question: "Ali, do you think Turkey wants a solution?"

Ali thinks a moment then says, "Erdogan only wants to be seen to want a settlement. Even just before the referendum, he was not negotiating."

"Strange, I have the opposite impression," I say. "I thought the Greek Cypriots were the ones not negotiating. I believe Turkey wants a solution so as to join the European Union. They wanted it at the time of the referendum and I believe they still want it now."

"Did they want a solution, or did they want to be *seen* to want a solution?" Andreas says, echoing Ali.

Ali says, "Now they are just using the credit they gained for supporting a solution in order to start negotiations with the EU." He slows down briefly to let a car overtake him. "That's a big thing for them. A major political gain for Erdogan."

"So you are pessimistic?"

"For this round of talks at least, yes," he says. "Turkey always wanted to control the northern part of Cyprus."

"That's debatable," Andreas says. "When they have a huge base in Incirlik, what do they need a base in Cyprus for?"

"Didn't they want to protect the Turkish Cypriots?" I ask.

"The coup was just an excuse," Ali says.

"But it was a very valid excuse," Andreas says.

"Yes, but why did they stay for forty years?" I say.

Ali says, "I believe we came to this because in 1950 the Orthodox church of Cyprus held a referendum asking: Do you want to unite with Greece? The Turkish Cypriots did not vote. There is evidence that only forty-two out of a population of fifty thousand voted. A lot of Greek Cypriots didn't vote either. But from those who did vote, ninety-six per cent voted for union with Greece. This was the beginning of the separation of the two communities."

"It all goes back to *enosis*," I say. "Turkey did what it did as an answer to *enosis*."

After the Bellapais turning, it becomes less populated until it's just countryside with olive trees, carob trees and low growing shrubs. The sea, as we drive along the coast, is calm and mellow and seems to blend into the sky. The coastline here consists of jagged volcanic rocks interspersed with smooth white ones. There's something vaguely familiar about it, though I can't quite put my finger on what—a family boat trip, perhaps, a Sunday picnic, a deserted beach with a lagoon. I make a mental note to come back with Stelios and explore the area one day.

After about an hour and a half we arrive at Davlos, which is called Kaplica now. Greek Cypriots get incensed that the Turkish Cypriots changed place names, our propaganda claiming it was all part of their plan to 'Turkify' the north. Surely it's natural to name the places you are living in with words in your own language. We park the cars and pile out, and head instinctively towards the sea, gathering at the beach bar, which is now deserted, the plastic chairs piled on top of the tables. One by one we take them down, while someone goes up to the restaurant in search of a waiter to take our order. Mustafa has caught up with us and joins us in time for coffee.

"From now on we should make Mustafa lead the way," Andreas announces loudly. "Since he's always getting lost, we are bound to have a group adventure!"

"One time we had a meeting in Nicosia," Hasan remembers, "but Mustafa drove all the way to Limassol!" Everyone laughs, including Mustafa.

We drink our coffee entertained by more stories of poor Mustafa's absentmindedness. But when we get back into the car, I'm disconcerted to find that Mustafa is indeed leading the way.

The road takes us back through the mountain range in order to come out onto the eastern coast. Above us hidden in the rocky crags, sits the castle of Kantara, with spectacular views in all directions, east along the Karpas peninsula known as the panhandle, south towards Famagusta bay, and west along the Kyrenia coast.

"We used to have a house in Kantara and would come here in the holidays," Ali says.

"So did my brother-in-law's family," Andreas says.

We pass a sign. "Balalan," Ali reads. "What was the original name?"

Andreas has a map that gives both the Greek and Turkish place names. He looks it up.

"Platanissos," he says. "It used to be a Turkish Cypriot village. The next village is Leonariso. Just a minute, let me tell you the name in Turkish." He consults the map again. "Here it is. It's called Ziyamet."

"Ah, Ziyamet," says Ali and his wife in unison.

"A friend of mine was telling me that there was always trouble in Platanissos in the '60s," Andreas says. "He comes from a nearby village and remembered that one time they couldn't go to the beach because to get to it they had to go through Platanissos. Imagine that! Not being able to go to the beach because of the troubles!" He pauses a moment thinking about it. "The same thing happened on the western side of the island, in Morphou. There were two small Turkish Cypriot enclaves there, Lefka and Gaziveren, where Suleyman lives now. I used to go and visit my grandmother in Morphou and sometimes kids used to throw stones at us as we went by. In Gionyeli too."

"In 1958, I think the British dumped a busload of Greek Cypriots near Gionyeli," says Ali. "They then told the Gionyeli people that the Greeks were coming to kill them, so the Turks found the Greeks and massacred them."

"The Greek Cypriots were from Kontemenos," adds Andreas. "It was one of the big incidents of the '50s. But I don't think the British did this on purpose."

"How come, then, the Gionyeli people knew… " says Ali.

"Is it so difficult to jump to conclusions? Suddenly you see a group of Greek men in your village—isn't it normal to believe that they're coming to kill you, especially when you're already tense, when you already have this anxiety… "

"It was a setup," Ali insists.

"I'm not sure it was a setup," I tell him, fed up with all the conspiracy theories that have always enabled us to shirk responsibility for the consequences of our actions. "It was probably bad timing. Or incompetence more likely. Maybe the British just got orders to drop them off anywhere, because there were other incidents breaking out at the time, and they needed the soldiers elsewhere. From what I read, that's what I believe happened."

"Some things we can never be sure of what happened," Andreas says. "That's why we need a Truth and Reconciliation Commission, where we can each apologise for our mistakes and forget about the past. That's the only way we can build a future."

"Our recent history in Cyprus is full of misunderstandings," I say. "All these mutual suspicions created the problems and made us jump to conclusions about each other."

"But was it really misunderstandings, "Andreas says, "or was it because we Greek Cypriots did not accept the independent country we had been given? Do you know what they did on the first anniversary of independence? They held a gathering in the central square of Nicosia to celebrate the referendum they had held in 1950 in favour of *enosis*! I mean, how can you have a new country and still be talking about *enosis*? Makarios should have told the people, we tried for *enosis* but we got independence. It's just as good, if not better."

"And we should have learned to live with it," Ali agrees.

"He didn't have the vision," Andreas continues. "He allowed himself to be swayed by the nationalists. Instead of standing up to them, he went along with them, saying he too was in favour of enosis. Because basically he was. Every time my father met him, he would come back furious, saying, this man is playing with fire, all he talks about is Greeks. My father was very farsighted. I remember when I was fifteen I had to fill out a form they had given us at the English School, and I asked him what to put for nationality. I was going to write Greek Cypriot, but he shouted at me, he said 'NO, NO, for goodness sakes, get it into your head, you are a Cypriot! Don't ever write Greek Cypriot anywhere.' I remember that to this day. Greek Cypriot is not a nationality. But people insisted on it. And they still do."

There is silence in the car as we mull over the events of the past. We are now back on the south side of the mountains, the flat plains spreading out ahead of us, fields of red and yellow wild flowers like decorative carpets in between the olive trees.

"Why is Mustafa slowing down?" Andreas says after a while. "Is he lost again?"

We have reached a crossroads and Ali and Andreas are not sure which way to go. Ali thinks we should turn left but Andreas spots a sign.

"Kaleburnu!" he cries. "We're on the right track. With Mustafa as our leader, we needn't worry about a thing!"

"This is probably only the second time I've come down this way," Ali says.

"Well, it's not as if this road leads anywhere important," Andreas says, as we go through successive sleepy villages with hardly anyone in sight.

A little further down the road another signpost appears.

"I think we're in Ziyamet," I say consulting Andreas' map. "The next village must be Lythrangomi, with that famous church, the one from where they stole those mosaics."

Sure enough round the very next bend the church of Kanakaria materialises beside us and, before I have time to take it in—pale stone walls, tiled dome on top of tiled dome, and a belfry—we've already driven past. The church became famous in the late '80s for one of the most widely publicised cases of art theft in the world. After 1974 its priceless 4th century mosaics were removed from its apse and sold on the black market. The mosaics, each measuring about two square feet and composed of hundreds of jewel-like bits of glass, marble and stone, are unique specimens of Byzantine art that survived an edict by the Emperor of Byzantium imposing the destruction of all images of sacred figures. Cyprus, being a backwater of the Byzantine Empire, didn't comply. They depict Christ as a young boy, various apostles and an archangel.

"They are said to rival the mosaics of Ravenna in beauty," I tell them. "The antiquity smugglers managed to get over a million for them, but I'm sure they must be worth a lot more."

They were sold to an inexperienced Indianapolis art dealer, Peg Goldberg, who fell in love with them. She then tried to resell them herself to the Getty museum in 1988, but the Getty alerted the Cyprus authorities who sued for their return and won in a landmark court ruling that opened the way for recovering stolen archaeological treasures worldwide.

"It changed the global art market and made it more difficult for museums and auction houses to sell artefacts whose provenance they cannot prove," I say.

"Where are the mosaics now?" Ali asks.

I tell him they have since been repatriated and are on display in the Byzantine Museum in Nicosia. "It's a shame we can't see them where they were supposed to be, but they are still worth seeing. I have, and can tell you they truly are magnificent."

"Derince," Ali says, as we pass yet another signpost hidden behind some bushes.

"Derince is Vathilakas," Andreas says. "Avtepe/Ay Symeon is next. That's where we have to try and find the field with the tulips. Ay Symeon was originally a Turkish village but they all spoke Greek in this area."

"Salise's grandmother also spoke Greek," Ali says and his wife, who is quiet and serious, smiles at us.

"Really? Where was she from?" Andreas asks her.

"From a small village in Paphos, Istinço," Salise replies.

"But are you all from Istinço?" I ask, knowing that Hasip and Ali's family were from there too.

"Our families knew each other," Ali says. "But we met later. My mother left the village when she was three years old, and my father when he was seven. They were friends in Nicosia."

"And when they found out that they were both from Istinço, the love affair blossomed," Andreas teases.

"Istinço is like the word Istanbul, which comes from the Greek 'Is tin Poli' meaning 'to town'," Andreas says. "So 'is tin Tzio' means 'to the village called Tzio'. In Turkish 'Çö'." He pauses a moment, then adds, "There were more donkeys than people there."

Yet another signpost appears, this time with a picture of a tulip on it.

"Aha! You see, we're on the right track," Andreas says. "It says *Lale*."

"*Medosh* tulip," I read under the picture. "I suppose it means tulip of the meadows."

"In Greek *metoshi* means outpost, or branch," Andreas says.

We turn off the main road and onto a very uneven dirt road. We are shaken vigorously in all directions, as Ali flies over the bumps and swerves to avoid the larger ruts in the road.

"I remember this road, from last time we came," Andreas says, his voice vibrating with the motion of the car. "It goes on like this for quite a while."

I try to keep from feeling nauseous by looking out of the window. "I don't see any tulips whatsoever," I say.

"They only grow in one specific spot," Andreas says. "A small field of a few hundred metres. I hope we can find it."

The fields are green thanks to the recent rains, and tall yellow clusters of wild mustard line the road. Here and there occasional wild poppies add accents of red. The dirt track seems to go on forever.

"Sarper is probably worried about lunch," Andreas says looking at the time. "We told the restaurant we'd be there round one o'clock and it's already quarter to. But I suppose it doesn't matter if we're a little late…"

Eventually the road peters out, ending in a large field. We discover that we are not the only ones with the same idea. Two other cars are also parked in the field. One of them has diplomatic number plates. The word quickly spreads that it belongs to the new British High Commissioner. Typical, I think, the British always seem to know where the best spots are wherever they are in the world. The High Commissioner and his family are in the process of getting back into their car to leave and we respectfully nod hello as we head towards the tulip field, picking our way over stones and around shrubs. Even Hasip attempts the walk, wobbling precariously as he goes.

Andreas slows down to make sure he's alright. "Hasipaki, are you managing it?" he asks him, using the Greek diminutive to express his concern. "Soon we will go back for *yemek*."

"Yes, that's a much better idea," Hasip says, panting.

It's not long before we spot the tulips, like dark drops of blood protected by sheaths of green leaves dotted all over just one small area. It's towards the end of the season so there aren't that many of them left, but enough for us to marvel at.

"Are these Greek Cypriot tulips or Turkish Cypriot tulips?" Hasip asks when he finally gets there.

"They are definitely Turkish Cypriot tulips," Hasan says, "because they were born in the TRNC."

"Certainly not," Andreas says. "They have been here since Mycaenian times, so they must be Greek."

We spread out all over the field to examine the tulips, with each clump of tulip surrounded by a clump of coffee club members, some bending over to examine and photograph the flowers with their phones, others posing for a selfie with the tulips in the background. We are surrounded by the typical Cypriot maquis of low growing scrub, and ancient volcanic rock formations dating back to the beginnings of time before humans roamed the earth. A few birds fly low over the bush tops catching airborne insects and filling the air with their songs. Further down, I can just make out the blue of the sea in the distance, from where it is believed the first human beings came and settled on the island, the earliest remains of whom were found in caves on these eastern shores. I feel angry with my compatriots for not wanting to come here and see their land for themselves. They don't want to feel like tourists in their own land, they say, in one of their meaningless slogans. Of course they feel like tourists if they hardly ever come. Besides, how are they less of a tourist when they visit Paphos or the Troodos mountains? Clearly it's the existence of the border that makes them feel like that, ironic because it's us, here, who refuse to recognise the border, by crossing and acting as if it does not exist. At the end of the day, all states are but figments of our imagination, a story we tell each other and persuade each other to subscribe to. Their story is one of two separate communities living in separate areas. It's not mine. Mine is of one country as a whole, one people—Cypriots, with a shared past, not always a friendly past, but about which we must find a way to agree so that we can move forward as one.

"You must admit," Andreas says, "that Mustafa managed to get us here after all and find the tulips."

"Even though we really meant to see the tulips in Paphos," Hasan says.

Having examined the tulips for about half an hour, we decide that we have seen enough of them and can now go and eat. Ali is now leading the pack to find the restaurant in the village of Kaleburnu/Galinoporni, although he's not sure of the way. But in Cyprus you can't go far wrong, just as long as you head in the general direction of where you want to go, you're bound to end up in the right place in the end. When we get to a fork with a signpost to the village, Ali wants to ignore it, thinking the other way is a shortcut.

Andreas disagrees. "It's better we follow the sign so we don't get lost," he says. "Otherwise Mustafa will make fun of us."

The village is perched on a hillside and feels like it could be a village in the Troodos mountains without the greenery. The restaurant owners are waiting for us and welcome us warmly in both Greek and Turkish. A group of men sitting on the narrow veranda playing backgammon, stop for a moment in mid dice throw as we go by, staring at us as if we are aliens. Inside, two long tables have been laid out and no sooner do we all sit down, than plates of *kleftiko*, potatoes and salad are carried out and placed before each of us.

Sarper is fussing round the table making sure everyone has what they need. "Is there enough food? Is everyone happy? There is also chicken if anyone doesn't want *kleftiko*..."

"If you don't like the food, you can blame Sarper," Andreas tells everyone pointing a finger at him. "*He* is the organiser."

After lunch some people want to set off home as it's a long way back, while the rest of us want to stop for coffee at Bogaz near Famagusta. The convoy is therefore smaller now, though Mustafa is still with us. We catch glimpses of the sea to our left as we drive south while to the right fields of corn or barley sway in the breeze.

At Bogaz the late afternoon sea is flat. We sit down at one of several seaside restaurants which at this time of year are empty and watch the boats bobbing up and down. A long table is prepared for us again and a waiter takes our order. Mustafa, his wife and a few others go for a stroll along the beach. I sit down with the rest enjoying the chatter, the sound of the silvery waves lapping gently against the shore, and the view of the bay. Every now and then my eyes drift towards Famagusta at the far end of the bay where the ethereal cluster of high rise apartment blocks and hotels of Varosha (which in Turkish means suburb), shimmers along the coast. In its heyday it was the island's main tourist resort, thanks to its shallow turquoise waters along a long beach of golden sand. Today it lies frozen in time, empty and deserted, dubbed a 'ghost town', since all of its predominantly Greek

Cypriot inhabitants fled in 1974 when the town was bombed by Turkish jets. The Turkish Cypriots subsequently never populated it, fencing it off instead and keeping it as a bargaining chip in expectation of a future deal that never came.

"Thank you for the organisation, Sarper," Andreas says, when we get up to go. "But next time please make sure there are more *lale*."

We say our goodbyes, as from here everyone is to make their own way back to Nicosia.

"Try not to get lost, Mustafa," Hasip says as he gets into his car.

The road back takes us past Trikomo/Iskele, the village of my maternal grandmother and General Grivas. They were at school together. "This man will destroy us," she once told me prophetically, remembering what a troublemaker he was growing up.

We drive along the main Famagusta to Nicosia road with Ali telling us a bit about Denktash. He says he was never on good terms with anyone who wanted a settlement in Cyprus, and quarrelled with almost every Turkish president from Ciler to Ozal. In the final analysis, he says, he harmed the Turkish Cypriot community. "The suffering that our community went through all those years was because of Denktash."

As he talks I think about how our leaders' nationalist policies drove us apart. Granted, it's easy to say with hindsight, as they weren't to know how things would turn out and each no doubt did what he thought was best for the people, but ultimately they proved to be short-sighted.

Back home the first thing I do is google Kaleburnu. Wikipedia says:

"The name of this village in Greek means tranquil-morning. It derives from the words γαλήνη (galini), which means tranquility and πωρνόν (pornon) which in the Greek Cypriot dialect means morning. Locals speak both Turkish and Greek. The correct interpretation of πωρνή (porni) in the Cypriot dialect is morning (the Greek πρωινή /proini), so the name means tranquility of the morning."

8 STORIES WE TELL OURSELVES

When my son was in Middle School he came home one day telling me that his history teacher had behaved very strangely towards the end of the class. He had juggled a few oranges, thrown a pile of exercise books on the floor, crumpled up some paper and run round the desk hollering. Their task for homework was to write a paragraph about what happened in the last few minutes of class. The next day in class, to their surprise they found that everyone had a slightly different version of events. That's history, the teacher said. Our job as students of history is to gather all the different sources and versions of events together and reach a consensus as to what occurred in the past.

Cyprus has one of the longest recorded histories going back at least 10,000 years. While no one contests events in the distant annals of time, when it comes to our recent history, consensus is less apparent. From independence onwards our interpretation of what happened varies according to who is telling the story, with Greek Cypriots telling a different version of events from Turkish Cypriots.

The dominant narrative on the Greek Cypriot side is that independence was imposed on us and therefore we were not morally bound to it; the 1960 constitution was unfair and biased in favour of the Turkish Cypriots and we were justified in trying to amend it; Turkey had a plan all along to partition the island; they encouraged the Turkish Cypriots to undermine the Cyprus government, mount a carefully planned rebellion, and withdraw into enclaves. The coup was staged by the CIA; we are victims of Turkey's expansionist and partitionist plans.

The Turkish Cypriot narrative holds that the Greek Cypriots never regarded us as equal partners in the new state of 1960; the Greek Cypriots provoked the conflict by first delaying implementing the constitution to which we were co-signatories and then attempting to scrap it; the Greek

Cypriots all along planned to unite the island with Greece and exterminate us; we are victims just reacting to the violence started by the Greek Cypriots. Turkey came to save us.

Did Makarios ever intend the 1960 constitution to work, or did he continue to harbour dreams about *enosis*? Did Turkey have a plan to partition the island, and sit patiently like a cat waiting for its prey, until the Greeks made a mistake? Did the Turkish Cypriot leadership help things along by putting up obstacles to prove that the new constitution was unworkable?

The truth was probably six of one and half a dozen of the other. As an American observer noted, "It was neither a carefully planned Turkish rebellion, as the Greeks maintained, nor a systematic attempt to exterminate the Turkish population, as some of the Turkish spokesmen alleged." We all overreacted.

Clearly the creation of the Republic of Cyprus in 1960 was a big disappointment for both sides. Nobody was happy with it. Greek Cypriots felt that, as a majority, their wishes had been ignored. They hadn't fought for independence, but for *enosis* and they didn't get it. Likewise, the Turkish Cypriots didn't get partition and their own state. The Greek Cypriots felt that whatever wasn't enosis was unfair, the Turkish Cypriots felt that whatever wasn't partition or total equality was unfair. Nobody thought that maybe a Cypriot nation might not be such a bad thing.

We remained conscious of our Greekness or Turkishness and our respective leaders never stopped reminding us that our first loyalties were to our own communities, our own groups. So the 1960 constitution brought into being a state but not a nation. The concept of a Cypriot identity did not exist.

Both leaderships did their best to create mistrust between us. Like a couple of misbehaving children, each side tried to prove that the constitution wasn't working because it was all the other side's fault. Problems arose that could have been solved but weren't because there was no will to co-operate and compromise. Disputes over separate municipalities and taxation created a deadlock in government. But over and above the unworkability of the constitution, it was the emotional attitudes that prevented us from getting along.

The Turkish Cypriots, still fearful of the majority, did not disband the paramilitary organisation TMT after independence and, as things deteriorated, the Greek Cypriots created their own gangs of armed irregulars. Each side's paramilitaries had secret documents outlining their action plans, which surfaced creating panic. First came the Akritas Plan, which reads like the rules of a secret schoolboys' club. It outlined how they would try and change the 1960 agreements so that Greek Cypriots could rule as the majority and then pave the way for *enosis*. Recognising that the

Turkish Cypriots would react, the plan also acknowledged the need for military preparations in order to quash them.

To the Turkish Cypriots, the Akritas plan seemed like a genocidal plot. They prepared their own plan. A TMT document surfaced which revealed that their objective in response to the efforts to annul the constitution was to break away from the Republic by setting up their own separate state, which would be recognised by Turkey, supported financially by Turkey, and whose population would be boosted with settlers from Turkey. They would only implement their plan if the Greeks tried to amend the constitution and their efforts would be focused on provoking the Greeks to do so by making it difficult for them to implement the constitution. They predicted the Greeks wouldn't need much provoking as "with their behaviour" they would give them "plenty of opportunities". They were right.

Makarios foolishly underestimated the danger from Turkey. He brazenly thought he could handle it and against the advice of both Britain and Greece who urged him to continue to negotiate, proposed thirteen amendments to the constitution, thereby playing straight into Turkey's hands. While these amendments streamlined the government and also removed certain aspects that emphasised the importance of whether a Cypriot citizen was Greek or Turkish, they also resolved all issues in the Greek Cypriots' favour. In the eyes of the Turkish Cypriots, the amendments demoted them to a minority rather than 'co-founders'. To them it seemed the Greek Cypriots were preparing for *enosis*, a view that the various statements from Makarios and his ministers seemed to support.

Things came to a head in December 1963, '*Kanlı Noel*' (Bloody Christmas), as the Turkish Cypriots officially commemorate it every year. On 21 December a Greek Cypriot police patrol, ostensibly checking identification documents, stopped two Turkish Cypriots, a man and a woman (a prostitute and her pimp) on the edge of the Turkish quarter in Nicosia. An argument broke out, a hostile crowd gathered, shots were fired, and the two were killed.

From then on things quickly got out of hand as fighting spread to the rest of Nicosia. Gangs of Greek Cypriot nationalist fanatics, led by people like Vasos Lyssarides and Nicos Sampson, a known murderer who bragged openly of killing a number of men and who had been sentenced to death for the EOKA murder of seventeen British soldiers before independence, waged attacks all along the line separating the Turkish quarter of Nicosia from the rest of the town. Most of the fighting occurred in the suburbs of Kaimakli and Omorphita where many Turkish Cypriots lived. On Christmas Eve it spread to the other main towns and, in the first months of 1964, several people were killed in Limassol and Paphos as well.

After that bloody Christmas, TMT started forcing Turkish Cypriots, ostensibly for their own good, to move from their homes to areas they protected, sometimes even using threats, shootings and arson in order to get them to do so. From being spread all over the island they ended up crowded into enclaves occupying only three per cent of the island. The largest stretched from the north of Nicosia up into the Kyrenia mountains, including the castle of Saint Hilarion from where they could survey the whole of the north coast all the way to Turkey. The Greek Cypriot paramilitaries cut off electricity, water and food supplies to the enclaves, leaving the Turkish Cypriots to live in squalid conditions. All in all about twenty-five thousand Turkish Cypriots had to leave their homes. About eight hundred Turkish Cypriots were moved from the Omorphita area alone.

Hasip and his family were amongst them, he tells me one Saturday when I ask. His father, Dervish, was a successful carpenter from the Nicosia suburb of Ortaköy, and his wife, Bahire, was from Istinço in Paphos. He bought some land in the Nicosia suburb of Kaimakli in the mid 1950s on which he built homes for his large family.

Hasip was nine years old when the fighting began. Around forty Turkish Cypriots had sought shelter in their house, one of the few made of concrete at the time, including women with babies. There was no milk and very little food, but they got by with the help of some of their Greek Cypriot neighbours.

"Our good Greek Cypriot neighbours brought us some eggs, bread and other food. Our bad ones would shoot at us while we were playing in the street," he tells me one late summer's day in the Han. "I remember it vividly. Though I don't want to remember it. My family suffered a lot in that period." He pours some water into his lemonade to dilute it and gives it a stir with his straw before taking a sip.

At one point, he says, a group of between twenty and thirty Greek Cypriot thugs led by Nicos Sampson surrounded the house holding machine guns. His older brother Ali, barely eleven at the time, happened to be at a neighbour's house from where he watched the scene unfold in horror and fear, as Sampson's men rounded up around fifteen Turkish Cypriots, including his father, stuffed them into trucks and drove them away.

The men were taken somewhere nearby in Omorphita and made to line up against a wall. They were given a cigarette each, supposedly their last before being executed. Fortunately for them, two British officers happened to drive by, saw what was going on and began arguing with the Sampson band. This probably saved the Turkish Cypriots, who were subsequently taken to an ice cream factory where they were severely beaten. Later, a Greek Cypriot police officer accompanied them back to their homes, ordering them not to leave, while a British soldier was sent to guard them. Dervish sent a message to the leader of the Turkish Cypriot community at the time, Dr. Fazil Küçük, informing him that they had become hostages, but Dr. Küçük sent a message back saying that there was nothing he could do to help them. They were stuck in the house until mid January 1964 when they were able to go into the walled part of Nicosia, where the Turkish Cypriot paramilitary could protect them. There they moved into Dervish's workshop from where they eked out a living surviving as best they could.

I soon discover that every Turkish Cypriot has a similar story to tell.

"The years between '63 and '68 were very bad," Suleyman says when I turn to him. "Our family was hit very badly because my father had died just before the '63 events and my poor mother had to look after all of us, as well as all the other people who came to stay in our house. Whenever there was trouble, all the relatives used to come to our house seeking safety. It was the same in '58. They stayed for months even though our house was very small. Some of the people who left ended up getting shot. It was very, very difficult for us. Even if you had money there were things you couldn't buy. Food, for example."

"I remember it clearly," Hasip says. "Everyone had a day allocated to them to collect their weekly rations. I used to be the one to collect the rations for the seven of us. Every Friday I would put it all in a cart which I used to push all the way to the *pantopoliyo* (market) and back. From '63 to '67 we relied on the Red Crescent to survive. Every month a ship would come from Turkey from the Red Crescent." He turns to Hasan, who has been quietly listening next to him. "You remember that too, Hasan, don't you?"

Hasan nods. "I used to run after the truck to get bread," he says. "Every family was allowed only a certain number of loaves."

"Our rations consisted of two kilograms of rice, two kilograms of flour, one kilogram of jam, two kilograms of sugar and a bottle of oil. And one gallon of heating gas," Hasip continues. "No bread. This is what we used to live on. And the other side ignored this. Can you imagine, a hundred and twenty thousand citizens of this country, suffering, not having enough food, gasoline, cement, paint, car batteries? For eleven years! And the majority of Greeks closed their eyes." He shakes his head and looks at me. "Maybe they didn't know."

I look away. While I was too young to be politically aware, I wonder about my parents. Didn't they know? Did they know and not care? For us, Greek Cypriots, this was a period of growing prosperity, a new wealth that came from improved agricultural practices, increased exports, and the development of the construction, manufacturing and tourist industries. Our new middle classes lived in large, comfortable houses, had two cars, telephones, a TV, and all the latest labour-saving appliances. We were sent abroad to pursue higher studies, preferably in the UK and the United States, but also Greece, and came back to cushy jobs in the civil service or in the family business. Did everyone just turn a blind eye? While my parents were partying in Kyrenia, weren't they aware of the forced starvation of a whole population? That there were pockets of humanity amongst them who we were being deliberately and inhumanely squeezed out? Even if they knew, did they just shrug helplessly wondering what could they could do when this was the government's policy, the policy of the president himself, a so-called man of God?

"Makarios used to say, 'let them boil in their juice'," Mikis says. He too shakes his head in disbelief and stares absently out onto the courtyard. "We wanted you to boil in your juice."

"For *enosis* to happen he had to get rid of the Turkish Cypriots," Kokos says, the word 'Makarios', as always, animating him.

"It was like a *bayram* holiday for us whenever one of our relatives in the villages managed to send us a basket of food, especially if it included a chicken," Suleyman remembers. "In the villages they didn't have a problem with food because they could grow their own, just like they always did, but they did have a problem with security. After '68 things relaxed a bit."

"We used to go around cutting things down to turn into furniture," Hasip says. "Anything we could get our hands on. We weren't even allowed shoelaces."

"Why not shoelaces?" Andreas says.

"Who knows?" Hasip says. "Maybe because with open shoes you couldn't run very far!"

"Who decided all these things, anyway?" Mikis wonders. "Makarios?"

"Probably," Kokos says.

"Those enclaves were like small prisons," Andreas says.

"It was like living in a cage," Hasan says.

"The Turkish rebellion, we Greek Cypriots call it," Kokos says. "Just like that, out of the blue, you guys rebelled!"

"No one wonders why we rebelled," Hasan says.

"All Greek Cypriots should take a minute to try and imagine what it was like being a Turkish Cypriot in 1963," Andreas says. He runs his hands through his hair and surveys the courtyard. A few people are milling around, chatting, or just walking by.

"It wasn't a Turkish rebellion, it was a Greek rebellion!" Mikis says having gone quite red in the face. "There was even a plan. They sent people to the schools to recruit the older kids. They wanted to create special forces that would kill all the Turks and unite with Greece. It makes my blood boil to hear someone say that the Turks rebelled."

"Our history books don't even mention the period after 1963," Andreas says.

"Yes, we don't want the truth of those uncomfortable events to come out," I say. "It's as if we're totally deaf to your version of our story. And the same thing happened on your side. After 1974 you didn't hear our side of the story. Instead our suffering was completely downplayed and presented as us getting what we deserved."

"I just want to forget about those days," Suleyman says, making a gesture as if to rub it all out. "I hope my children and grandchildren never experience anything like that. And I hope the same for yours."

"Makarios was following Grivas' policy but implementing it differently," Kokos says. "Grivas wanted to throw the Turkish Cypriots into the sea. Makarios wanted to make them leave on their own. Grivas wanted to use violence, something Makarios couldn't be seen to be doing, so he used him as his front man. In actual fact he wanted the same thing. His dream was to kill the Turks while they were sleeping."

"Makarios created the first EOKA and he put Grivas as its head," Mikis says. "*He* was behind the so-called Akritas plan. *He* created the paramilitaries to tackle the so-called rebellion of the Turkish Cypriots, which he himself provoked by not implementing the constitution."

"His interior minister, put a bomb at the statue of one of our heroes in order to create anti Turk feelings," Kokos says. "Who do you think put a bomb at the Bayraktar mosque?"

"That was our lot," Hasip says. "To make it look like it was your lot and make Turkish Cypriots afraid so Denktash could control them."

"Ok, you're right," Kokos concedes. "It happened twice. The first time it was Denktash, but the second it was our lot." The late summer heat causes a few beads of sweat to form on his forehead which he wipes away with the back of his hand.

"And what about the babies in the bath?" I ask. "Who killed them?" An article has appeared in the papers recently about one of the events of those days—the murder in 1963 of a mother and her three children. A photograph published at the time showed her lying dead in a bathtub with her three dead children thrown in on top of her. The article hints that the killer was actually a Turkish Cypriot and that the Turkish Cypriot authorities at the time had taken the opportunity to deliberately set up the photo blaming the Greek Cypriots in order to whip up fear and hatred amongst the Turkish Cypriot community against them.

"Nobody knows," Hasan replies shrugging.

"There are a number of witnesses," Sarper says sitting across from me, "but for some reason they refuse to talk. They're scared. If it was Greek Cypriots who did it, why would they be scared?"

"The article is nonsense," says Mikis. "Our lot did it, there's no doubt about it. Sampson's 'heroes'," he mimes a pair of speech marks, "went in and shot them all."

"Makarios wanted to kill the Republic of Cyprus," Mikis says. "His speeches prove it. He's on tape as having said that 'as long as this damn race, the Turks, continues to exist in Cyprus, we will never be able to achieve our goal of *enosis*.' Someone wrote about it in a book." He lowers his voice, "Makarios banned the book and ordered all copies to be destroyed."

"He was a dictator," Kokos says. "He had spies everywhere. He knew everything that was going on."

"Both he and Grivas knew that if they went for *enosis* the Turkish Cypriots would react," says Mikis. "As we would have reacted, if we had been the minority and you wanted union with Turkey."

"Of course, you would," Hasip says.

"It's quite simple, really," Mikis continues. "Makarios thought, since the Turks wouldn't accept the thirteen amendments to the constitution he wanted to make, he would have a paramilitary army ready to impose it. So when the Turkish Cypriots moved into their enclaves, he was happy to trap them there so that they would become exhausted psychologically and then either give up and accept his terms, or emigrate."

"Is that the way to handle your minority?" Andreas says. "Force them to ask for help from abroad?"

"The truth is you Turkish Cypriots are now in the arms of Turkey. And I'm not sure if you can ever get out. Of course the question is, who put you there? *We* put you there! We were pushing you for years, and you were saying, no, no, please, we don't want to go, we want to stay with you, but we wouldn't listen. And now we complain that Turkey won't let you go. Turkey will *never* let you go".

The Turkish Cypriots round the table nod their heads vigorously.

"That's exactly what Lanitis warned us would happen in 1962 before it all blew up," Mikis says. "He said if we neglect the Turkish Cypriots, they will, out of necessity, be forced to depend more and more on Turkey, which is exactly what happened."

Nicos Lanitis, I'm well aware as I sit there watching the clouds roll over the courtyard, wasn't a politician, but a concerned businessman and citizen who in many ways proved to be visionary. I try to remember the details. Didn't he call on Greek Cypriots to be generous and give more than what they receive? Yes. That and tolerance is the fundamental rule of being in a responsible position, he said. If the Turkish Cypriots provoke us, we should not react. We must gain their trust. He also said we must teach Turkish in Greek Cypriot schools and Greek in Turkish Cypriot schools and that the two communities should see each other as one people, people of the same country. He was duly pronounced a traitor, of course.

"It was when the Turkish jets bombed the island in '67 that things got better for us," Hasip says.

"No, the Turkish jets didn't bomb us in '67," Mikis corrects him. "You're thinking of '64. After the inter-communal violence in December

1963, the Turkish Cypriots brought in shiploads of ammunition and soldiers from Turkey through Kokkina, the only place they had access to the sea. About five hundred men arrived every night. Because the Greeks were also bringing in men from Greece. The Cyprus government then launched an attack on Kokkina and Turkey retaliated by sending its fighter jets to bomb Greek positions."

Kokos says, "For three days in August 1964 Turkish warplanes bombed the Tylliria area. They hit residential areas and a hospital. Over fifty people were killed, including nineteen civilians."

"But wasn't it '67 when they bombed Geçitkale?" Hasip asks still trying to get his facts straight, making me realise how much confusion still reigns about our recent history.

"No, they never bombed Kofinou," Mikis says. "They only bombed the area around Kokkina and Mansoura near Polis. And that was in August 1964. Turkey almost invaded then. We were only saved at the last minute by the UN Security Council. After that the UN were sent to the island."

"And they're still here, half a century later," Hasip says. "Keeping the peace, supposedly."

Kokos says, "The incidents at Kofinou, when Grivas started massacring the Turkish Cypriots there, happened in 1967. Turkish jets just flew overhead. They buzzed Nicosia and four ships appeared in the sea off the coast of Kyrenia. They didn't bomb anything then. They just wanted to scare Makarios."

"It was a shot against the bow," Hasip says.

"That's when the penny finally dropped," Mikis says. "Makarios realised that Greece would never stick its neck out for Cyprus and get involved in a war with Turkey. From that point on in his speeches he acknowledged that sometimes in life one has to accept 'what is feasible rather than what is desirable'."

"After behaving as if Turkey was four hundred miles away instead of forty, Makarios finally learned his lesson," Andreas says. "Have you heard of the term Finlandisation? It means mind your neighbours. Finland's neighbour was the great Soviet bear who was out of control. The Finns kept a low profile for seventy years until eventually Russia collapsed. You just don't poke the bear when the bear is seventy million people, militaristic, aggressive, undemocratic, and in many ways problematic, while you are just a dot in the Mediterranean. Makarios was an idiot, a megalomaniac. He did not behave maturely to protect his people."

"Of course Finland lost some land too," Mikis says.

"Twice Makarios had an opportunity to solve the Cyprus problem and at the last moment changed his mind holding out for more," Kokos says. "Once with Harding in the '50s, and again when Clerides and Denktash reached an agreement in 1973."

"But the opportunity was missed," Mikis sighs.

"Because Makarios scuppered it," Kokos says. "After all, he was winning!" He bangs his hand on the table to emphasise his point.

"If the Greeks hadn't been stupid enough to stage the coup, he would have succeeded," Hasip says.

"Yes, he was almost there!" Mikis cries. "He just needed another two or three years."

"Almost there," Hasip agrees, "because the Turkish Cypriots were leaving in their hundreds. Emigrating to Australia."

Kokos says, "Makarios would give the Turkish Cypriots free tickets to go to Ankara to study on condition that they would not come back after they graduated."

"Just before the coup Makarios had started becoming more realistic," Mikis says. "He realised that *enosis* would have to come gradually, otherwise Turkey would intervene. However, there were others who were more nationalistic than him, who were impatient and wanted *enosis* there and then."

"They wanted to throw the Turks into the sea," Kokos says.

"Their target was the same, just the strategy was different," Hasan says.

"Relations between Makarios and the Greek junta deteriorated," Kokos says. "He knew the Greeks wanted to stage a coup in Cyprus. He also knew, and the Greeks knew too, that Turkey had threatened to invade the island if Greece were ever to attempt to bring about *enosis*. Makarios just didn't believe the Greeks would be stupid enough to stage a coup and risk war with Turkey. So he provoked them."

"He didn't realise that they were very stupid indeed!" Mikis says.

"But how could they have been that stupid?" I ask. "I always thought it was because the Greek colonels got assurances from America that they wouldn't let Turkey invade. Isn't that why we hate Kissinger?"

"They were playing with fire," Andreas says. "How can you blame the Americans? They were looking after their own interests. After all, it may have suited them if Cyprus became two states. The same thing happened in '63 when Makarios sent one of his ministers to sound out the British about the thirteen amendments. They told him," he puts on a British accent, "'Well, that might be a bit of a tricky situation'. Except Makarios interpreted it to mean that the British weren't too negative to the idea. And went ahead with it, with dire consequences."

We are silent for a while thinking of these consequences. Ahmet comes to collect the dirty cups and take more orders. A small group is standing in the courtyard to take a photograph but quickly moves on to get out of the heat of the sun.

"What happened to your houses, Hasip?" I ask eventually.

"Two of them were burned down," he says.

"Greek Cypriots?" Kokos asks.

"We don't know. I believe the '63 burning was the Greek Cypriots, but the '68 burning was the Turkish Cypriots—TMT and Denktash. He didn't want the enclaves to collapse, otherwise he would have no power over the Turkish Cypriots. It doesn't matter which side the gang of thugs came from. They were all thugs."

Mikis agrees. "They both had the same mentality."

"Overnight things changed for us. We had to run for our lives," Hasip says.

He tells us that in 1968, when Makarios finally saw reason and lifted the economic sanctions against the enclaves, easing relations between the two communities, Hasip's father was able to go back to his house. He found it had been completely ransacked. Everything was gone, all doors, windows, even the tiles on the floor and roof were gone, as was the electrical system and, of course, all the furniture. Nothing but the shell remained. He began the task of rebuilding it. Other Turkish Cypriots also started doing the same.

"Then just when we had moved in with all our clothes and all our possessions, even our school books, they burned it down all over again!" Hasip says nodding gravely.

The night before they were due to move back into the house in February 1969, they received news that it was burning but by the time they got there it had burned to the ground. Some people said that Turkish Cypriots had set fire to it in order to put them off returning. Others that it was Greek Cypriots for the same reason. Whoever it was, neither the Greek Cypriot nor the Turkish Cypriot fire brigade went to extinguish the flames. Everything burnt to a cinder. Dervish had to start from scratch, having lost everything yet again.

Like Hasip's, my family also lost property in '63, three plots of land in the northern suburb of Kermia /Ortaköy. All in all, starting in the 1950s, and then again in the 1960s and in 1974, almost half of Cyprus' population (roughly half of Turkish Cypriots and a third of Greek Cypriots) lost their property.

Andreas says, "When I was seventeen I used to ride my bike into the Turkish quarter in Famagusta in order to buy some doner kebab. My mother would say 'Are you going to the Turks again?' Not that she had anything against them but because it wasn't safe, she was afraid."

"All this talk of 'our Turkish Cypriot brothers'," says Mikis, "it's just our propaganda machine pretending we used to get on well before '74. They show the image of the church next to the mosque in the village of Peristerona as if to prove it. We may have lived intermingled all over the island, but we existed separately. Villages tended to be either Greek Cypriot or Turkish Cypriot. Our friendliness was superficial. We rarely intermarried, we never truly understood each other."

"It's a big myth," Kokos agrees. "Especially in the towns. Less so in the villages."

"We used to look down on Turkish Cypriots," says Andreas. "But we paid the price."

"The nationalists and partitionists poisoned us," says Kokos. "Now the way back is twice as hard."

"Things didn't work out in 1960 because we had Makarios and Denktash," Hasip says finishing his coffee. "Now we have many Makarioses and many Denktashes."

"Unfortunately the fanatics won," Mikis says and sighs.

"Was it possible for Greek Cypriots to enter the enclaves?" I ask, having little recollection of them.

"No it was impossible," Hasip says. "Turkish Cypriots never left the enclaves and Greek Cypriots never came in. Only after '68 could some Turkish Cypriots leave. Nicosia was the biggest enclave. There was an enclave in Famagusta, and Kokkina."

"So the convoy that used to take us to Kyrenia, used to go through the enclave?" I ask.

"Ah, you remember the convoy?" Hasip laughs at the memory.

"I remember going on a picnic up in Bogaz and looking down at the convoy going by!" says Hasan.

Hasip laughs. "Hasan used to watch Andreas driving through Gionyeli with the UN convoy taking people from Nicosia to Kyrenia."

"It wasn't me," Andreas says. "I used to live in Famagusta and never visited Kyrenia. It was Marina he used to watch."

"Yes, you were watching me," I tell him. "I used to travel to Kyrenia with the convoy." I clearly remember hurrying to get ready by ten o'clock in order to join the line of cars in a spot in Ayios Dhometios just so as to travel the twenty minutes it took to drive through the mountain pass with a UN escort. Twice a day the convoy went, once in the morning and once in the afternoon, there and back. How ridiculous it all seems now, though at the time I thought it was normal. Just the way things were. I remember looking out of the car window at the Turkish Cypriot kids in the streets of Gionyeli. Sometimes those kids threw stones at us as we drove by. I never wondered why.

"Can you imagine, from 1963 to 1974 we never saw Kyrenia again," Hasip says. He sits back in his chair and grimaces at the idiocy of the situation.

"And then, to complete the story," Andreas adds ruefully, "from 1974 to 2003 *we* never saw Kyrenia again."

9 SMYRNA

War is one way things can go wrong. We all live in the shadow of war. We think that because we're living in the twenty first century and in a civilised country, nobody is going to kick our door down, murder our wives, husbands and children, drag us off somewhere and hold us hostage. And yet, we may be going off to work in the heart of the world's most advanced city, and suicide bombers may drive two planes into our office tower, or detonate a bomb in our city's subway system. As Eleni's first husband, the writer Christopher Hitchens, who I met when he was covering Cyprus for the New Statesman, once wrote, "politics can force its way into our lives in such a vicious and chilling manner." No matter where we are.

My father, who was fond of quoting various theories about life, used to say that most people will experience war at least once in their lives. He was unlucky. War touched him three times—in Smyrna, Berlin and Cyprus. He was only four when Smyrna, the city of his birth in western Anatolia was burned down, so the horrors of that experience really belong to my grandmother.

Smyrna was one of the most cosmopolitan cities in the world when politics forced its way into my grandmother's life that September in 1922. As far back as the Romans, it had been an enchanting, glittering place; the finest city in Asia, Strabo called it. Chateaubriand said it reminded him of Paris. Flaubert loved the sunsets there. Homer was born there and so was Aristotle Onassis.

In my grandmother's day, it was considered by some to be the apogee of western civilisation, a mingling of East and West, the epitome of racial tolerance and acceptance of diversity, everything that mankind can aspire to. Greeks, Turks, Jews, Armenians, Levants and Europeans all lived there. The American community called their quarter "Paradise". Others, however, thought that it was decadent and due for a fall, which it duly did, becoming in the process a showcase of all the horrors that man can perpetrate against man.

Even though Smyrna was under Ottoman rule, it had been spared the oppression on Greeks exercised elsewhere in the empire. The Greek majority, almost twice as many as the Turks, controlled the city's economy and culture. Everyone spoke Greek there. It was the city of the infidel, of the *giavur*, its Greek population twice that of Athens. Lives intertwined, communities freely borrowed from each other's customs, helping themselves to each other's words and expressions.

In 1919 Greece landed an army of some 60,000 troops at Smyrna from where, egged on by the Allies as a reward for helping them during World War I, they drove inland with the intent of annexing part of the collapsing Ottoman Empire. But the nationalist government of Turkey and its army commander Mustafa Kemal, later known as Ataturk, pushed the Greeks back.

Perhaps my grandmother got the first indication that something terrible was about to happen when she saw the lines of disbanded Greek soldiers streaming past her window, the fallout from the defeat of the Greek army after three years of war. Perhaps her brother, or one of her two older sisters, ran to tell her about the columns of ragged refugees that were pouring down the narrow streets of the town. Perhaps the whole family leaned out of the window watching them go by. Her four-year-old son, my father, may have asked her why the children's clothes were torn, why they were crying, or why their mothers were begging for food and water.

In her early twenties, my grandmother may not have been politically aware enough to know this was the end of the Greek prime minister Eleftherios Venizelos' Big Idea, the *Megali Idea*. Four and a half centuries after the collapse of the Byzantine empire, he had wanted to create a Greater Greece, regaining lands that had been lived in by Greeks for millennia with Constantinople at its heart.

Perhaps my grandmother then went about her day as normal. She might have gone down to one of the large department stores, or to the butcher's and baker's. There she would have bumped into people she knew and discussed what they thought might happen. Would the Turks attack them? Should they try and leave town, or should they stay? She would have heard that some of the wealthy families were already packing their things and leaving. All very well to go, she might have thought, but go where? So, like most others, she stayed, choosing to stock up, standing in line along with everyone else in a panic to fill their pantry with food. Just in case.

At the back of my grandmother's mind may have been thoughts about a return to the days when conquering Islamic armies sanctioned three days of pillage following the capture of a resisting town. She may have voiced her fears to her husband, who may well have told her that she was making a fuss about nothing and that Smyrna would fall peacefully into Turkish hands, after which it would be business as usual. After all there were twenty-one battleships of the Western powers in the harbour—eleven British, five French, several Italian, and three large American destroyers. Surely these ships would deter the Turkish army from committing excesses. My father may have sneaked a peek at those waiting battleships with their huge turrets in the bay from an upstairs window at the top of his house, or he may have marvelled at them from Smyrna's famous quay. Never had ships like these gathered in the bay. And so many of them.

Most people thought that the city would be safe. They continued to go to the brasseries and beer houses, the theatre and the movies. They went on their promenades along the quay dressed in all their finery, enjoying that warm autumn day and the beautiful wide open blue bay, normally full of sailboats, like swans crisscrossing the water. I almost have a memory of it myself, just from my grandmother's descriptions.

What happened next, Giles Milton writes in his book *Paradise Lost* on the events leading up to Smyrna's destruction, "must rank as one of the most compelling human dramas of the twentieth century. A humanitarian disaster on a scale that the world had never before seen, as the entire population became the victim of a reckless foreign policy that had gone disastrously wrong."

Even though the Turks were coming, Greek newspapers were printing stories about a tactical retreat of the Greek army, which would defend Smyrna from the advancing Turks and keep the city safe. My grandmother and the rest of the inhabitants of Smyrna must only have realised the danger they were in when they noticed that the last Greek troops, the Greek administration and the police force, quietly left town. They were undefended.

On the morning of Saturday 9 September the Turkish cavalry rode into the city. Perhaps my grandmother's blood ran cold as she watched from the windows of her house. They were a magnificent spectacle, cantering along the waterfront, banners flying, the horsemen sitting high in their saddles, their scimitars unsheathed and glinting in the sun, black fezzes on their heads. Did she believe them when they cried, "*Korkma*! *Korkma*!" Don't be afraid, as they rode by, watched by thousands of anxious inhabitants. By evening, the Turkish army was approaching the city from all sides. My father, too young to understand the danger, would surely have recognised the fear on his parents' faces.

The tension increased as the day progressed. Turkish irregulars arrived and began looting and pillaging. Violence broke out. Turkish soldiers took up positions all over the city, shouting threats and firing guns. The terror must have been palpable. I wonder if my grandmother slept a wink that night, what with all the screams and gunshots coming from the Armenian quarter.

The Armenians were the Turks' first target. Turkish irregulars broke into their homes, looting, raping and killing. They would break down a door, drag out any young girls they found inside, and two or three soldiers would take them to some shop nearby or across the street. There would be screams and sometimes a gunshot. It was a bloodbath. Many Armenians sought shelter in the Prelacy thinking there would be safety in numbers but the Turks came there too, hurling a grenade over the wall at the huddling masses inside. The Greeks weren't spared either. Everyone had a story to tell about neighbours attacked, friends and relatives houses ransacked, dead and rubbish lying in the streets. Young girls lying dead with their breasts cut off, clotted blood between their thighs. Gunfire day and night. Which of all the horrors that occurred during those days did my grandmother witness? She never told me.

The streets were full of Turkish soldiers who would go into the houses and come out with their scimitars dripping with blood. Did my grandmother catch sight of any as they wiped their swords clean on their boots and leggings? What did she feel as the looting and murder went on steadily under her eyes, as the soldiers broke down the doors of houses shooting the poor cowering inhabitants? At what point did my grandmother and her family decide to gather together some belongings, including their jewellery, and join the masses on the quay?

By now most foreign nationals had realised that it was no longer safe to stay in the city. The foreign consuls all started evacuating their subjects before it was too late. George Horton, the American consul, describes what he saw before leaving in his book *The Blight of Asia*. He says he watched Turkish soldiers unloading what appeared to be large barrels of petroleum, wheeling them into the Armenian quarter and spraying the buildings. Flames broke out soon afterwards. When asked what they were doing, they replied that they were under orders to blow up and burn all the houses of the area. Many others witnessed similar scenes, but despite scores of impartial accounts testifying that the Turkish army deliberately set fire to Smyrna, to this day, most Turkish historians deny accusations of genocide and even claim the fire was an act of sabotage on the part of the Greeks and Armenians.

At first the wind was blowing from the sea but in the early hours of Wednesday 13 September the wind changed direction. It wasn't long before the various separate fires spotted by witnesses became one large conflagration raging throughout the Armenian quarter. At this point my grandmother and her family may have climbed up onto the roof terrace of the house and seen the vast dark clouds of smoke arising from a wide area of the city and realised they had to go. Perhaps it was the fire that finally made them leave their home.

Although Smyrna's streets were lined with imposing, stone-built mansions, they were more flammable than they looked. The fire spread easily. Leaping flames, crumbling masonry and burning cinders soon started raining down from the sky. If she hadn't left earlier, surely this was when my grandmother and her family joined the masses on Smyrna's wide quayside. Despite being two miles long and slightly wider than a football pitch, it was still too small to accommodate more than half a million people. As more and more people arrived, the entire waterfront turned into one solid mass of humanity.

Once there, though, my grandmother and her family were trapped. As one survivor described it, they were caught between three deadly elements—fire, sword and water. On the one side was the burning city, on the other the deep waters of the bay, while at the northern and southern ends of the waterfront Turkish soldiers sat waiting preventing them from fleeing. Amid piercing shrieks and blows, a smoke so hot that you thought you were on fire, many fell into the water, or perhaps jumped.

Every now and then the word would spread amongst the crowd, perhaps the result of wishful thinking, that Greece was sending ships to save them. Perhaps my grandmother and her family stared out onto the bay hoping and praying for a boat to take them away. In vain. No ships came. By the time dusk fell the fire had reached the waterfront. The flames leapt higher and higher. The screams of the frantic people on the quay could be heard a mile away.

The night of 13 September 1922 in Smyrna must have been one of abject terror and horror. Shrieking women calling to their dead children. Children calling for lost parents. Young girls of fifteen or sixteen dragged away. People clinging to the quayside, Turkish soldiers chopping off their arms. People throwing themselves into the sea to escape the horror. The sea thick with corpses. Turkish soldiers pouring buckets of liquid over the refugees and setting them on fire. A wall of unbroken fire with flames a hundred feet high. Loud explosions at intervals. People nearest the city being massacred. The stench of human flesh. All the while people wondering, the ships, the ships, where were the Greek ships? How my grandmother held on to her child and remained with her family is a miracle.

Yet none of the European battleships anchored in the bay did anything to help the people on the quay. From time to time during the night one of the battleships would shine its searchlights over the masses on the wharf as a way of preventing some of the crimes. The fire was so strong, they could feel its heat. They could hear the screams from the quay. On board one of the British ships, the Iron Duke, the sailors urged the captain to help, but he said he had orders to remain neutral. Instead, in order to drown out the sounds from the shore, he ordered the ship's band to strike up tunes. Other ships followed suit. What must my grandmother and the rest of the people on the shore have thought that night as the sound of Caruso in Pagliacci wafted over the water from the ships while their homes burned and they struggled to stay alive?

In the end the British captain gave in and sent a boat to the shore. The French, Italians and Americans followed suit. Was my grandmother amongst those desperate people who threw themselves on the boats, so many that the crew had to beat them back to get away?

Thursday continued in the same vein. The ships managed to save another 20,000 souls from the quayside, barely a handful of the masses on the quayside. The fire was still burning fiercely even though many parts of the city had been reduced to rubble. Nor did the savagery show any signs of abating, as groups of armed Turks prowled through the crowd, every now and then striking at someone and kicking their body into the sea. Still the people on the quay waited for Greece to save them. At one point the people all joined voices in prayer, praying for ships. It all seemed in vain.

My grandmother and her family would probably not have survived, had it not been for the courage and resourcefulness of an American. Five foot three, a hunchback with glasses but with a ready smile and an engaging personality, who easily made friends with everyone he met, Asa K. Jennings was an employee of Smyrna's YMCA. When all the American citizens were evacuated, he alone stayed behind to do what he could to help. Realising that no boats were coming, he was seized with 'an uncontrollable urge', as he later described it, to do something. He drove to the Turkish army camp and got a meeting with Mustafa Kemal himself, persuading him to agree to allow the refugees to leave, all except for men of military age.

He rowed over to the French vessel, Pierre Loti, but the captain refused to help, saying he was bound by his government's neutrality. Then he rowed over to an Italian cargo ship, the Constantinople, where he managed to bribe the captain to take two thousand people.

He began boarding people on Thursday 21 September, watched over by the Turkish army in case any men tried to get away disguised as women. "It was heart-breaking to see the grief of loved ones when soldiers pulled the men back from the ships", wrote Jennings, but he could do nothing to stop them. By late afternoon they were all aboard. As soon as the ship set off, the refugees fell on Jennings, kissing his hands and feet in gratitude.

He took them to the island of Mytilene, where he found twenty-five Greek passenger ships just lying there empty and jumped on the opportunity to use them to evacuate the remaining refugees from Smyrna. But the Greek general wanted a written guarantee that they would be protected by the American military as well as an assurance that the Turkish authorities would allow the ships to return to Mytilene. Jennings rushed back to Smyrna and got a written agreement from the American commander. But even this was not enough for the Greek general.

But just then a Greek battleship, the Kilkis, arrived in the harbour and Jennings persuaded the captain to send a telegram to Athens asking them to allow the twenty ships to evacuate the refugees. The Greek government vacillated. They too wanted guarantees. In the end Jennings took matters into his own hands with an ultimatum. He threatened to send an open message, without code, saying that the Greek government would not permit Greek ships to save thousands of refugees awaiting certain death. The bluff worked. The Greek government put all the ships in the Aegean under Jennings' control. Still the captains hesitated about entering Turkish ports. They feigned mechanical problems. At this Jennings informed them that he would be sending naval engineers aboard every vessel that claimed to be unseaworthy and if they were found to be lying they would be court-martialled or even executed. All the ships sailed at midnight with Jennings leading the way.

He describes the scene when he arrived back in Smyrna. "At the water's edge, stretching for miles, was what looked like a lifeless black border. Yet I knew that it was a border not of death, but of living sufferers waiting, hoping, praying for ships—ships—ships! As we approached and the shore spread out before us, it seemed as if every face on that quay was turned towards us, and every arm outstretched to bring us in. indeed, I thought that the whole shore was moving out to grasp us. The air was filled with the cries of those thousands, cries of such transcendent joy that the sound pierced to the very marrow of my bones."

Jennings' ships were allowed to dock only at the end of the pier, a narrow walkway that was not designed to cope with large crowds. The walkway was enclosed by metal fences and divided into three long sections, each of which had its own narrow gate. These gates were guarded by a double line of Turkish soldiers, while at the entrance to the pier there was a large crowd of senior officers. The purpose of these fences was to force the refugees to pass through the narrow gates where they could be carefully scrutinized and all the men who appeared to be of military age detained for "deportation to the interior."

As soon as the first ship docked, the crowd surged forward in a frantic rush to get on board. The Turkish soldiers beat them back with the butts of their guns to make them come more slowly. But they seemed insensitive to pain. The greatest fear was of not making it onto the ships. Those who fell were trampled, the sick were abandoned to their fate. Many were pushed into the water. The crush was worst at the first gate where there was a bottleneck. Women lost shoes and clothes, hair was torn out, couples separated. Mothers lost their children and called for them frantically, children fell off the pier and drowned and old people died of exhaustion.

At the gates soldiers seized the wealthier-looking women and robbed them of whatever they had left. Any men they caught trying to escape with their families were roughly beaten and dragged away. Families so close to freedom were separated for ever. Mothers and children would cling to the father and son weeping, begging for mercy but found none. The Turkish soldiers beat the men back into the groups of prisoners to be deported and drove the women into the ships, pushing them with guns, straps or canes, herding them like animals shouting "*Haide*! *Haide*!"

The sight of the fleet must have filled my grandmother with both relief and dread. Relief that she would finally be rescued but dread that her husband would be left behind. The only thing my grandmother told us whenever we asked about our grandfather, was how a half-naked Turk with a sabre intercepted them and took her husband away.

"Take the child, Calliroe," were his last words to her. "Go to Athens. I'll find my way to you later." He never did. Nor did she ever find out what became of him.

All in all it is estimated that approximately a hundred thousand people were killed and another hundred and sixty thousand were deported into the interior, many dying under the harsh conditions or executed along the way, a forced march that resembled the deportation of the Armenians seven years earlier. Most, like my grandfather, were never seen again.

As the ship took her and her family away out of the bay, did my grandmother look back wishing she would never set foot in Smyrna again? Perhaps that was the point when she finally broke down, thinking of her husband and what would happen to him. Perhaps my father tried to comfort her as she sat quietly weeping, in the realisation that something unbearable had just happened on earth. Perhaps, like the American consul, George Horton, she too felt a sense of shame that she belonged to the human race that could perpetrate such horrors.

The war between Greece and Turkey ended in 1922 in what Greeks call the Asia Minor Catastrophe, a disaster arguably greater than the fall of Constantinople in 1453, for it marked the end of the three thousand year Greek presence on Anatolia's Aegean shore. In 1923 the Treaty of Lausanne ratified the compulsory exchange of populations between Greece and Turkey, involving the movement of some one and a half million people. The Greeks were eliminated from Asia allowing them to stay in Turkey, with guaranteed minority rights, only in Constantinople/Istanbul and on a couple of islands. In return, the Turks were turned out of their homes in Crete and in the whole of Greece's territories except for Western Thrace, where they were promised similar minority rights.

In 1930, when Venizelos and Atatürk, on behalf of the two countries and cultures, lavishly celebrated the end of a century of murderous feuding, Arnold Toynbee wrote in Chatham House's Annual Review for 1930 that "this terrible process of segregation [of Greeks and Turks]—a process which had inflicted incalculable losses of life and wealth and happiness upon four successive generations of men, women and children in the Near East—had at last reached its term."

Only Cyprus was left out of this grand reconciliation between old enemies because, having been annexed by Britain in 1914 the moment Turkey came into the war, it was not involved in the population exchanges. Indeed, as part of the 1923 Treaty of Lausanne, Turkey renounced forever any claim to sovereignty over the island in favour of Britain.

Laurence Durrrell wrote that for the Greek of today, the East had become a memory that he touches from time to time, "like a man touches every now and then with his fingers a healed wound."

Greeks still try to keep its memory alive down the generations with a self-deluding little poem:

"Πάλι με χρόνια με καιρούς,
πάλι δικά μας θα 'ναι!
(Once more, in the fullness of time,
they shall be ours again)."

It's been ninety years without Smyrna. And it's been forty years since my father's third experience of war, and my first, and hopefully last, when we lost our house in Kyrenia and barely escaped with our lives.

10 AYŞE GOES ON HOLIDAY

The eerie banshee wail of the sirens wakes me at daybreak as it does every year on the anniversary of the invasion. A cry of collective pain that echoes down the years over a wound that still has not healed. "Black Anniversary" for us in the south, the "Happy Peace Operation" and a cause for celebration in the north.

This morning's *Phileleftheros* carries an article by one of President Makarios' aides in 1974. He recalls that a few days before the coup that brought on the invasion, Makarios had said in an interview to a foreign paper that he did not believe that the Greek junta would dare carry out a coup in Cyprus, because it would inevitably result in Turkey invading, something the junta was not in a position to handle. Afterwards, the aide suggested to Makarios that perhaps it would be better if they did not have the interview translated into Greek and sent to the local papers as they usually did, so as not to draw attention to it in case the junta viewed it as provocation. Makarios told him that what he had said in the interview was the truth and not a provocation at all. "Don't worry, there won't be a coup," he had said confidently. "And even if there is, I promise to let you know twenty-four hours in advance so you can take your precautions." His mistake, the aide says, was that he credited the junta with a sense of patriotism and believed that their fear of Turkey invading would hold them back. In any case, he adds, they had received 'assurances' that all problems would be solved by Monday. Monday was the day the coup took place. Five days later on 20 July, Turkey invaded.

Today, Turkish Prime Minister Tayyip Erdogan is in the north to take part in the celebrations. Huge posters of him line the main roads in the north. They read: "Our past was one, our future is one, we are one heart, happy peace and freedom holiday, Recep Tayyip Erdogan, Turkish Prime Minister." At least ten thousand people have been gathered in the streets to welcome him, the result of an intensive campaign. However, some Turkish Cypriot organisations have also come to protest. They carry banners saying, "*Asihtir*", or "fuck off", reflecting a general feeling within the community of tiredness with being under Turkey's thumb. Police use force against the protesters resulting in injuries and detentions. The head of one of the protesting organisations says in an interview that Turkey should have withdrawn its troops after restoring constitutional order in the island in 1974 but instead put the northern part of Cyprus under military control and sent in settlers from the Turkish mainland. As a result of this military act, the Turkish Cypriots have been living in slavery for thirty-seven years and face the danger of extinction. He adds that if the Turkish Cypriots aren't freed from Turkey's chains, they will disappear.

Speaking at the main commemoration ceremony, Erdogan answers the protesters.

"On the one hand Turkish Cypriots oppose the population transfer from Turkey, on the other they don't have many children. Cyprus needs more people, so every family should have at least four children," he says. Then he says something that even the most hardened optimist (me) finds chilling. He says: "Turkey has no intention of withdrawing any of its troops from the island. The Greek Cypriots lost their chance by rejecting the Annan Plan in 2004. Time is running out. The Cyprus problem is approaching its end. We have other alternatives if necessary."

"What's up with Erdogan?" I ask the following Saturday at the Büyük Han.

We're in the middle of a heat wave and people around the table are trying to keep cool, in any way they can. Hasan is sitting at the top of the table practically in the entrance trying to catch the slightest bit of through-draft. Next to him Hasip is eating some refreshing *muhallebi*. Mikis is fanning himself with his newspaper and Sarper is wiping the sweat off his brow with a handkerchief. Suleyman is in his usual place against the wall looking as cool as a cucumber. Andreas isn't here yet.

"Hubris," Mikis sighs. "It happens to all leaders when they stay in power too long. It comes from the Greek, meaning to be arrogant and not accept the limits of human abilities and defying the gods. It leads to nemesis."

"*Re*, Hasip, have you started?" Andreas calls out from half-way across the courtyard as he approaches the table before even sitting down.

"Started what?" Hasip asks looking up at him in surprise.

"Didn't you hear Erdogan? You need to start having more children."

"Yes, but if you're not careful soon there will be more of us," Hasip says, turning back to his *muhallebi*.

A colourful troupe of performers swarms into the courtyard behind

Andreas. They take up positions in the centre and begin to dance and play music. Some of their members flit round the tables handing out leaflets.

"What does the leaflet say?" Andreas asks. "Can somebody please translate?"

Sarper volunteers. "They are the *Baraka* (the Shed) Theatre company," he reads. "And further down it says, "nobody is more deaf than the man who doesn't want to hear.""

"These are the guys who put up the banner saying "*asihtir*" to Erdogan," Hasip says with some awe. "They've got guts." He looks at the leaflet. "It says here that they are a bunch of youths who want to change the country. The world is big enough for all of us, and we should live in harmony, it says."

"And they don't get arrested?" I ask.

"Oh, they do, they do," Hasan says matter of factly. "They get arrested, they serve some time and get out again. Our laws are very democratic, you see. Even when Erdogan himself orders them to be arrested, our government can't do anything."

"But isn't it rude of you to say '*asihtir*' to the country that came to save you?" I ask. This Turkish swear word, freely used by Greek Cypriots, is considered to be such an insult that it is rarely used in the north.

"After they saved us, they should have gone back home," Hasip says, crossing his arms indignantly.

July 20 1974 is one of those momentous times in a group's history, the kind where for some reason it is important to know where each and every one of one's friends were at the time and what they were doing. It's as if knowing somehow links one to the tragedy as well as to the other person simply by virtue of the sharing.

"So what were you guys doing in 1974?" I ask the Turkish Cypriots.

For a moment they don't answer. Hasip puts his spoon down and Hasan leans back in his chair thinking.

"Hasan and I were both in the army together," Hasip says. "In Nicosia. Based in the suburb of Kaimakli."

"We have always been together for as long as we can remember!" Hasan laughs. "We grew up together, went to school together, and ended up at university in Manchester together. We were together in the army as well."

"We shared everything, blankets, clothes, our cups, everything." Hasip pauses to swallow another mouthful. "I remember one time during the war we were looking for something warm to wear."

"What did you want something warm for?" I ask surprised. "It was summer and there was a heat wave!"

"Yes, but at night when we were on guard duty it was cold."

"Everyone else was running around looting, but we weren't interested, we were just looking for a coat or something warm," Hasan says, amused at the exploits of their younger selves. "We broke into a house and looked around. It was dark so we used a lighter because that way you couldn't be seen, whereas if you used a match the flare would give you away. I opened a cupboard and found a lady's coat with a fur collar. Hasip found a long coat. So we tried them on."

"We looked very funny in those ladies coats," Hasip says, grinning as he remembers how they posed in front of a mirror.

"But did you have to fight?" I want to know.

"In one of those battles," Hasip says, "I was just given a Sten gun with only six bullets. But it was faulty and fired all the bullets at the same time. One pull and they were all gone. "

I take a sip of my lemonade and wait for them to continue. Few people are hanging around in the sun of the courtyard today, preferring to seek the shade of the surrounding restaurants.

Hasan takes up the story: "Hasip and I were with a professional officer who was using a Bren gun, which we didn't know how to use. Our job was just to hand him the magazines. Then it jammed and he took it down and tried to fix it. Suddenly it went off and I saw Hasip keel over saying: 'I am deeeaaad, Hasan'." He rolls his eyes and sticks out his tongue. "I said, 'Hasip, what happened?' He said, 'I am dead, Hasan'." He laughs and looks at his friend.

"Well, I saw some blood, I thought I had been hit," Hasip says, looking around to make sure everyone could see that it was an understandable mistake. "A bullet must have just scraped me."

Hasan laughs again and remembers another incident. "Another time Hasip and I were sitting under a carob tree. Suddenly there was an explosion next to us. It was so strong we felt the blast. I watched Hasip keel over and I shouted, 'Hasip are you alright?' Again Hasip said, 'no Hasan, I am deeeeaaad'. But there was nothing wrong with him at all! So Hasip died twice in the war!" His shoulders heave with silent laughter and he points a finger at Hasip.

Hasip ignores him. "Ali, my brother, was in a worse place than us; he was in Kaimakli," he says. "I remember there was a car nearby and it smelled really bad. There were dead bodies in it." His words instantly evoke a memory in me. I too know that smell.

I turn to Suleyman who is absent-mindedly watching the comings and goings in the courtyard. "How about you, Suleyman. Were you in Cyprus in 74?"

"Well, unfortunately I was a soldier, too," he tells me. "I had to fight… I was twenty years old."

"With Hasip and Hasan?"

Suleyman laughs. "They were hiding under the bed, both of them…" He looks at them with mock derision. Then continues, "I was at Ay Kassiano, in Nicosia where there was *real* danger.... Actually I had a very bad experience. I was using a bazooka and I was ordered to shoot. This was just behind the *pantopolio*, the market. When you fire a bazooka, first you hide while you prepare the bazooka, and then you have to put it on your shoulder and stand up. So in order to fire, for a moment you are visible to the enemy from the waist upward. You are an easy target. So I got everything ready, got up, pulled the trigger... and the stupid rocket didn't fire! What's more, the manual says that sometimes there may be late ignition so you're expected to remain standing for a minute or so in case it ignites. You can't sit down because it might go off and you'll end up killing yourself. So I had to stand there trembling and sweating like hell. That one minute was like a lifetime for me. I saw my whole childhood go by in front of my eyes until my assistant tapped me on the shoulder. He said, 'one minute is over, you can sit back down now'. I changed the bazooka and the next time it went off successfully." He pauses. "I may have killed someone that day... I don't know if I did .... And I don't want to know... " He looks away lost in thought for a moment, then snaps out of it turning on me abruptly. "But WHY DO YOU ASK such questions on such a beautiful day?" He laughs and takes a deep breath composing himself again.

"I think Suleyman was the one hiding under the bed," Hasan says. "Our company was the only one that fought. All the rest were in their barracks. We went all the way to Küçük Kaimakli."

"Why didn't you let the Turkish troops do the fighting for you?" Mikis asks.

"The bastards didn't come to Nicosia!" Suleyman says.

"Yes they did! They were parachuting from the sky!" I say.

"Only north of Gionyeli," Suleyman says. "They just sent one tank to Nicosia... to boost morale!"

"They had confidence in you!" Mikis says. "They knew Suleyman had the bazooka, and Hasan the Sten gun..."

"Which wasn't even working," Hasan says.

"A funny thing happened after the checkpoints opened," Suleyman says. "I went out to dinner one night with a Greek Cypriot journalist friend of mine. We discovered that her husband was an officer in '74 who was also posted in Ay Kassianos. We started talking about the events of that day. He knew everything that I described down to the last detail, and I knew everything he described, as well! Turns out, we were both in the same place, me on one side and he on the other!"

"Amazing!" Mikis says. "How far apart were you?"

"Fifty metres. But we couldn't see each other because there was this stupid tree in the way. We were both trying to burn it down so that we could get a better shot of each other. We tried everything. We even threw Molotov cocktails at it but they didn't work. So at one point I jumped out, walked to the tree, poured a can of kerosene over it, set it on fire and walked back to my position." He laughs at the memory. "And the Greek Cypriots, like true Cypriots, didn't shoot at me! Because I was doing them a favour as well, you see. After we burned down the tree we continued shooting at each other. That's war Cypriot-style!" We all laugh. After a while Suleyman shakes his head and continues, "I was born in 1954. At the age of four I experienced British tear gas. At the age of nine I lost my father and witnessed the intercommunal fighting of 1963. At the age of sixteen, I had to take up arms, I was in the army in the evening and at school during the day. At the age of twenty I had to fight in a war. My whole generation, both in the north and in the south all more or less experienced the same things. How can we be normal people? I mean think about it!"

"Hasip even went to prison," says Hasan. "We were posted along the ceasefire line in Küçük Kaimakli and Hasip recognised a Greek Cypriot friend of his on the other side. He offered him a Coke. Someone saw him and told the commander that he was helping the enemy so they put Hasip in prison for a bit."

Now it's Hasip's turn to shake his head as he remembers his Greek Cypriot friend. "I met Dinos again after the war in Manchester. He told me that both his brothers were killed. I felt terrible. I didn't know what to do. I felt as if I was the one who had killed his brothers. He said he would never come back to Cyprus again and he never did."

"Luckily I didn't come across any of my classmates," says Hasan. "We were the class of '73, and had all been drafted in the army. Can you imagine shooting your classmates?"

"I have to say that even in the heat of those days," Hasip says, "I was very careful not to shoot someone, in case I killed another Cypriot. Because I always felt myself a Cypriot. And in September when I went to the UK I hugged all my Greek-speaking friends."

Suleyman remembers another story. "Between the first operation and the second, we were still on duty, even though the fighting had stopped. When we were off duty we used this empty house to rest and wash. One night I was there sleeping when I felt my friends shaking me awake. Get up, get up, they said, the second operation has started. I said, what operation? They said, the fighting has started again. So I got up and was just walking down the stairs when a mortar shell fell on top of the house landing on the bed that I had been lying in. That shocked me!" He laughs nervously. "I've said it before and I'll say it again, … we … are … not… normal … people!"

"Ayşe came on holiday," says Hasip. "That's what we say when we talk about the invasion. It was the code message Turkey's foreign minister, Professor Turan Güneş, sent back to Ankara from Geneva giving the go ahead for the invasion when he realised that neither Greece nor Britain were willing to do anything to restore the status quo after the Greek coup. It read: 'I will be delayed here for a while. Let Ayşe go on holiday'. Ayşe was the name of his daughter."

"The problem is Ayşe liked our country too much for our sake and stayed," Hasan adds ruefully.

"We say it was Attila who came," Mikis says, referring to the Greek Cypriot code name for the Turkish army.

We sip our drinks in silence, the ice cold lemonade refreshing on a hot day like today. Suleyman gets up to go and one by one so do the others. Soon only Hasip, Hasan and I are left.

"But what about you?" Hasip asks. "You haven't told us where you were during the war."

"Oh, it's a long story," I say.

"Tell us, tell us," Hasip and Hasan both say together and settle down to listen. "We have nothing better to do." So I tell them.

On the day of the coup, my family and I (apart from my sister who was abroad) were at our house in Kyrenia. My father had left early that morning to go to the office and ended up stuck in Nicosia for a couple of days because of the coup. A curfew had been imposed, so we were a houseful of women, only venturing out once to drive to the supermarket in town to stock up.

There we bumped into everyone we knew, as the whole of Kyrenia had the same idea, loading up our trolleys with rice, pasta, toilet paper and canned food. Neoclis, the owner, was delighted at the business. He had a facial tic, which made him grimace every now and then, and it was particularly pronounced that day under the pressure to serve everyone. The few black greasy strands of hair he had left, which he normally combed from one ear right over to the other in a comical attempt to hide his bald pate, were flying in all directions.

On the way back home we were stopped at a checkpoint. Men with guns ordered my mother to get out of the car and open the boot. They were young boys, not much older than me. They peered inside, looked through the plastic bags and let us go.

My mother sat glued to the radio day and night. When they announced the new president on television she shrieked in shock and indignation. "Nicos Sampson! Of all people!" My grandmother watched crestfallen. When I looked up from the book I was engrossed in to see what all the fuss was about, I saw an ordinary man, though somewhat too young, I thought, to be president. The fact that he was surrounded by gun-toting men in uniform should have told me something, but I was eighteen and not in the least bit interested in politics. So I didn't know that this was the man who had led armed gangs that attacked the Turkish Cypriots, including Hasip's family in the sixties, earning him the nickname of "the butcher of

Omorphita", the area of Nicosia where Hasip and Kokos grew up in.

Half way through the news, the doorbell rang, making us all jump out of our skins. We weren't expecting any visitors, especially as the curfew was still on. We huddled together in a panic, thinking it might be soldiers from the army camp across the bay and wondering whether or not to open.

"Who is it?" my grandmother eventually asked in a tremulous voice. But it was only Koulla, our live-in housekeeper, who had locked herself out by mistake.

The following day rumours started spreading that Turkey was preparing to invade, as it was entitled to do by the Treaty of Guarantee in order to restore constitutional order. The moment my father got back from Nicosia, my mother started nagging him.

"The Turks are coming," she said, following him round the house. "We must leave. Everyone's left Kyrenia already."

"Nonsense," he said pouring himself an ouzo. "They're just sabre rattling."

"But the BBC said they are going to invade," my mother insisted. "The Turkish fleet has already set sail."

My father had heard all this too many times before. "Every time the Turkish admiral puts on his hat, do I have to leave my home?" he said dismissively, taking his ouzo out onto the veranda, where he made himself comfortable with his feet up on the railing. "And where would we go? To Nicosia? Why would it be safer there?"

My mother had it all planned. "We could go to my brother's in Limassol."

"And how do you know they won't land in Limassol?"

"Oh for goodness sakes, why would they go to Limassol?" she said crossly. "It's on the other side of the island."

"They might go to Famagusta," my father argued, as though for argument's sake. "Famagusta has a big port. They might be more interested in that."

"But Kyrenia is just forty miles away!" She lit a cigarette in exasperation and drew on it nervously, trying to think of better arguments to persuade him. "If you don't come, I'll go on my own," she said finally.

My father tried to reassure her. "Don't worry, nothing's going to happen. The big powers will never let them invade. It would be madness." He put his hands behind his head and looked out across the calm blue sea at the dark smudge of the Turkish coastline hanging like a threat just over the horizon. Despite not being reassured, my mother agreed to stay.

Just before the sun went down, I joined my father for a dip in the sea. As we stood on the water's edge, I started telling him about *Jaws*, the book I had just finished reading, all the while gazing worriedly down into the dark waters beneath my feet. So engrossed was I in fending off thoughts of sharks lurking in the depths, that I didn't notice the real threat up in the sky. When I realised that my father wasn't listening to a word I was saying, I followed his gaze and saw two planes flying by overhead at an enormous speed. They looped towards the hills, curved round over the town of Kyrenia and seconds later disappeared in the direction of the Taurus mountains. It was at this point, my father later admitted to me, his heart sank, but it was too late to leave: the curfew was on.

The next morning a toothache woke me at five. I got up to open the shutters but the light was already too strong, so I quickly shut them again without looking out. Had I done so, I would have seen the Turkish warships lying in the flat silvery sea at one-mile intervals all along the coast.

The first person up in the house that morning was Koulla, our housekeeper. As usual she went downstairs to the kitchen to make herself a cup of coffee. It wasn't until she stepped out onto the veranda that she came face to face with the warships and stopped short. Turning towards the army camp across the bay, she saw groups of soldiers also staring out to sea, as if they were about to watch some curious performance in which they played no part. She immediately put down her coffee and rushed upstairs to wake my mother. Normally the first one awake listening to the BBC, on this day she was fast asleep.

Then came the first explosion. Back in my bed, I froze, but tried to calm myself. It was probably just the workers dynamiting Snake island for the foundations of a new hotel they were in the process of building, I reasoned. A split second later my mother burst in, grabbed my arm and pulled me out of bed, sheets and all.

"Stop it," I said crossly. "What are you doing?" Most unlike her, she said nothing, just continued to drag me, feet still tangled in the sheets, into the corridor away from any windows. Koulla was already there and my father also appeared pulling on a pair of trousers. Soon we were joined by my grandmother and aunt Ourana. Another explosion. We heard glass shards tinkling as they fell on the floor.

"Into the car," my father ordered. I quickly put on a pair of shorts and a T-shirt and rushed to the garage. I got into the car and sat in the front passenger seat sharing it with my mother, while the old ladies and Koulla squeezed in the back.

"Are we all here?" my father asked about to drive off.

"Niove!" my grandmother exclaimed in a panic. "Where's Niove?"

Her older sister was still inside the house. Koulla rushed back inside emerging a few minutes later with the old woman in her nightie stumbling half dazed towards the car, having been woken from a drug-induced slumber.

"Have we got everything we might need?" my father asked. The only thing I had taken was my diary. Aunt Niove had her German passport, and my mother her radio.

"What about your jewellery?" my father asked my mother. She looked at him blankly. "Go get it," he ordered, "you never know when we'll be back."

The jewellery box having been retrieved, we were about to drive off when aunt Niove remembered, "My wig! I can't go anywhere without my wig!" We waited a few tense minutes longer in the garage with the gunboats menacingly in front of us and fighter jets screaming by overhead, as Koulla went back in to fetch the wig. Meanwhile another gorgeous Kyrenia day dawned around us, soft pinks and pale blues reflected in the mirror-like sea. It was like a "perfect deception", as Durrell described a similar historical day on the island that started the EOKA campaign against the British in the fifties.

At last all seven of were in the car. My father waited for a lull between the planes, took a deep breath and sped off in a cloud of dust along the dirt road, hoping against hope that the gunboats wouldn't notice us as we shot up to the top of the hill with its perilous incline and back down again on the other side. At the main road he jolted to a stop.

"Left or right," he said and conferred briefly with my mother. The fastest way back to Nicosia was left but that meant driving past the army camp and that was under attack. My parents remembered an Englishman they knew who lived near the village of Trimithi in the Kyrenia mountain range and decided to head there thinking he would give us protection.

"Let's hope we're making the right decision," my father said as he turned right.

The main Kyrenia road was eerily empty. We saw no one, met no other cars. Here and there came bursts of rifle fire, while heavier artillery shells thumped into the mountainside. The planes roared loudly overhead. We felt like a moving target on the road, so as soon as we could, we turned up into the hills, my father driving with one eye up in the sky. When he saw a plane he veered off the road, screeching to a halt under a carob tree. We looked at him as if he'd gone mad. "So that we're not a moving target," he explained. The planes screamed by overhead, so fast and so loud, now here, now there, it was hard to tell which direction they were coming from, even with my face squeezed onto the windscreen. One flew so low above us I thought it would scrape the roof of the car. The planes were accompanied by the crackle of gunfire, but whether it came from the sky or the ground, I couldn't tell.

We eventually made it to the Englishman's house, a sprawling Mediterranean styled villa, with tiled roof and wooden shutters, sitting all on its own above the village, in the shadow of St Hilarion's craggy cliffs. Up here it was peaceful, so we got out and rang the doorbell. No reply. We trouped round the house to find a way in, but all the windows and doors were shut tight, the garden slightly overgrown. Clearly the owner was away.

Round the back I spotted an external staircase leading down to a boiler room and made a mental note just in case we needed somewhere to hide.

"We'll wait here, it should all be over by lunchtime," my father said, basing his assumption on the ability of Cyprus' army to withstand the military might of one of the largest territorial armies of the world.

We sat in the car in the peace of the pine trees surrounding the house, and watched, as though at a drive-in cinema, as down on the coast, the Turkish invasion unfolded before us, gunboats unloading their deadly cargo of soldiers and tanks in perfect formation like a colourful parade, to the accompaniment of explosions at varying degrees of proximity and the rat-a-tat of gunshot fire. We were in the middle of a heatwave and the sea was like a mirror. Normally I would be waking up about now and going into the pool for a swim, complaining to my mother how bored I was. Instead I had front row seats to history. I wished I was still bored.

Hasip and Hasan certainly aren't. They are both leaning towards me from across the table for once not saying anything. I take a sip of lemonade and continue.

As the day wore on it became clear that we wouldn't be going home any time soon. The bombing intensified. We realised we needed to shelter inside the house. I found a bathroom window that had been left slightly ajar and managed to squeeze in through the external wooden bars and opened the front door for the rest of the family.

Inside we saw an English country style living room with chintz curtains, lots of comfortable sofas and armchairs and two enormous Chinese floor vases. A staircase with a stained glass window led upstairs to several bedrooms and bathrooms. We found the phone was still working, so we called my uncle in Limassol. "Leave it to me," he said, "I'll get you out." How he was going to do that though was unclear. What he did, he later told us, was pour himself a stiff glass of scotch, put on his most British of accents and, using his position as Honorary Consul for Belgium, call the British bases. They put him through to the War Office where he was told that, much as they would like to help, their contingent based at St Hilarion castle was also under fire. They couldn't move to save anyone, they said.

Meanwhile my father decided that the area below the staircase was the safest place to be in case a bomb fell on the house. So we collected cushions from the living room sofas and lay them down on the floor so that we could sit more comfortably. Behind us underneath the staircase was a wedge-shaped cupboard in which two bottles of gas were stored. We were a little concerned because there was a distinct smell of gas when you opened the door, which made us wonder whether they were leaking. But as there was nothing we could do about it, we tried not to think about them.

Under the staircase was where we stayed, never wandering too far, not even to the kitchen for a drink of water. The kitchen cupboards were bare, apart from a couple of tins of cat food. "If the worse comes to the worst..." my mother said. Not that any of us was hungry.

We hardly spoke all day long. What was there to say? We were each of us focused only on the waves of explosions, distant at first, then getting closer and closer as the gunboats methodically shelled the land from east to west and back again, thinking any minute now we would be hit, then past us, when we would relax slightly, all the time wondering, when would it all stop? Occasionally we would turn on the radio that my mother had brought with her. Military music came from the state radio station, occasionally interrupted with announcements at how our brave soldiers were forcing the enemy to retreat in Nicosia. Not a word about what was happening in Kyrenia.

At one point in the afternoon we heard voices just outside the front door near where we had parked the car. We froze. Two men were discussing something in Greek. We gave no sign of life pretending there was no one in until eventually they left.

Under the stairs was also where we slept, huddled together, dreaming dreams of explosions and war, grateful the next morning when we woke that we had made it through to another day.

On the second day we faced a different kind of threat. A forest fire had broken out in the hills above us from the bombing. The wind was blowing it in our direction and it was getting closer and closer. Every now and then one of us would go upstairs and look out of a window to check on it. As the day progressed we could hear it crackling, we could smell it, and we could even feel its heat. By late afternoon it had reached the field next door and we started entertaining thoughts about leaving the relative safety of the house. Then the wind changed and the fire died down.

On the third day my mother heard on the BBC that a ceasefire had been agreed, which would come into effect at six that evening. I started counting the hours, but as the day wore on, the bombing got worse. We no longer felt safe under the stairway.

I wanted us to go into the basement but my parents were reluctant to venture outdoors to reach the stairs leading down to it. From time to time I would go to a window and peer out through the shutters trying to calculate the risk. "Stay away from the window," my mother would warn me and I would pull back, only to look out again a little later. I saw yellow fields and the blue sea twinkling in the distance, nothing visually threatening. Only the thuds and booms and crackle of gunfire indicated things were not safe out there.

By the afternoon the explosions became almost constant until finally my parents agreed to try the basement. One by one, as in some Hollywood movie, we each made a dash for it, braving what we expected would be a hail of bullets. None came. No one saw us.

The basement was a small room about four metres by six with a concrete floor and concrete walls. At the far end, opposite the door, sat the boiler. We tried to get comfortable on the uneven floor, the old ladies heaving themselves down with difficulty. We sat down and waited.

Six o'clock came and went. Gradually the bombing subsided though we could still hear occasional gunfire. At some point the old women could no longer take it on that hard floor so they decided it was safe enough to go back up into the house. Koulla went with them. I thought it was too soon to leave the basement and decided to stay a while longer. My parents stayed too.

As daylight faded we heard a new sound. Men shouting, coming down from the mountain and shouting. Shouting and shooting. Getting closer, louder. Suddenly they were everywhere. All around us. I held my breath. A massive explosion rocked the house, followed by the sound of boots above us, around us, inside the house. Another explosion, a smaller one. What was happening? Were the old ladies and Koulla alright? Any minute now, I thought, they would see the stairs leading down to the basement.

"We're going to die." I threw the words out hoping for some reassurance, like a rope ladder thrown over a wall in the hope of escape. My parents said nothing, as if they hadn't heard, as if I hadn't uttered those words. There was nothing they could say, of course. Nothing they could do.

Then from somewhere outside came my grandmother's voice, loud and deliberate, clearly intended for us to hear. "Oh, where are they taking us? Where are they taking us?" Then nothing.

Silence fell over the house, punctuated by occasional gunshots and distant voices. Darkness fell. Nobody moved or spoke for a long time. Then we heard footsteps approaching, coming down the stairs. We held our breath as we watched the handle of the boiler room door being turned, the door opening, and an ashen-faced Koulla coming in.

My parents greeted her ecstatically. "Koulla, you're alive! How did you escape? What happened?"

She told us the Turks had taken the old ladies. "They didn't see me." She had spotted them coming from one of the bedroom windows, heard them shouting to each other as they came. She ran downstairs, warned the old ladies and quickly hid in the cupboard under the staircase, the one with the gas cylinders, grabbing a cushion with her as she went. The old ladies remained seated on the sofas in the living room where the Turks found them. From her hiding place she heard Niove saying "German, German", and knew she would be brandishing her passport. She heard the soldiers searching the house. One soldier opened the door of the cupboard where Koulla was hiding but didn't look behind it even though he must have felt some resistance. Perhaps he thought it was the cushion, which was sticking out a bit behind the door. He shot once into the cupboard. The bullet missed her by a few inches. The next thing she heard was my grandmother calling out as they left.

We went back up into the house and inspected the damage. The Chinese vases lay in pieces on the floor and the sofas had all been slashed. The stained glass window lay shattered on the landing. My father said it must have been from a hand grenade, which caused the explosion we had heard. We crunched upstairs to investigate. My mother started shutting all the windows, as by now darkness was falling. As I looked out from one of them, I saw soldiers approaching again.

"They're coming back!" I shouted. "Stop shutting the windows. They'll know someone's here."

This time we didn't have time to go back down into the basement so we crouched in the first bedroom at the top of the stairs. We didn't even shut the bedroom door.

The soldiers entered the house again. Then we heard the voices of the three old ladies. They had brought them back. My grandmother was going, "Aah, aah". Heavy boots began stomping all over the house again.

"I'm going to shout and let them know that we're here," whispered my mother.

"No, don't make a sound," my father urged her.

For a brief moment she was quiet. Then, "No, it's better we tell them we are here rather than they find us hiding or they'll come in shooting."

"Shush," I hissed.

"I'm going to call," she insisted and stood up to go to the landing. I jumped onto her holding her down and covering her mouth. We struggled a moment silently, my father saying, "Stop it, stop it, sh, be quiet."

We were silenced by the sound of footsteps crunching on the glass on the stairs. We saw a torchlight flicker on the wall outside the open bedroom door. Once again we held our breaths. Even my mother didn't move. Then whoever it was changed his mind and went back downstairs. We waited. The house seemed quieter but we couldn't be sure they had all gone. We could hear the old ladies in the living room talking amongst themselves. My mother got bolder.

"I'm going to call," she said again and before we could stop her she was on the landing. "Mehmet!" she yelled. "Mehmet."

"What? Are you upstairs?" came my grandmother's voice. "We thought you were still in the basement."

"Mehmet!" called my mother, as my grandmother's face appeared.

Fortunately the Turks had gone, so we all came down and joined the old ladies in the living room where we quizzed them to find out what had happened.

"They were speaking in Turkish," my grandmother said.

"Of course they were speaking in Turkish," Ourana interrupted.

"They're Turks, what did you expect them to speak." My grandmother ignored her.

"But you could understand, couldn't you, because you speak Turkish!" My father beamed at his mother encouragingly. She gave a sad little martyrish smile and continued.

"They took us into a field and made each of us sit under a tree. Then they started digging."

"They were digging our graves!" Ourana interrupted again, her eyes like saucers to emphasise the potential horror of the scene.

"At one point," my grandmother continued, "Niove's nightie rose above her legs, you know how she always is, and one of the officers came and pulled it back down. 'No, madame,' he said, 'soldiers here'." She wagged a finger in imitation, while giving her sister a disapproving look.

"And then Ourana started making her will," Niove jumped in. "She started telling me what she wanted to leave to who—her gold bangles to the girls, her ermine coat to Julia…." She snorted. "As if I was going somewhere she wasn't."

"But you had a German passport," Ourana said defending herself.

"What difference would that make?"

"They wouldn't kill a German national," she said as if this were a universally acknowledged truth. "It would cause an international incident!"

My father put an end to the argument. "But why did they bring you back?"

"They probably got fed up with Ourana," Niove said derisively. "She wouldn't stop talking. The soldiers kept on saying 'Shut up, shut up'. And still she wouldn't stop."

We laughed and looked at my grandmother for confirmation. She smiled weakly and shrugged her shoulders. "Who knows?"

The next day the BBC informed us that the British had sent an aircraft carrier, HMS Hermes, to evacuate British citizens from Kyrenia. We decided we had to get on it, even though none of us had a British passport. We filled some bottles with water, got back into the car and my father turned the key. Nothing. The car was dead. He got out to look under the bonnet and found the battery was missing. That's when we remembered those Greek voices we heard outside the front door that first day. They must have stolen it. We had no other choice now but to go on foot.

Out in the open after three days in hiding, I felt exposed, vulnerable. As we walked down towards the coast, I became acutely aware of my surroundings. All my senses were on high alert, as if I were on some kind of drug, in a state of altered consciousness. The colours of the trees and bushes seemed a brighter clearer green, as if it had just rained and washed away the dust, the sky seemed to dazzle and the sounds of the countryside were clearer and louder than normal. I picked up everything, the twitter of the birds, the sizzle of cicadas, which normally I may not have noticed. Mostly I was aware of an eerie silence. Occasionally in the distance came gunshots, too far away to worry about, but spread out enough over the landscape to make me more aware of its depth and breadth and my place in it. It was as though I was in a Sensurround movie, or a three-dimensional game, a game of life and death. Lose focus and it would be game over.

The old ladies struggled in the heat. They had to stop frequently to rest and take a sip of water. After a while, a bright red open-roofed MG came by. My father flagged it down. The driver was a British expat with red bushy hair and thick sideburns. He looked at us suspiciously. As politely as possible my father explained to him about the heat and the old ladies and asked if he would be so kind as to take them down to the next village in his car.

"Dreadfully sorry, old chap, this isn't my war. I'm not getting involved," the man said and drove off, leaving my father to stare after him muttering something about the different kinds of people there are in this world.

We continued to make our way slowly downwards until we reached a cluster of houses. Some people came out and spoke with my father and before I knew it they had made a two-roomed house with three double beds available to us. They even slaughtered a chicken for us to eat. Koulla boiled it and left it on the kitchen window to cool where unfortunately a cat passed by and gobbled some of it up.

The villagers all gathered round my father and held endless political discussions. One problem they faced was what to do with a young Greek Cypriot soldier they had found in a ditch who had been wounded in the head. They had buried his uniform and were nursing him back to health. In the evening the men decided to head up to the nearby village of Trimithi to get supplies. My father wanted to go with them to see if he could find a battery for the car, but my grandmother put her foot down.

"You're not going anywhere," she said firmly. "If you go, we all go."

No amount of arguing would change her mind. She was adamant. So he stayed, albeit reluctantly at having to give in to a woman.

My grandmother's instincts turned out to have been right. None of the men who went to that village came back that day. They ended up as prisoners of war in a jail in Adana, Turkey. Weeks later we saw them on TV being interviewed by the BBC. There was old Yacoumis and the rest of them beaming at the cameras being asked, "Is there anything you want to know from the outside world?" and replying, "Yes, what did Manchester United do?"

Around lunchtime the following day there was a commotion. The Turkish army had surrounded the village. They entered the village square, guns at the ready, vigilant and alert, a soldier at each corner. We watched them warily and they us. The officer, who spoke perfect English with an

American accent, addressed the village headman who called my father to translate. Everyone was to come out of their homes and gather in the square. My mother turned to me and ever so slightly gave me a nod. I understood that she wanted me to go back inside the house and get her jewellery. I slipped back into the door and was just bending down under the bed to reach the box when I saw a pair of army boots follow me in. I froze and looked up. The soldier pointed his gun at me and then under the bed, as if to say what's under there? Thinking quickly, I pushed the box as far under the bed as I could and picked up my diary instead. I stood up and, as nonchalantly as I could, presented it to him. For a moment neither of us moved staring at each other. Then he motioned that I should give it to him. I handed it over and watched him flick through the pages intently, as if this was the most interesting book in the world. As if he could read it. My heart beat fast as I stood there, like a pupil caught redhanded writing naughty notes in class. Except this teacher held a gun which was pointed at me. He's a human being, I thought naively, we're both human beings, surely he wouldn't. After what seemed like an eternity, he handed me back my diary and let me join the others outside.

I never got a chance to retrieve the box as we were all ordered to leave the village immediately. They made us walk down to the main road to Kyrenia, a few minutes away. There we gathered on the pavement outside a shop with shattered windows. The Turks then proceeded to draw up lists of names according to nationality. "We need it for the Red Cross," the officer said, but it seemed they were trying to separate the men from the women and children. There was much shouting and arguing and this went on for ages. At one point word went round that some of the Turks had gone back to the village. Shortly afterwards a couple of shots rang out.

What seemed like hours later a UN jeep went by. My father immediately jumped out into the road and tried to flag it down. The driver slowed down but didn't stop, looking back briefly as he continued down the road. But a little later the jeep returned, accompanied by a small armoured personnel carrier. The chief officer got out and asked what was going on. He said he became concerned when he saw us because there had been rumours about a whole village having been massacred on a beach further down along the coast and didn't want to let something like that happen again. A young English woman was sitting in the UN jeep with her four year old son. She had been holidaying in one of the villages and had spent the three days of the war out in the countryside using her Girl Guide knowledge to survive. My parents and a few other villagers persuaded the UN to accompany them back to the village. When they came back my mother told me that they had found the soldier had been shot dead. Her jewellery box lay under the bed empty. Only two pieces were saved, a brooch and a diamond ring that my father had taken out of the box and slipped into his pocket when we were still up at the Englishman's house.

From that point on the UN took over and arranged for everyone to be taken back to the Dome hotel in Kyrenia which they had turned into their headquarters. Koulla and I got to ride back in the personnel carrier. The UN soldiers helped us climb into the hatch and told us to stand half in half out. "Hang on," they said, and sped off, swerving frequently to avoid the craters in the road. There were no other cars on the road. Along the way we passed some shops with broken windows. Some people were coming out laden with things. Here and there were the blackened bodies of burnt cars. Near the army camp next to the turning to our house, I saw a car in a ditch by the side of the road as flat as a newspaper. A putrid stench emanated from it, a smell I had never smelled before or since, or ever want to again.

Up ahead a battalion of Turkish soldiers came towards us, marching in formation in the middle of the road. "Which side of the road do we drive on now?" the driver asked his mate, slowing down. "In Turkey they drive on the right." They joked about it a bit, debating whether to play chicken or not, then chose to stick to the left. The battalion adjusted itself accordingly.

The Dome hotel was like a crowded airport terminal during a strike. There were people everywhere, sitting and lying against every bit of wall they could find, along the corridors, the great rooms, in the bar, the halls, the games rooms. Seven thousand people in all, we were told, had sought refuge there. Somehow, my father managed to get us all a room on the second floor where, from the tiny balcony overlooking the hotel's entrance, I would watch the UN cars coming and going. In the evenings I would listen to the sounds of the night, no longer the buzz of traffic, but mainly of cats and dogs howling in the distance as they foraged for food.

My father found many people he knew in the hotel. They had set up a committee in charge of food, at first using up whatever was in the hotel's fridges and when that ran out, Neoclis, who with his tic and greasy hair, was also there, made several trips together with the UN to bring whatever hadn't gone bad in his shop back to the hotel. Each day the committee and the UN would draw up lists—lists of people with Greek passports, lists of people with Cypriot passports, lists of people with foreign passports. A few foreign correspondents managed to reach the hotel to interview people. The German magazine *Stern* sent a reporter to interview Aunt Niove, the only German national there, but judging from the desperate look in his eye as he tried to make head or tail of her answers, I doubt he got much sense out of her. The German ambassador was the first to come to pick up his citizens—none other than Aunt Niove again. But she point-blank refused to go. "What am I going to do in Nicosia on my own?" she said and sent the ambassador away empty handed. The next day everyone tried to persuade her that she must go and a few days later the ambassador was summoned back again. Just before she left, Aunt Ourana took her sister aside and again told her how she wished to dispense of her worldly possessions. This time my grandmother joined in as well.

We rose and slept with the sun, as there was no electricity, of course. I would often sit on the rocks by the hotel pool and stare at the mountains and coastline that I loved so much, wishing that I would never see it again, so desperate was I to get away.

Finally, after about two weeks, the UN told my father that they had arranged for a bus to go to Nicosia and that my grandmother, aunt Ourana and Koulla were on the list of people going back. "Lucky you," I told my grandmother. "You'll be able to go home and eat well and have a bath." She pretended to be happy at the thought, but we all knew she hated being separated from her precious son.

Meanwhile, Hasan has made himself comfortable across several chairs as usual, feet on one and an arm on another. Hasip is playing with his glass of lemonade nodding for me to continue. The Han seems quieter as most people have stopped to have lunch, but not even Hasip is hungry yet.

The next day, I tell them, the UN announced they had arranged for another bus to Nicosia and this time we were on it. My mother and I got on and waited for my father who was busy chatting to the UN head of command. When he got on the bus, he looked anxious. As he took his seat next to my mother, I heard him tell her in a low voice, "Do you know, what the UN chief asked me to do? He asked me to call UN HQ when we get to Nicosia and tell them we arrived safely. Apparently he hasn't received any word about what happened to yesterday's bus."

My father's anxiety increased when he noticed that the rest of the passengers on the bus were all mainland Greeks, perhaps the families of Greek army personnel. We were probably put with them since my father had a Greek passport, but he wasn't at all happy about being on the same bus as people who might be considered to have been coupists. Then an armed Turkish Cypriot police officer got on board, sat in the front and the bus set off. My parents kept on looking back to see if we had a UN escort but there was none.

As we drove into Nicosia, I listened to my parents in the seat behind me quietly pointing out buildings and places to each other that they hadn't seen since the early '60s.

"Look there's Christis' factory…"

"And there's the Severis flour mills…"

They also recognised the Seray hotel in the heart of the Turkish sector of Nicosia where the bus stopped. Here the Turkish Cypriot police officer ordered all the men over the age of fifteen and below fifty to get off the bus. This caused an uproar. People objected, they begged and pleaded and argued. But there was nothing for it but to obey. I watched as a woman clung desperately to her teenage son. My father told them he was fifty-six, but that didn't seem to make a difference. He lowered his head and reluctantly got off the bus along with the rest of the men. My mother sat stoically and said nothing.

The bus set off again with only women and children on board. It weaved its way through the old part of Nicosia pulling up at a two-roomed house with a courtyard, which we were told was a school. A couple of Turkish Cypriot policewomen appeared. They ordered us to take off any jewellery we were wearing and hand it to them for safekeeping. We had to stand in line while they searched us. The courtyard was empty. A trail of liquid—urine—flowed across it and green bottle flies buzzed around it. At the far end were two classrooms. Inside one I could just make out a group of people. They seemed to be waving to us.

"That looks like *yiayia*!" I told my mother, barely believing it myself.

"Don't be ridiculous," she said. "Your grandmother is relaxing and having a nice bath at home."

But no, as we soon discovered, my grandmother was indeed in there, along with aunt Ourana and Koulla. They were delighted to see us. They had spent the night there on the floor with just a blanket. We would be joining them. No one knew how long we would be staying there or why. It soon dawned on us that we were prisoners. The Turkish Cypriot policewomen seemed nice enough, but they were essentially our guards. I went up to the iron gates of the yard and looked out onto the street. How hard would it be to escape their attention and run? I began to plot my escape.

As it happened I didn't have long to plot. By evening the rumour spread that we were to be released. We were put back onto buses and driven to a checkpoint in the heart of the old town, not far from where we were being held. There to my surprise we met up with my father. He had been put in a real jail and given a blanket and a bucket in which to urinate. He had finally managed to convince his captors of his age and they had let him go.

Despite warnings that we might be shot by the Greek Cypriots when we tried to cross, we crossed anyway. I went first. As soon as I stepped over some invisible line, a gaggle of men with long hair and scraggly beards patted me on the back and cheered. We were promptly bundled into trucks and taken to Antonakis Bar, one of the oldest nightspots in the old town, where we had the most delicious plate of spaghetti I ever had.

The next day we went to my uncle's house in Limassol. There life was normal, as if the rest of the island were not being torn apart. The only indication that things had changed was the fact that my uncle was told to fire his Turkish Cypriot housekeeper. I don't know who told him that and what they threatened him with, all I know is that he and my parents discussed the situation at length and with much anger and indignation every evening. In the end he complied.

News of the Turkish army's second push, almost a month later, which left them holding the eastern beach town of Famagusta, was a distant story. Turkey now held over a third of the island. The Turkish Prime Minister, Bulent Ecevit declared "we are now in a situation where the foundations have been laid for the new Federal State of Cyprus."

Most of the tables around us are empty now. Ahmet is sitting down at the far corner waiting for more customers or just relaxing after a busy day. Yusuf is tidying up some of the chairs, stacking the extra ones near the entrance. Hasip and Hasan are uncharacteristically silent.

"We gave them Marina and got Sevil," Hasip says eventually. His future wife came from Limassol and was amongst Turkish Cypriots who had been rounded up and held in a stadium there for whom my family and I were exchanged. We were both part of an overall exchange of populations that our leaders had agreed on.

"You were very lucky," Hasan acknowledges. "You were in the worst area under St Hilarion."

We're quiet for a while contemplating the role of fortune in one's existence, until Hasip decides to lighten the mood.

"You should have called us!" he says. "We would have saved you!"

We all laugh. Beyond our table, a few people are wandering about in the courtyard, the sun beating down relentlessly on the cobbles.

11 WORDS, FOOD AND POLITICS

A report by the European Commission of Human Rights that came out shortly after the invasion, brings home exactly how lucky I was. It lists human rights violations that occurred in Cyprus at the time of the Turkish invasion. In it witnesses describe killings of civilians in their homes, streets or fields, as well as of people under arrest or in detention. Women of all ages were raped, while in some areas, enforced prostitution was practised. All the women and girls of an entire village were rounded up and put into separate rooms in empty houses where they were raped repeatedly, some of them in front of their own children, others in public. In some cases after being raped, the victims were stabbed or killed. People were whipped, had their heads knocked against walls, their teeth broken, their chests and hands jumped and stepped on, cigarettes stubbed on their skin, their bodies beaten with electrified clubs and pierced with bayonets, dirty liquids poured on them. Most of the acts described occurred after the ceasefire when Turkish armed forces were not engaged in any war activities. One witness, a schoolteacher, one of two thousand Greek Cypriot men deported to Turkey, described how he and his fellow detainees were repeatedly beaten after their arrest, on their way to Adana, in jail in Adana and in prison camp at Amasya. Another witness described conditions in detention camps in Cyprus at the Pavlides Garage and the Saray prison in the Turkish quarter of Nicosia (where my father was held), as reported to him by former detainees. Food, he said, consisted of one-eighth of a loaf of bread a day, with occasional olives; there were two buckets of water and two mugs which were never cleaned, from which about a thousand people had to drink; toilets were filthy, with faeces rising over the basins; floors were covered with faeces and urine.

Not included in this report were human rights violations committed by Greek Cypriots against Turkish Cypriots, which came to light later. In Tochni/Tashkent near Larnaca, eighty-five people were massacred. The men were first arrested and put on two buses and then killed, the women were gathered in a house and raped. The remains of the men on the first bus were eventually found in Gerasa and those of the second bus in Pareklisia. Their surviving wives now live in Vouno, a village in the north, which has come to be known as the 'Village of the Widows'.

In the tiny Turkish Cypriot villages of Aloa, Maratha and Sandallari near Famagusta, Greek Cypriots rounded up all the men and sent them to prison camps in Limassol. They then established themselves in the village and subsequently raped many women and young girls. This continued until 14 August 1974 when Turkey launched the second operation towards Famagusta. At that point the men decided to flee and not wanting to leave behind any witnesses, they killed everyone, about ninety people, including the elderly and babies, their bodies buried in a mass grave with a bulldozer.

One Saturday I wake up to the sound of rolling thunder and heavy rain, but by eleven it has more or less stopped. I hunt for an umbrella and set off for the Büyük Han.

When I enter the courtyard I don't see any of my friends in their usual place under the arches. Has no one come? Where is our table? Did the rain put them off? What happened to rain or shine there's always someone here? Then I notice friendly hands waving at me from the cobbles. They have moved the table into the sun, leaving our usual place under the arches, which now looks empty and cold.

As I look for a place to sit, I'm told I have a choice—"*güneş karşı* or no *güneş*"—facing the sun or in the shade with my back to it. There is also *ortada*, or in Greek, *kai ilio kai skia*, half in the sun and half in the shade. I choose to sit facing the sun and drag a chair next to Hasan.

"*Güneş nazi cekiliyor*," he tells me as I squeeze in. "The winter sun can be tolerated." Indeed it can and it soon makes me take off my jacket.

"We have decided *yağmur bitti*, there won't be any more rain," Andreas says a few seats further down, pulling up a chair on which two other umbrellas have been placed and indicating that I should add mine. A chorus of "*yağmur bitti*" echoes down the table.

"*Vroshi telos*," Hasan says, starting another chorus of 'no more rain' but this time in Greek. He smiles pleased with himself.

"*I vrochi eteleiose*," Andreas corrects, enunciating every syllable. "That's proper Greek." Hasan practices it.

"Yesterday was something else," Hasip says. "We experienced so much rain it was unbelievable."

"Yes, but yours was pseudo-rain," Andreas says.

"*Re Ahmet, polli vrochi simera*," Hasan tells the coffee shop owner, as he distributes the coffee from his tin tray.

"Did you hear that?" Andreas proudly tells Ahmet in Greek. "He's learned to speak Greek!"

Ahmet hovers behind him silent and serious, slowly trying to get his head round all the many goings on. "I heard," he says grumpily, "but I wasn't sure what language he was speaking."

"You see Ahmet's Greek is *'villageois'* Greek," Andreas says. "He comes from Vatily, he knows nothing. He only knows Cypriot Greek. So when Hasan spoke proper Greek he got confused."

"He's not like us aristocrats," Hasan says and sniffs haughtily.

Ahmet takes a few more orders and leaves.

I notice a bunch of bananas in the middle of the table. "From which republic are these bananas?" I ask.

"Funny you should say that," Hasip says, "we were just having a big argument with Suleyman here, whether ours is a bigger banana republic than yours. Before we met Andreas, we always thought that the country was better managed on your side than ours. Nowadays we're not so sure."

"Yes, but we were the original banana republic," I say.

"I'm afraid that's not correct, my dear," Suleyman says, shaking his head at me. "You forget that we set up the first banana republic together."

"True, but you took the banana that we planted together and left and planted your own."

"We're both equally stupid," Andreas says.

"Meanwhile, pass me one banana, please," Hasip says reaching for one.

"The Turkish Cypriots authorities excelled themselves today," Andreas says after a bit. He speaks loudly so the whole table can hear. "They gave me a speeding fine from last year. Should we write a letter to the newspapers complaining about how long it takes them to issue a fine?"

Hasan thinks a moment then says, "No, because people will wonder why. You see this is very normal behaviour on our side."

"The car insurance to go to the north is a hundred euros for the whole year," Mikis says from further down the table, unfolding a piece of paper that he had in his pocket and storing it in his wallet. "They told me that as a favour, *hattirika,* they would charge me seventy euros. In Turkish, the guy said, *hattir icin.* I know *hattir* means favour, because we use it, but what is *icin?*"

"*Icin* means 'for'," Hasan explains.

"Oh, for your *hattir*! For your sake!"

"Yes, it means especially for you," Hasan says. "We Cypriots say a lot of things like that, but we don't actually mean them."

"Yes, it's a complete lie," adds Andreas. "It's the famous Cypriot marketing strategy. Except it doesn't work any more. People have wised up."

A white haired man with a round smiling face arrives at the table. People greet him as *'daskalos'*, teacher.

"Kyriakos *daskalos* comes from the village of Afania," Andreas informs everyone, doing the introductions. "It's the same village that Sevtap comes from, the lady whose restaurant we are going to for lunch today."

"Yes, she was a very beautiful young girl in 1974 when we left the village," Kyriacos says wistfully. "I may even have been a little bit in love with her sister." He smiles bashfully and adds, "but our families wouldn't let us marry."

"Kyriakos," Andreas continues, "likes to teach, but unfortunately in doing so he also has a tendency to get himself arrested." We all look at him curious to hear more.

Kyriakos laughs and obliges. "After the checkpoints opened I would often visit some people I knew who lived in the Karpas. There I became quite good friends with the village headman, the *muhtar*. One day he asked me if I could teach him and a few of his friends to speak Greek. I said of course, so we got together at his house one evening and I started to teach them the basics. Gradually word spread round the village and more and more Turkish Cypriots joined our group until eventually it got too crowded in the *muhtar's* living room. We started looking for somewhere else where we could meet and someone suggested we use the village school, which was closed in the afternoons. 'You're the *muhtar*,' they said, 'open it.' So he did. But then one day the police arrived. They barged in and made us all step outside while they searched the place. We did as we were told, not thinking too much about it. Then a policeman said that they had received information that this man, and he pointed at me, had put a bomb in the building. The next thing I knew, they had put me and the *muhtar* in jail for the night. Fortunately the next day it was all cleared up. They let us go, apologising. Maybe some nationalists wanted to put an end to the Greek lessons and tried to scare us."

Suddenly someone comes up from behind me and covers my eyes. I turn round to see the big smile and pretty face of my friend Ipek. She's wearing an attractive brightly coloured dress that brings out her olive skin. Everyone has stopped talking and turned to look at her. She returns the look, politely smiling all round and nodding hello to a few people like Sarper, who she already knows. Andreas invites her to join us. He pulls over a chair from a nearby table and, like the *muhtar*, or community chief at some state function, makes everyone shift along to make room for the new guest.

"Ipek's father used to play football with Centinkaya," Sarper tells us. "He played centre half."

"Really?" Andreas says. "So he must have been a very well-known footballer."

"People used to say, you might be able to pass the ball, but not my father," Ipek says proudly.

"Does he still play?"

"No, now he owns a sports shop and I work there with him."

"The most exciting matches were always the ones between Cetinkaya and Apoel," Andreas adds.

"Cetinkaya was always a very nationalistic team," Hasan says.

"Both teams were," Andreas says.

"Some of the players became MPs," says Sarper, knowledgeable as usual. "They controlled TMT through the football team. Turkish Cypriot teams withdrew from the Cyprus Football Association in 1955, following the beginning of EOKA. The last match to take place was between Larnaca side Pezoporikos and Cetinkaya in the semi-final of the Cyprus Cup."

"For fifty years the problem has been in our heads," Mikis mutters.

"Do you play football too?" Andreas asks Ipek.

"No, I play tennis."

I explain that we both love tennis and met at the Field Club in Nicosia, where we played a couple of tournaments against each other.

Ahmet appears for more orders. "Ah, Mr Ahmet, we have brought you a new customer," Andreas tells him in Greek. "Her father was a very famous football player. He played for Cetinkaya. But you aren't with Cetinkaya, are you. You are with…"

"Fenerbahçe," Ahmet says.

Andreas remembers his manners. "What are you going to have, Ipek? Would you like some *rizogalo*? What about a *muhallebi*? Or *sütlü*?" He turns to Hasip and Hasan. "That means tea with milk, right?" Hasip and Hasan nod their heads and glance at each other, trying to suppress their smiles.

Ipek thinks a moment. "Mmm, I love *muhallebi*," she says, hesitating. "But I think I will have coffee."

Andreas throws his head back and laughs. "You're a typical Cypriot. Offer a Cypriot something he wants, and he's bound to say no. That's why there will never be a solution to the Cyprus problem. Even if it's the best deal in the world, we are bound to say no!" He leans forward and picks up the olive bread that someone has brought from the middle of the table. "There's also *zeytunlu*. Is that the right word, *zeytunlu*?" He looks at Hasip and Hasan for confirmation. They nod vigorously and assure him that it is, it is. Andreas eyes them suspiciously.

"Are you teaching me wrong things?"

"Who us?" says Hasan.

"Never!" says Hasip.

Andreas isn't so sure. "I don't trust you," he says. "You let me order 'Türkçe kahve', meaning Turkish-speaking coffee instead of 'türk kahve', Turkish coffee, for five years without telling me it was wrong."

"Until Sevil spoilt our fun," Hasip laughs remembering how his wife had told them off for not correcting him. "We went 'sh, sh,' to her, but it was too late."

Just then Mikis, who has been engrossed in his newspaper, lets out a derisive snort. "The UN is saying that it's either now or never for a solution to reunite Cyprus on the basis of federation. They say this is the endgame and that they aren't going to bother with us forever. They want our leaders to reach an agreement one way or another. Of course, the Greek Cypriot press are attacking Alexander Downer again."

"They want to kill the messenger," Andreas says laughing. "As if the UN will replace Downer just because the Greek Cypriots don't like him."

"And even if they did change him," Mikis says, "we're bound to hate his replacement too! If he doesn't support our views one hundred percent, we assume he's on the side of the Turks. It's been like that for years."

"Unfortunately, I have to get back to Gaziveren," Suleyman says, collecting his hat and camera.

"You see, he is *villageois*, after all," Andreas says. "He lives in a village."

"Are you joining us for lunch, Ipek?" Andreas asks.

"No," Ipek says. "I have a tournament this afternoon."

"I see now why you are a *champignon* of tennis," Andreas says.

"The word is *şampiyon*, Andrea," Hasan says grinning triumphantly.

"Oh, ok, *şampiyon*," he says, brushing away his mistake with a wave of his hand, almost hitting Suleyman in the process.

"*Re* Andrea," Suleyman objects. "Why do you talk like this, with your arms?" He copies Andreas' gesticulations. "You almost hit me!"

"Because I am a Cypriot *köylü*."

"Go have your coffee on the Greek side, you rude Cypriot. *Theo mou!*"

"*Thee mou*," Andrea corrects him. "Come on, let's go and eat."

We all get up and go in our different directions. Andreas, Hasip, Hasan, Mikis, Kyriakos, Kokos, Sarper and I, set off through the streets of old Nicosia for the restaurant.

Round the corner from the Han we stop at Hasan's shop to say hello to his blonde blue-eyed wife, Nurdan, who graciously agrees to run the shop on her own on Saturdays so that Hasan can be with us. She kisses us all one by one as we troop in and fill up the shop's two aisles, slightly overwhelmed as she tries to answer all our questions on the price of nuts and Turkish delight, while also attending to her regular customers.

We then continue through the pedestrian part of the old town along the busy streets filled with shoppers idly going in and out of shops and waiters serving people sitting at tables in the street, and on to the Selimiye Mosque, once known as the Ayia Sophia church, one of the largest and oldest surviving gothic churches in Cyprus, which to my grandmother was as venerable as the Ayia Sophia church in Istanbul.

Sevtap's restaurant is situated in the grounds at the back of the mosque. It consists of five or six tables placed in the shade of tall pine and cypress trees or under large umbrellas. It's very quiet and peaceful and only a couple of the tables are occupied. A tiny annex serves as the kitchen. A low wall surrounds the mosque on the other side of which is an empty lot, surrounded by old buildings.

The usual debate ensues over where to sit—in the sun, or under the trees, under the umbrella, or near the building—until we finally join a couple of tables together and place them close to the sandstone wall where it's warmest, dragging over an umbrella as well, just in case there's more rain.

"*Merhaba,*" Andreas says to a young girl who has come to help. "Seftap?" he asks using the inflection of his voice to ask the question where language fails him.

"*Gelecek,*" the girl replies.

"Ah, *gelecek*. She's coming," Andreas says. He turns to us. "Shall we go inside and see what there is today?" He saunters off towards the kitchen followed by a few of the others. Hasip, Hasan and I take our seats at the table.

"What are you having, Hasip?" Hasan asks.

"*Köfte,*" he replies. "Sevil never makes it for me, because it's fried." He sits down at the head of the table. "Hasan, you go in and order for me, please."

"Sure, I will go and order for you," Hasan says and promptly sits down next to him. "Or better still, why don't you go and order for me as well? *Köfte*, chips and salad, please."

"Okay," says Hasip pleasantly without moving. "I'll wait until *kargaşalık* finishes ordering because I'm sure, with him in there, they must be going crazy!"

I offer to convey both their orders for them and follow the others to the kitchen to see what there is today. Inside the kitchen annex it's dark and narrow. I squeeze past Mikis and Kokos trying to decipher the menu written on a blackboard near the entrance.

"Ah, *türlü*," Mikis says recognising a word. "That must be mixed vegetables."

Andreas is in the back peering at the dishes of steaming food behind a glass counter.

"Is that *louvi*?" he asks. The girl, who has followed him in, looks at him blankly. Clearly the word for black-eyed peas is not the same in both our languages.

Just then Sevtap herself emerges through the doorway.

"*Hoşgeldin, Hoşgeldin!*" she says smiling at everyone and wiping her hands on her apron before taking it off. "*Kopiaste.*" She, like Ahmet, is a bilingual Cypriot. While age has worn her features, she is still a striking beauty, with her green eyes, reddish hair and high cheekbones.

"You look very beautiful today. *Çok güzel,*" Andreas says putting his fingers together in a gesture of admiration. "Did you go to the *kuaför*?"

Sevtap laughs and brushes him away embarrassed. Then she notices Kyriacos. They both blush and embrace warmly. As the proxy representative of her sister who was once in love with this man, she is endearingly shy.

"What delicious things do you have today, Sevtap?" Andreas asks in Greek.

Sevtap goes through what's on offer, "*koutsia, dolma, louvi, köfte, makaroni poulli.*" A selection of pulses, meatballs and the hearty peasant dish of Cyprus, boiled chicken and pasta with grated halloumi cheese.

"*Ehei molohia?*" Kokos asks. M*olohia*, a spinach-like green cooked in tomatoes, surprisingly is unknown in the south. There is *molohia*, so Kokos orders some.

"Are we going to order separate dishes each, or a selection for everyone, in the middle, *ortaya*?" Andreas asks. We all agree on *ortaya*, in true Cypriot fashion preferring a little bit of everything, rather than committing to one dish.

"We're eight," Andreas tells Sevtap. "*Oxto. Sekiz portion.*"

Sevtap never writes anything down, yet remembers everything. Back at the table Andreas decides where everyone will sit. "You sit there, Kyriakos will sit *karşı*, opposite, and I will sit here."

A man has joined us who I don't know but who I see sometimes at the Han. He's also called Andreas, is our age, dressed all in denim, with an open friendly face. He sits down at the end of the table opposite me and next to Kokos. Of course, the conversation turns to the Cyprus problem, with Kokos and he both vying with one another to see who knows our recent history better and in greater detail. I listen to them riveted, barely registering the usual banter going on down the other end of the table. On one aspect this new Andreas definitely has the edge.

"Do you know how many Greek Cypriot missing persons there are from the sixties?" he asks. Ever since 1974 the Greek Cypriot propaganda machine has broadcast far and wide that one thousand six hundred and nineteen Greek Cypriots had disappeared as a result of the Turkish invasion and that Turkey refused to tell us what happened to them. Meanwhile the Turkish Cypriots have responded with demands from our side to tell them what happened to their missing from the sixties. That there are also Greek Cypriots missing from that time is news to me.

"A few dozen?" Kokos replies.

"Forty-four," the new Andreas says with precision. "And Turkish Cypriots?"

"Many more, I would guess," Kokos says. "A couple of hundred?"

"Four hundred and ninety-five."

The waitress arrives with the drinks and almost immediately afterwards brings the food, two plates of each dish that we ordered, which she distributes evenly, one at each end of the table so that everything is in reach of everyone.

A couple goes by along the path by the side of the mosque who Andreas recognises. "*Kopiaste*," he calls to them. "Come and join us. All the food here is pseudo food." They laugh and wish us *bon apetit*.

Hasip serves himself a huge portion of *köfte* and digs in with relish. "Ate, *kaliorises*," he says.

"What's he saying?" asks Andreas puzzled.

I laugh. "He's mixing up *kali orexi* with *kolosorises*." Bon appétit with welcome.

"I was just trying to show off to Hasan that I know one word more than him."

"Those showers we had earlier on were almost tropical," says Mikis looking up at the sky. "It's called convection rain."

"You know that *köfte* is not very healthy, Hasip," Andreas says concerned about his friend's health.

"… it reaches a cold area there, it condenses, forms clouds. Cumulonimbus, they're called," Mikis continues.

"Everything good is harmful," Hasip sighs munching away.

"In thirty years we will all be dead anyway," Kokos says, his mouth full.

For a while the only sound we can hear is that of cutlery. Here in the grounds of the mosque it is quiet. No sounds of traffic disturb us. A few cats wander about under the tables meowing for a morsel of food. Overhead the sun goes in and out of the clouds casting patterns of shade and light on the ground around us.

"Our side never admitted that there were Greek Cypriot missing in the sixties," the new Andreas continues, "because if they did, they would then have to admit that there were also Turkish Cypriot missing. And for obvious reasons they didn't want to do that."

Nevertheless, he tells us, a few years ago the Missing Persons Committee started investigating and relatives gave samples of their DNA. His father-in-law, whose brother was amongst the missing, went too.

"They found his brother's body last year," he tells us. "The Turkish Cypriots were building a road near the village of Mandres when they found human remains. Someone said, 'stop, there's people buried here'."

He speaks fast and intensely, barely pausing to take a breath, let alone to take a bite of the food on his plate. He's like a man who knows an important truth and wants everyone to know it. He describes how the Committee had unearthed the bodies of six people buried in a makeshift grave there. Their arms had been tied behind their backs and their skulls smashed. They also found the remains of coats and jumpers.

"Clearly this had been a winter, not a summer, occurrence," he says and looks at us meaningfully to make sure we've understood, but then spells it out anyway. "1964 not 1974."

He goes on to tell us that these murders were in return for Turkish Cypriots having been killed by Greek Cypriots in the '60s. They had rounded up these Greek Cypriots and approached Makarios asking him to return the Turkish Cypriots they know they had taken. Makarios called his henchmen, who denied they were holding anyone.

"The Turkish Cypriots weren't stupid; they figured we had killed their people."

He then tells us that after the war in 1974 he read an article claiming that Denktash had wanted to return the bodies of about two hundred Greek Cypriots that had ended up in the north. "But guess what? Our government wouldn't take them!"

Kokos nods knowingly. "We didn't want them because it would ruin our story, the pretence we were keeping up for propaganda purposes that we had all these missing persons which the other side refused to acknowledge."

The new Andreas pauses and takes a few bites of his food. At the other end of the table, the others are chatting and joking as usual. Eventually he says, "You know what I would do if I were president? I would tell the Turkish Cypriots, I want to understand your side but I want you to understand mine too. For one thing, I would acknowledge that the Turkish Cypriots also have refugees, just as we do."

"Oh yes," says Kokos. "Three times they were refugees. Greek Cypriots often forget that we aren't the only ones with a refugee problem, that the Turkish Cypriots too lost their homes and were displaced, living in tents and refugee camps eleven years before we did."

"But we must also acknowledge the murders that took place," the new Andreas says.

He is interrupted by a plate being passed down to our side of the table. "These dolma are called fake dolma," Sarper says.

"They are pseudo-dolma," Andreas says.

"*Yalanci*," Sarper adds. "Without meat. They're called fake dolma because they're stuffed with rice instead of minced meat."

"They have the same word in Greece—*yalantzi*," says Mikis. "It's a dish that the Greeks from Istanbul brought with them when they were kicked out of the city."

"We're only interested in words at this table," says Hasan. "Not so much food."

"No, we like the food, too," Hasip objects.

The new Andreas serves himself and continues. "I was an officer in the army in 1974. One night in August, after the second operation, I took my unit out to a restaurant. About twenty of us. All sitting at a long table eating and drinking. My men were all at one end and a bunch of reservists were at the other. They were older than us. At one point I heard one of them boasting. He said, 'up in Aloa, at Sadallari...' He stresses the names of these villages, filling them with significance. "At Aloa, at Sadallari, I shot a Turkish Cypriot woman carrying her child. She fell and the child, who was two or three years old, started running. So I grabbed it by its little legs and threw it into the ditch.' Those were his words!" He looks at us to see our reaction. We are silent. "I still shudder whenever I think about it. I turned round and looked at him. "*Re malaka*,' I told him, you did such a thing and you're bragging about it?' He turned to look at me, surprised. I guess he didn't expect anyone to react like that. He probably thought I would say 'bravo', pat him on the back, or say he was a hero or something. Then his eyes narrowed and he said, 'Got a problem, kid?' He gets up, picks up a chair and throws it at me! I went for him and before you knew it a fight broke out between my lot and his. I threatened to tell his commanding officer, but my men tried to hold me back. They said he was some kind of big shot lawyer and that he might make trouble for me. But later the guy came up to me and apologised. He said, 'Look, everyone brags that they did something in the war, I just said the first thing that came into my head.' I believed him." He takes another bite of his food. "But the following summer, when I returned to the island as a student, I read an article in the papers that made me realise that the event the guy had been boasting about had indeed happened after all. The article said that Denktash, accompanied by the UN, took Clerides, who became acting president after the invasion, to the villages of Sadallari, Aloa and Marathasa to show him where about eight or so Turkish Cypriots were buried in a mass grave. They had been thrown into a rubbish dump. Women, children and old men. The men had previously been taken to Limassol. Only one person survived by playing dead, and he was the one who showed them where the bodies were. I later found out that one of the killers had already told Clerides what had happened. He told him that he had thrown a medallion depicting the Akropolis on top of the bodies. Clerides spotted it and tried to claim that perhaps these were actually the bodies of Greek Cypriots. But Denktash would have none of it. He told Clerides to cut the crap, we can check if the boys have been circumcised, if you like. At that Clerides apologised and agreed to investigate."

He stops to take a sip of his beer. "Why do you think the Turks killed our people, the ones who are missing? Like in Asha, for example. Because they heard about the massacres *we* committed. In Tochni eighty-five men died. Three people did it. Later the Turkish Cypriots resettled their widows in the village of Vouno. The Village of Widows, they call it. I went there. I sat in the village coffeeshop with a friend of mine. We ordered two *metrios* and tried to strike up a conversation with the *kafedji* but he didn't speak any English or Greek. So he went to fetch an old man who spoke perfect

Greek. "Welcome, *horkanoi*, fellow villagers,' the man told us. We offered to buy him a cup of coffee, but he said, 'You come to my village to buy me a drink? Certainly not, I'll buy you one.' We said fine, go ahead, so he sat down. I asked him if he was from Tochni and he said yes. Then I asked, 'how did you manage to escape?' Just like that, straight out. My friend kicked me under the table, but the old man saw him and said, 'don't kick your friend, it's good that he asks, so he can learn the truth.' He told us he had three sons and three daughters. Two of his sons were nineteen and twenty-one when they were killed. Working as builders. He, himself, was a cook for the UN at Zygi where the British had a small contingent. The night it happened he had to go to work at five in the morning, but he had a bad feeling and wanted his whole family to go with him, or at least just the men. Just in case. The boys said, 'come on, dad, what's going to happen? Who should we be afraid of, our friends, the *horkanoi*, our fellow villagers, with whom we play football every day?' So they stayed, and he went off to work on his own. When he came back they were all dead."

The sun has gone behind a cloud and a slight breeze has picked up.

"I think it's going to start raining in twenty minutes," Mikis says, anxiously looking up at the sky.

"I don't mind the rain," Andreas says. "Besides we're under an umbrella." The sun has disappeared and the clouds are looking ominous.

I don't fancy the idea of having to walk back to the checkpoint in the rain and chew a little faster. Hasip is pleased with himself because he's had the foresight to park his car in the empty lot next door so he won't have far to walk.

"Someone told me that the parking lot over there was once for camels," Andreas says.

"There used to be a *han*, there," says Hasan. "It was called the *Develer Han. Develer* means camel."

"So if you had a camel you came here and if you had a horse you went to Büyük Han?" I ask.

"And a donkey you stayed out," Hasip says.

"If you had a donkey it meant you were a *köylu*," Andreas says.

Mikis tries to forget about the weather and pours himself some more beer. "Did you know that Greek Cypriots wouldn't be caught dead drinking Turkish beer, Efes," he says.

"And yet half our names are Turkish," says Andreas. "We just add the suffix 'is' on the end to make it sound Greek."

"What a lot of stupidities we've done in this country," says Kokos.

"What do you mean 'done'?" Hasip cries. "We're still doing them!"

The new Andreas says, "If it was my sons who had been killed, I wouldn't want to see a Turkish Cypriot in front of me ever again in my life. And yet this guy was so friendly to us. When we finally got up to go, he said, 'You're never going to come back, you know. Our *horkanoi* came once when the checkpoints opened and then never again. What's the matter with them? Why don't they come? Are they gifting all the land to us? Shouldn't they be coming here every Sunday and drinking coffee with us? Showing us that this land is theirs?' I promised him that we would come back and about a month later we did. The man wouldn't let us leave. He took us to his daughter's house, where they laid on a feast for us. We chatted and laughed and they were very friendly. We are still in touch to this day. We've become good friends."

"How do you explain his attitude?" I ask perplexed.

He shrugs his shoulders. "He believes in divine justice," he says pointing to the sky. "That there's someone up there watching over us. When one of the killers got cancer and died a very painful death, he said it's Allah above."

Vouno, or the Village of Widows lies very near the giant flag on the mountainside. Someone once told me that in the early years after the war the widows would light eighty-five candles in memory of their loved ones. Then someone decided to make the lights more permanent using electricity from a nearby army camp. I imagine it would have been an easy step for some nationalistic soldier in the camp to think of turning those random lights into the shape of a flag just to bug the Greek Cypriots. How easily things can be misunderstood. What had started out as a cry of pain, turned into an insult, causing even more pain, in a never-ending spiral going down the generations.

Andreas suggests we order some *katmer* for desert, the traditional Cypriot pancake. "You cannot resist Sevtap's *katmer*. It's made with the *tsippa*. "

"What is *tsippa*?" Hasip wants to know.

"It's the skin that forms when you boil milk. It's used in *katmer* to improve the taste."

"It's something our politicians don't have," mumbles Kokos under his breath. *Tsippa* in Greek also means to have backbone.

As if she has read our thoughts, Sevtap brings a plate stacked high with pancakes and places it in the middle of the table. We reach out and take one each, rolling it up like origami and wrapping one end in a paper napkin, so as not to let the honey drip all over us. Unsurprisingly a drop falls onto Hasip's T-shirt as he takes a bite.

"Oops!" Andreas says. "Now Sevil will know Hasip had *katmer*!"

The new Andreas says, "The truth is we killed their people and they killed ours. That's the truth. We have to put it out there and accept it and then it will be history."

I wonder what it will take for such a thing to happen. For the time being these events, as well as those of the sixties, are hardly ever spoken of, rarely acknowledged, as if a dark cloak of collective amnesia has been thrown over those days by our respective propaganda machines, which urge us never to forget that we had been victims of crimes, while totally ignoring crimes we ourselves had perpetrated as if they had never happened.

"The sky is looking ominous," Mikis says looking up. "We'd better hurry up."

As we walk back to the checkpoint, Kokos points out places he remembers from when he was growing up in this neighbourhood. "Over here was a guy who used to make *halva*, and over there was bakery. Down that road was the *han* of Ayios Antonis. It's an army camp now. That road comes out at Ermou street. J & P's very first offices when they created the company were here. I don't remember the Büyük Han, though. It may have been closed." We turn towards a narrow street teeming with people at the end of which is a dead end. "Over here is Kykkou street. It turns into Ermou." Once one of the busiest shopping streets in old Nicosia, Ermou street straddles the buffer zone in almost its entirety, its shops now practically rubble, with weeds reclaiming the road. "My dad's shop used to be over there," Kokos says pointing down another street. "There's a square there from where buses used to leave for Kyrenia. One of these shops used to be Ouzounian's shop, who used to sell Raleigh bikes before he started importing cars."

We stop a moment at Hasan's shop to say goodbye. I notice that the boxes of Turkish delight have his name on them.

"I didn't realise you were a brand name, Hasan!"

"Yes of course," he says proudly.

"Did you know that Turkish delight lasts a long time?" Mikis says. "It's because sugar has an enzyme that kills microorganisms by osmosis. It suffocates them by absorbing all their water. That's why if you want to preserve something you put it in sugar."

"And the biggest coincidence of all," Kokos says, "is that Hasan's shop used to be my grandfather's shop!"

He and Hasan look at each other and smile.

12 LIFE IN LIMBO

The end of our war did not mean we had peace. Instead we existed in a state of perpetual ceasefire; it was neither war, in that there was no shooting or loss of life, but nor was it peace, in that things hadn't been sorted out. It was like a chronic illness that you're aware is there, festering beneath your day-to-day existence, causing you some discomfort, but not enough to stop you from getting on with your life, allowing you to keep on pretending there's nothing wrong, rather than to seek a doctor's remedy.

I coped with the loss of Kyrenia by resolving, Buddha-like, never again to own anything, or at least never to become attached to possessions. I told myself, accumulating things and investing them with my emotions is a meaningless pursuit. Stuff invariably disappears, gets lost or gets stolen. It's a source of disappointment, and certainly not worth the sorrow. I decided that I would never again be tied down to a home or even a country, I would be a citizen of the world, free as a bird, nothing would touch me. Needless to say, my resolution didn't last long. As a student in the years immediately after the war, the best I did was to make sure everything I owned fitted into one suitcase, admittedly a very large suitcase, as I recall dragging it on and off numerous trains and planes. But that was about it. I have since come back to the island, got married, acquired a family and even a house of my own, despite the niggling little worry in the back of my mind, like most Greek Cypriots, that one day Turkey will come and get us all!

Neither Hasan, Hasip nor I were on the island during those first few months after the invasion to experience the stark realities in our country firsthand, as people came to terms with the aftermath of those three short days of war. Everyone was shell-shocked and jumpy. The slightest bit of bad news, the odd shot that rang out here and there, made people certain that the Turks were in the process of making another push to acquire the whole of the island. Some folks had prepared 'flee bags' with necessities, ready at a moment's notice to jump into their cars and leave home.

While the transfer of populations had been comprehensive and abrupt, it still continued well into the autumn months. It was a common sight in those early days to see cars and pick-up trucks loaded to the hilt with people and their belongings—clothes, baskets, furniture, pots and pans and the inevitable mattress balanced precariously on the top. Celia, who was still at school here, witnessed it one evening. During dinner with our parents at a roadside restaurant on the Nicosia-Limassol road, she saw a convoy of buses drive by.

"Who are those people?" she asked astonished at this unusual sight.

"It's the Turkish Cypriots," my father told her. "They're leaving."

"Why are they leaving?" she said. She couldn't understand why, since the war was over, they had to go.

A report by a group of US Senators who visited the island on a Study Mission in early September 1974 provides a picture of conditions prevailing at the time. Driving along the roads of southern Cyprus, they wrote, is to drive through an "endless refugee camp", as over two hundred thousand people sought shelter under trees, along the roadside, in cars, in open fields, under small lean-to huts made of pine branches and sticks, and in tents provided by International Relief agencies. Every available public building and accommodation was filled with refugees—schools, churches, monasteries, and civic buildings. District towns were flooded with them, while small towns and villages doubled or tripled in size and idle men swelled the unemployment rolls.

Pockets of people from both communities did not make the move, remaining stuck on the 'wrong' side of the divide, either by choice or circumstance. A large number of Turkish Cypriots remained in Turkish villages in the south or in the Turkish quarter of the larger towns, the American report says. For example, in the mixed village of Kalokhorio, where the Turkish quarter had not been disturbed, having hoisted a white flag above the mosque as a signal of the lack of hostile intentions, there was no indication of any harm being done to them. However, other Turkish villages did feel beleaguered and isolated.

"Objectively nothing has changed in these Turkish villages, except the fear that something has changed," a United Nations official said.

In the north, the situation was equally abnormal. For one thing, there was the sudden presence of an army of occupation, approximately forty thousand men strong. For another, there were refugees on this side too, as thousands of Turkish Cypriots fled from the south to the north. To their surprise, the Americans noticed that the refugees the Turks most often mentioned were not those from the current conflict, but rather the twenty five thousand Turkish Cypriots who had been displaced as a result of the

1963 intercommunal violence. They mentioned "one deserted and run down area bordering Nicosia, called Ormorphita," as being a symbol of the neglect they felt the Greek Cypriots had subjected them to eleven years previously. As Denktash told the Study Mission, "the many drops of Greek injustice to the Turkish minority has, over the years, filled the ocean in which we are all now drowning." The sense of Turkish Cypriot grievance is real and runs deep, the report says, as they felt the current suffering of the Greek Cypriots, although quantitatively far greater, was in principle the same as that which they had suffered in the past.

The Study Mission also mentions that some twenty thousand Greek Cypriots were stranded in the north, particularly in the Karpas peninsula. Also about four hundred and fifty Greeks still remained in the waterfront Dome Hotel in Kyrenia, while Bellapais, in the hills east of Kyrenia, had become a virtual prison for the local population. In the abandoned city of Famagusta and its suburb Varosha, which had once housed forty thousand people, the streets were empty, no life stirred. Only a few old people were left hiding in their homes, some too feeble or ill to move, others afraid to come out in sight of the Turkish army, emerging under cover of darkness to scavenge for food and supplies. On whatever side of the ceasefire line Cypriots found themselves at the time, all felt the same apprehension that conditions may change for the worse.

A book by Turkish Cypriot Vamik Volkan, *Cyprus—War and Adaptation: A Psychoanalytic History of Two Ethnic Groups in Conflict*, published in 1979, gives insight into life on the other side of the Kyrenia mountains after the invasion. A professor of psychology at the University of Virginia, Volkan is one of the world's leading theorists and practitioners on the psychological aspects of large groups and spent his life studying "our tendency to kill each other in large numbers." The conflict in Cyprus cost him the loss of a friend, who had been like a brother to him, an event that possibly shaped his future career.

His book focuses on the emotional and psychological effects that the Turkish invasion and transfer of populations had on his fellow Turkish Cypriots. While I was wanting to divest myself of all worldly possessions, amongst my compatriots, the Turkish Cypriots, there was a mad scramble to grab as many things as they could. So widespread was the looting of Greek Cypriot houses, factories and villages, that it was the main subject of discussion at social events. A euphemistic new word was coined for it, *buluntu*, meaning "something found". Volkan explains their preoccupation with material things and their desire to acquire supplies in some abundance without guilt, as psychological justification for having been deprived for so long. "See, we were deprived of all luxury for eleven years, and now it is our right to have them!" the argument would go. The general preoccupation with *buluntu* eventually ended, perhaps because the Turkish Cypriot authorities brought the situation under control, or because there was nothing more to be "found". The authorities put what remained in warehouses and offered for sale the television sets, clothing, canned goods, and other supplies left behind by the Greek Cypriots.

Interestingly, many Turkish Cypriots hung on to some object they had found in the Greek Cypriot homes they had occupied, particularly things like photo albums or wedding pictures. For the Turkish Cypriots these 'linking objects', as he calls them, acted as a kind of emotional bonds between them and the Greeks whose homes they now occupied. Volkan tells the story of a Turkish Cypriot refugee who, on entering the Greek Cypriot home that he had been allocated, was amazed to find his own photograph on the mantelpiece. It had been taken in 1936 during the annual sports day held at the American Academy in Larnaca and showed him and the former Greek Cypriot owner of the house receiving their trophies. He had his own copy of the picture, but had left it behind in his old home in the south.

The most common link to the Greek Cypriots was the great heaps of rubbish that lay about in empty houses or in the fields full of stuff the Greek Cypriots had left behind as they fled. Volkan recalls the reluctance of the villagers to burn the piles of rubbish, continuing to point out items in the piles such as broken toys or children's books with Greek writing, and puts it down to the guilt they felt at replacing the Greeks who had owned these simple family belongings, now rubbish."

The war had left the northern beaches of the island strewn with dead bodies, over which the authorities scattered quicklime as a hygienic measure, well into the spring of the following year, he writes. Even after the beaches were cleaned and the people resumed swimming there, signposts still warned that any suspicious objects should be reported. It was not unusual to find bits of green plastic in the water from the body bags used to carry the corpses after the war. People were nervous about swimming there and would often joke that the small fish that bit the bathers did so because they were so used to feeding on human flesh. "Nervous laughter would follow such a remark," Volkan says, the uneasiness of the Turkish Cypriot bathers yet another indication of their feelings of survivor guilt at enjoying themselves in a place of death.

When Volkan returned to the island a year later, he found most of the rubbish heaps had disappeared and "life had started coming back to the place of death", as people began to adapt to their new life. Three years after the war, when he returned to the island again, he flew in from Istanbul on a plane marked "Cyprus Turkish Airlines", landing at a new modern airport "vastly more impressive than any in Turkey", in a "new" country, the Turkish Federated State of Cyprus, though not one officially recognised by any country other than Turkey. In actual fact northern Cyprus had become an extension of mainland Turkey. Tourists consisted of mainly mainland Turks, as many Turkish conferences were held in the old Greek Cypriot hotels that now had Turkish names. Turkish Cypriots, who had been living abroad, mostly in England, also returned for visits.

But for all these improvements, psychologically speaking, Volkan writes, the Turkish Cypriots, were still living in a symbolic enclave. All they had done was replace the concrete walls that surrounded them in their pre-1974 enclaves with an 'invisible' one. In effect, they were still not yet recognised as equal to other human beings. They held passports unrecognised by all countries except Turkey, with the accompanying humiliation and loss of self esteem that having identities that were not accepted by others entailed. But now they at least felt safe and, like people everywhere, turned their attention to earning money, and taking care of their families.

This time Volkan found the "linking objects" that connected the Turkish Cypriots with the Greek Cypriots were no longer obvious, although they did surface every now and then. Occasionally someone whose home he was visiting would bring him the picture of the Greek who had formerly occupied his house and speak about him, but interest in these mementos was no longer as obsessive as it had been in the early days after the war.

What, I wonder, would he have made of the return to the Greek Cypriots of these "linking objects", when the borders opened in 2003? At the time I had thought these were touching gifts by the Turkish Cypriots to the owner whose house they had taken over. Now I realise that it was more than that. As they handed back the photo albums and other objects from a lost life, it was as if the Turkish Cypriots were saying, here, this is yours, I may not be able to give you your house back, but here are the photographs of your life back, I kept them safe, I've paid my dues over the years, now I can finally be free to get on with my life. For the Turkish Cypriots it was a kind of expiation.

Volkan was in Cyprus when Archbishop Makarios died suddenly of a heart attack at the age of 64. After escaping the coupists and fleeing abroad, Makarios had returned to the island a few months after the invasion to a hero's welcome in the south, immediately taking over from the Acting President, Glafkos Clerides, "one of the few realists amongst Greek Cypriot politicians", Volkan calls him. After the loss of Famagusta and almost a third of the island, Clerides had been on the point of agreeing a deal with Turkey. He declared in a speech that Greek Cypriot thinking had been based on "false assumptions, terrible mistakes and illusions", the main one being "that we could treat the Turkish Cypriot community as a simple minority without taking into account that it was backed by Turkey with a population of thirty three million." He openly acknowledged that it would be necessary to accept federation. But Makarios on his return slapped him down, saying he had been too eager to make concessions. Instead he espoused a dogma of 'the long struggle', repeated incessantly in speech after speech. We would not rest, the dogma went, until we had achieved "a just and viable solution", a Cyprus without Turkish settlers, without foreign troops and where all the refugees could go back to their homes.

The news of Makarios' death was greeted with general indifference amongst Turkish Cypriots. The few comments Volkan heard were disparaging. It rained on the day of his funeral, something very unusual in Cyprus in August, and he remembers how a Turkish Cypriot official commented that he bet the Greeks would say it was the tears of heaven (which they did), while the view on the Turkish side in accordance with an old Turkish belief was that rain accompanies the burial of a sinner to wash away his sins. Turkish Cypriots did watch the funeral on television, betraying their surface indifference, Volkan says, while the sounds of the twenty-one gun salute during the funeral drifting over from the south caused some people to fear that the Greeks were beginning to fight each other all over again and that they might be hit by stray bullets.

One thing about Volkan's writing bothers me—he refers throughout to "Cypriot Greeks" and "Cypriot Turks", rather than the more usual Greek Cypriots and Turkish Cypriots. At first I wonder if this is purely an accidental quirk in translation, but later I realise it may be a deliberate statement on identity, indicating his preference for Greekness and Turkishness as opposed to Cypriotness. In later writings he criticises attempts over the years by the international community to create a Cypriot identity that would unite the total population under the term "Cypriotism". He refers to such attempts as propaganda. Historically speaking, he says, there has never been a Cypriot ethnicity or nationality and even puts the word Cypriot in inverted commas. He fears, if this were to happen, the Turkish Cypriots would be integrated and assimilated by the Greek Cypriots. "Everybody being a 'Cypriot'," he says, "would minimise the existing ethnic identities of being a Turk or a Greek, would mean that the Cypriot Greeks, would be in power, would rule the total island and would put the Cypriot Turks once more in another invisible enclave, one called minority status." In his view, to attempt a common identity for Greek and Turkish Cypriots "was to chase an unreachable goal". "Both Greeks and Turks have their own long idealised histories, and to create one new 'nation' by fusing them, is as unrealistic as it would be to create a new nation that merged Arabs and Israelis," he says. He disagrees with one American diplomat who exclaimed at a meeting Volkan attended, "What is wrong with people who cannot get together and be a nation the way we have in America?"

In a more recent book, *Enemies on the Couch: A psychopolitical journey through war and peace*, published in 2014, Volkan also reveals that when the UN Secretary-General's Special Advisor on Cyprus, Alvaro de Soto, visited the island to start working on a solution in preparation for the Annan plan, he paid Volkan a secret visit to sound out his views on a possible solution. "I explained to him that offering a solution based on the concept of 'Cypriotism' would be most unrealistic. Instead I suggested the 'Swiss cheese border' approach that I had been presenting at various academic meetings earlier. Briefly, Cypriot Greeks and Cypriot Turks primarily look after their own internal affairs while maintaining a physical border between them. This border would also function as a psychological one and thus support both sides' large-group identities. However, this border should have 'holes' like holes in a block of Swiss cheese: people belonging to political, societal, artistic and other similar organisations would be able and expected to pass through such 'holes' and share their useful expertise and activities as Cypriots, and do their best together for the whole island. Then everyone would go back under his or her side's ethnic umbrella. This way there would be no space for humiliation. Such an approach would remove the Turkish side's 'isolation' by creating a common Cypriot state with two opposing sides existing peacefully under certain legal conditions."

While in the north people were adapting to their new life, in the south we clung to our beautiful memories of the homes and places we had lost, actively encouraged not to attempt to heal from our loss, through slogans like *'Den xechno'* (Don't forget), as every evening before the news images of places in the north like Kyrenia harbour, Famagusta beach, churches, villages and monuments would be flashed onto our screens, frozen in time as we had left them for ever more. We were ordered not to forget, told our national duty to our group was not to forget, and never to accept what had happened. The only way things could be put right is if we could all go back to the way things were, if all the refugees went back to their homes, if the Turkish army and the Turkish settlers left, if Cyprus became a unitary state once more. Since this was not likely or possible, we preferred to stay as we were, stuck in anger and denial with our memories intact.

At every opportunity officials and the media railed against Turkish intransigence that prevented a solution that would allow us all to go back to where we were before, never entertaining the thought that perhaps the other side didn't want to go back and that the reality was that there was no going back. We had a special vocabulary which we regurgitated, and woe betide anyone who went against the norm, as one visiting British politician did when he called the invasion an 'intervention', creating a horrified uproar in our politically sensitive waters, and leading him to accuse us of living under a 'tyranny of words'.

Three years after the war, Makarios finally agreed with Denktash that they would seek a solution based on federation. Subsequently they held round after round of direct talks, indirect talks, proximity talks, shuttle diplomacy and occasional head-to-head summit talks between the leaders of the two communities in order to hammer out the details. Talks would start, then they would falter, then start again, then reach a deadlock.

When the Turkish Cypriots proclaimed their own independent state, the Turkish Republic of Northern Cyprus in November 1983, it sent Greek Cypriots reeling. Our response was to add 'pseudostate' to our vocabulary. At first we would prefix it with the words 'so-called', but then for brevity, resorted to placing it in inverted commas, just to make doubly sure that we eschewed it, even though grammatically it negated itself. Inverted commas began to proliferate and covered everything official that came from the north, such as 'Foreign Minister' or 'Prime Minister'. They were even used to describe prawns that came from the north and were served at restaurants in the village of Pyla in the buffer zone, where Greek and Turkish Cypriots still lived together. Ironically, the name means 'gate', and it was through Pyla that goods and people could, to some extent, come and go between the two sides. The village became known for serving excellent fresh prawns at its restaurants, some of which were then sold to other restaurants in the south. At one point the Greek Cypriot press got wind of the story and created a self-righteous uproar about the ethics of eating prawns whose provenance was the pseudostate. In covering the story they made sure to place the word 'prawns' in inverted commas, as they were illegal and therefore 'unrecognised'. Occasionally they called them pseudoprawns, and sometimes even 'pseudoprawns'.

Throughout this time, if our papers were to be believed, we seemed always to be "at a crucial point in the Cyprus problem", without ever being so. Nothing ever happened. Cyprus was the personification of the Greek saying, 'nothing is more permanent than the temporary'. And we would each invariably blame the other side for intransigence and time wasting.

Thirty years went by in this state of limbo, Dante's first circle of hell. Then something changed.

13 YES AND NO

Christopher Hitchens used to say that the Cyprus problem would never be solved, as it would prove too dreary to work out all the details. But in 2004 we do work out the details through a plan for federation drawn up under the auspices of the UN Secretary-General Kofi Annan. The plan runs to over nine thousand pages, most of it legal texts, but when it dawns on me that this time a solution is more than just talk and I could even be getting my house back, or at least some kind of compensation, I become interested in reading it.

Fortunately the plan has been summarised in an easy to read "Citizens Guide" written by a team from both communities and issued by the Peace Research Institute Oslo. The plan seeks to strike a balance between the competing legitimate interests and human rights of both the dispossessed owners and the current users. It aims to minimise the dislocation of current users, and at the same time respect people's rights to their property. Through various territorial adjustments, it tries to ensure that as many Greek Cypriots as possible return to their properties under the administration of the Greek Cypriot federal state, while reducing the number of Greek Cypriot properties that would remain within the territory administered by the Turkish Cypriot state. With the plan, the UN estimates, more than half the Greek Cypriots who had been displaced in 1974 would get their homes back under Greek Cypriot rule, while under a quarter of the Turkish Cypriot population in the north would have to be relocated.

I read on to find specifics of how the plan affects people like me with property in an area that would remain under Turkish Cypriot rule. First of all, I don't lose my property. The plan recognises me as the rightful owner. I will have two options—compensation or reinstatement. If I apply for reinstatement, whether or not I get it depends on various factors—if the current user is dispossessed (Mr Denktash could possibly make a case for himself that he is indeed a dispossessed owner as he had a plot of land with two olive trees in Paphos), if he had made substantial changes to the property (doubtful), if the property is in a military area (at the moment it is, but it is unclear if it will still be so after a solution), if it was being used for the public benefit (Mr Denktash could perhaps argue that the house would be the residence of every Turkish Cypriot head of state) and if I am in the quota of people being reinstated (the plan allows about 20% of Greek Cypriots to go back, oldest first). If I am not given reinstatement, I would have to accept compensation. While obviously, I would love to have my house back, I would be willing to accept compensation for the sake of a solution and reunification of the island. Why, I'd even let them keep the house for the sake of a solution.

Politically, the plan proposes the creation of the United Cyprus Republic, a federation of two constituent states — a Greek Cypriot State and a Turkish Cypriot State — loosely based on the Swiss federal model. There's also provision for a Truth and Reconciliation Commission to resolve "outstanding issues from the past".

On the minus side, the plan allows both Greece and Turkey to maintain permanent military presences on the island, although this is tempered by the fact that troops will be phased out until only a token number remains.

It's not a perfect plan, but it's a compromise. It all sounds quite reasonable to me. I become favourably inclined to what becomes known as the Annan plan.

While the plan had begun to be worked on during the presidency of Glavcos Clerides, the man who Volkan viewed as 'the only Greek Cypriot politician who was a realist', he lost the elections to Tasos Papadopoulos, who while always having been against sharing power with the Turkish Cypriots, nevertheless promised to support a solution in order to get elected.

Things start heating up when in February 2004 the UN summon the Greek and Turkish Cypriot leaders, Papadopoulos and Rauf Denktash, to New York and ask them to commit to the peace process. Both try unsuccessfully to squirm out of it, while Turkey makes it abundantly clear that it is intent on a solution in order to pursue its ambitions of joining the European Union.

Talks to revise the plan continue in Cyprus and seem to be proceeding well. The UN Secretary-General's Special Representative in Cyprus, a swanky Peruvian diplomat called Alvaro de Soto, emerges from the meetings beaming at the cameras and saying discussions were fruitful and constructive.

Yet the two leaders next to him both look sullen. Papadopoulos looks miserable and mournful, giving the impression that he is being dragged through this procedure against his will. Short and skinny with a thin moustache, bulbous nose, slicked back hair, and shifty eyes, he reminds me of a typical cartoon villain, always intent on hatching some fiendish plan to outwit the opposition. A hardliner (he is rumoured to have been the brains behind the Akritas plan in the '60s to kill any Turkish Cypriot resistance to *enosis)*, he came to power with the support of the communist party, AKEL, whose leader Demetris Christofias, assured voters "he's a changed man." Papadopoulos believes Turkey doesn't really want a solution but is just playing a "communications game". He was counting on Denktash to scupper the talks in New York as usual, but when he didn't, because Turkey put the screws on him, he had to agree to the peace process or risk appearing the intransigent one.

Denktash is his usual openly negative self. He takes every opportunity in talking to reporters to reveal the issues that he had tabled at the negotiations and the replies he had received from Papadopoulos in order to prove that co-operation between Greek and Turkish Cypriots is impossible. He tries to scare the Turkish Cypriots that acceptance of the plan will mean the dissolution of the TRNC, that the Greek Cypriots will come and force them out of their homes, that they will destroy their economy, that half of all businesses will close down because of harmonisation with the EU, and that when the Turkish army leaves, the Turkish Cypriots will suffer the same fate as in 1963.

Papadopoulos follows the same tactic. In his statements to journalists, he reveals Denktash's extreme positions and his own "appropriate" response. The statements of the two leaders become material for the morning radio chat shows and create a climate of pessimism and despair, not to mention confusion and fear. Papadopoulos' party, DIKO, openly starts campaigning for a NO warning Greek Cypriots that the economy will collapse, that they will have to support not only the Turkish Cypriots, but the Turkish settlers, that the Turkish occupation will be legalised and that Greek Cypriots will lose their national identity.

As face-to-face talks are getting nowhere, Alvaro de Soto decides to change the format of the negotiations, reverting to proximity talks, having separate meetings with each leader and then telling the other what was said in the meeting.

How ironic, I think, watching their antics, that the two people who have to negotiate the solution and our future, are the ones who want it the least. Aptly they both get nicknamed "Denktashopoulos". Nevertheless, the process has taken on a momentum that neither of them are able to stop.

"It's going to get solved, it's going to get solved!" I tell my husband excitedly one evening at home, dancing round the kitchen table. "The Cyprus problem will finally be solved!"

"Give it a rest," Stelios says dismissively, munching his supper. "The Cyprus problem is forever."

The subcommittees discussing the new federation unanimously agree on a new flag. Blue, gold and red horizontal stripes. Denktash is not happy with it. He doesn't like the fact that the blue stripe is on top and the red stripe on the bottom and wants it the other way round. The Bishop of Kyrenia, who is of the same ilk, is even less impressed than Denktash.

"They put the blue on the top to remind us that we are Greek and red on the bottom to tell us that we will become Turks," he says in an interview.

A few days later we also get a national anthem. It gradually dawns on everyone that this may finally be it. There's no way back. The two leaders will have to agree. The New York deal they both signed stated that if they fail to do so, Greece and Turkey will step in and if they, too, fail to agree, then the UN will fill in the blanks and send the plan to separate simultaneous referenda on both sides.

Things look so promising that some rejectionist parliamentarians introduce a bill to require a seventy per cent majority for the plan to be approved in the referendum rather than the existing fifty per cent plus one. Fortunately it doesn't pass.

I become cheerfully optimistic, certain that the referendum will go our way. The whole population becomes glued to their television sets. Everyone becomes an expert, everyone has an opinion. At first the people on the talk shows sound reasonable.

"What's the alternative?" the wife of a former president, says. "Turkey will annex the north and Cyprus will be permanently divided. It means partition. With no compensation for our lost properties."

A handsome Swiss constitutional expert on the UN team appears on television to explain the plan. He is calm, sensible, and clear. My takeaway is that the plan is balanced and has taken both sides' fears into account. He is followed by a studio panel discussion.

"Who does this foreigner think he is?" says one of the guests on the panel, himself a lawyer and self-proclaimed constitutional expert, intent on rubbishing him. He spits and mumbles as he talks and I can't decide if he has a speech impediment or is apoplectic at what he has just heard. "What does he know about constitutional affairs?" he says. "He's too young!"

"Nonsense!" counters a former Attorney General, and one of the island's top legal minds who supports a solution. "You can't dismiss people just like that. I know this man personally. He is extremely well educated and has been to the best universities."

"Universities? Pah!" the man spits back. "He didn't even use any legal jargon in his interview!"

The other panelists are no better. They have already decided that the plan is unworkable and is bound to break down, just like the 1960 constitution. Reason and common sense doesn't sway them, as the former Attorney General explains that there are so many checks and balances in the plan that there could not possibly be a deadlock as in 1960.

Unfortunately he's outnumbered, giving the impression to viewers that his is a minority view.

A few days later, to my dismay, a number of opinion polls appear claiming that an alarming number (67%) of Greek Cypriots would vote 'NO' in the referendum.

To make matters worse, every now and then American and British diplomats warn that Cyprus will face serious consequences if the referendum doesn't get through, giving the rejectionists the opportunity to claim that the plan is all a foreign plot that must be thwarted.

The rejectionists hold a mass rally at which they all shout "NO! NO! NO!" and accuse everyone else of being traitors. More and more of them appear on the discussion shows spewing bile against "this cursed Annan plan" and calling on the people to "stand up for their rights at last". Anyone who supports the plan is accused of selling out, of being unpatriotic, or of being a *nenekas*, a surrender monkey. And worse, a traitor. "I bet you wouldn't be supporting the plan if you were from Kyrenia," screeches one woman caller hysterically. I can't understand why. What about the large populations of the towns of Famagusta and Morphou, who would be going back under Greek Cypriot rule? And what about the percentage who would also be going back but under Turkish Cypriot rule? Just because not all Kyrenians would go back, should nobody go back? How selfish of her! Even if I don't get my house back or compensation, I would still support reunification for the greater good of the island as a whole.

The Kyrenia refugees hold a large meeting at the conference centre in Nicosia. I naively decide to attend. Strident military music greets me as I enter the auditorium. At intervals, the music stops and a voice blares out over the loudspeakers.

"Compatriots!" the voice says. "A new unfair solution that does not serve anyone's interests is being put before us! Let us all fight together for a fairer European solution!" The military music resumes, only to stop a few minutes later.

"The plan is a concession to Turkey! The plan does not guarantee that Turkish troops will leave! The plan gives legitimacy to the illegal regime in the north!"

Above a long table on the stage hang two large posters, one of Kyrenia harbour and the other of a clock with the words "Cyprus zero hour". Elsewhere banners read: "A just European solution" and "A just solution for Greek Cypriots and Turkish Cypriots". Behind me a television crew is filming the proceedings.

I watch the people gather around me. Old friends greet each other. They seem dazed and downcast, as if yet another catastrophe has befallen them.

The voice over the loudspeaker cuts into the music again. "Compatriots!

NO, to a solution where might is right!"

There are hardly any young people in the audience. Those under thirty never knew the north, have no emotional attachment to it.

"Compatriots! *All* refugees should have the right to their property!"

I tune in to the chatter around me. A man in front of me is muttering to his neighbour. "Go back? What for? What sixty-five year old is ever going to go back? What's he going to do there all on his own with just his wife? No schools, no hospitals, no nothing." His friend nods grimly. Everyone looks miserable.

"Compatriots! The Annan plan deprives us of our human rights! We will not give up our rights for a just solution for all Cypriots!"

The man in front of me continues, "And whenever I hear them going on and on about this bloody black man's plan (Kofi Annan happens to come from Ghana) as if it's such a major achievement, it just gets on my nerves."

"Compatriots! We did not fight and were defeated. They fought us! We are struggling to hold our heads high!" The slogans don't even make sense.

There's a flurry of activity in one corner of the room and the Bishop of Kyrenia sweeps in, like Darth Vader with his flowing black robes and headgear. He sits down with his entourage in specially reserved front row seats to thunderous applause.

"NO to a solution that will recognise the Turkish invasion! NO to Attila's harmonisation with the EU!" says the loudspeaker voice.

A number of dignitaries take their place on the stage. I recognise the leader of one of the smallest but loudest of the rejectionist parties, which advocates the impossible position of a return to the unitary state of 1960.

"Compatriots! Compensation cannot give us back our dignity! This land belongs to us, not to the settlers from Turkey!"

None of the two main political party leaders are here. Is it because they are in favour of the plan, or are they just sitting on the fence?

"No more concessions! NO to partition with our signature!"

The Bishop of Kyrenia gets up to address the crowd. "The plan is a monstrosity that cannot possibly work," he says. "The second national catastrophe for Hellenism will come about if we accept this evil and cursed plan."

"It's a disgrace! A disgrace," shouts the crowd.

"We must trust in God to save us from this plan. By agreeing to this plan we will be signing our own destruction. Anyone who votes for this satanic plan will be doomed to a life in hell. Those who are trying to make the plan sound good are the very people who through their continuous concessions brought us here in the first place. We must shout a resounding NO to prevent the destruction of the Republic of Cyprus!"

"NO!" shouts the crowd obediently.

The Mayor of Kyrenia takes the podium. A mayor in exile, who has been symbolically elected to a post without a constituency for the last thirty years, he is yet another example of our state of denial. The first thing he comments on is the absence of the big parties, communist AKEL and right-wing DISY. "Even though all the political parties have been invited to attend our meeting they have not honoured us with their presence."

"Disgrace! Disgrace!" choruses the crowd.

I, on the other hand, take the fact that the two largest parties haven't turned up here as a good sign. Together they form almost 70% of the vote. I feel a glimmer of hope.

"History has taught us that when the going gets tough only very few people stay behind to protect the gates of Thermopylae," he continues. "It would be better to turn down an unjust and unworkable solution than say YES to a bad settlement, with all that it entails for our people and future generations. Everyone who remembers the shadow of Kyrenia castle, the Queen's Room in the castle of St Hilarion, the church of Glykiotissa, cannot possibly vote YES."

I feel a rush of blood to my head. Why the hell not? Surely that is the only way for these places to be part of our country again. I feel like marching up onto that stage, grabbing the microphone from the mayor's hands and addressing the crowd myself: "Have you all gone mad? Here you are with a chance to get your land and property back, to make the island whole again, and you are shouting NO? What's the matter with you all? Why are you listening to these people who have a vested interest in keeping the situation as it is? What more do you want?" Almost immediately I see myself on the evening news being carried away arms flailing, ranting and raving, to chants of "traitor, traitor" from the crowd.

I do nothing, but don't last much longer in that place.

The next day an article by the Bishop of Morphou appears in the papers. Morphou is a town on the west coast that in the territorial readjustments would be returned to the Greek side under the plan. The Bishop of Morphou, a young up and coming priest, his long dark hair tied back in a priestly yet fashionable bun, with kind eyes and a gentle manner, is the only senior clergyman who is openly and fearlessly a YES. In his article he advises His Holiness from Kyrenia to consider the future of the island and put his weight behind a solution based on the plan. "I'm going back to Morphou whether it's under the Annan plan or the *Aman* plan," he says with a pun on the word *aman*, meaning for mercy's sake. He writes bluntly, even crudely, and makes for an amusing read. His position is all the more astonishing in that he lays the blame for the country's predicament squarely in the hands of the clergy, particularly Archbishop Makarios and his henchmen, whose mistakes have brought us to this point.

"Unfair? What's unfair about the plan, you idiots?" he writes. "They're giving us back what they took from us, that which we lost as a result of our stupidity. And the only reason they're giving it back to us is because it so happens that it suits their interests, not because they love us, or respect us, but in return for something else. And what do we do? Instead of grabbing it and shutting up, we start whingeing and complaining as always […]. Fellow Cypriots, you need to understand that we've made a mess of everything. You need to understand that we've been defeated as a state […]. Forget about what's fair, stop your whining and remember that unfairness is the rule and not the exception. Admit that we have screwed up because of stupidity and because of the corruption of our leaders. Welcome the Annan plan with open arms, as you would manna from heaven…"

Greek Cypriot society becomes polarised into YESes and NOs. Essentially, it's an ideological clash between Greek Cypriot nationalism and Cypriotism, each side convinced theirs is the best guarantee for the group to survive against the existential threat posed by Turkey. The most ardent NOs are predominantly Greek Cypriot nationalists, who see themselves as the natural evolution of ancient Greece, by virtue of having the same language, culture, religion, and values. They view federation as diluting their Greekness and therefore a threat to their identity, allowing Turkey to meddle in the island's affairs. On the other hand, the YESes, like my friends and me, view Greek nationalism as responsible for having brought about the current state of affairs in the first place. While not denying our Greekness, we consider Cyprus has its own character, independent of either Greece of Turkey. Emphasising Greekness excludes the Turkish Cypriots. We feel we can still be Greek, but within an independent Cypriot state which has links to Greek culture but also common ground with the Turkish Cypriot community. We view reunification as the only way the Greeks of Cyprus can survive, whereby both Greek Cypriots and Turkish Cypriots can have a common identity, as Cypriots.

Sometimes the YES/NO divide cuts right through friends and family members. I'm not surprised that one friend who's scared of anything new or the unknown, turns out to be a NO. I hear about a business owner who has fired any employee who was a NO because "it proves they're not intelligent enough to think for themselves." Lawyers are particularly prone to being NOs. "It's probably because as lawyers they are over-sensitive to agreements going wrong," Stelios reasons. Soon we realise that four out of five people we know are all NOs. Even people who stand to regain their property are NOs. Some are NOs because "foreigners are imposing this plan on us." Has everyone gone mad?

At the heart of all the rejectionists' arguments is the feeling that the plan isn't fair. 'It isn't fair' resonates from all corners of society. It isn't fair that not everyone will be getting their property back. It isn't fair that the 80% majority Greek population should share power with the 18% minority

Turkish population. Until one exasperated YES politician replies on one of the chat shows, "But life isn't fair. Unfair things happen all the time. Do we sit there bemoaning our fate? No, we accept it and move on!"

It all reminds me of an experiment conducted in 1982 by two German professors on ultimatum bargaining and described by Ori and Rom Brafman in their book *Sway: The irresistible pull of irrational behaviour*. The researchers placed a random pair of strangers in separate rooms and told each one that they had been paired with a partner, whose identity they would not know and with whom they would not be allowed to communicate. The pair would be given a combined sum of $10. One of the two would decide how to split it, and the other would decide whether to accept the split or not. If the receiving partner accepted, both participants would get the money, but if he didn't, neither of them would. Most people decided to split the sum equally and the receiving partners accepted it. However, in some instances the splitting partner decided to give himself more. In this case the receiving partner would reject the offer and walk away, leaving them both empty-handed. This happened no matter how great the sum of money offered was. At the heart of this behaviour, the writers say, is a deep belief in fairness, one that we will defend no matter what, even if the decision is irrational.

Greek Cypriots feel that they have lost a third of the country's territory and even though a large number of people who had lost property would be getting their homes back, specifically the large populations of the towns of Famagusta and Morphou, they feel it's unfair that not all the refugees could go back. This may be seen as irrational, because at least with a deal they get something back, whereas with no deal they get nothing. Later in the process when the Turkish Prime Minister Tayyip Erdogan boasts the Turks had got everything they wanted, you could just feel the collective Greek Cypriots giving him the finger and saying, oh yeah? We'll show you. You've got nothing. Of course we would get nothing too.

As days go by, it becomes increasingly clear that the Presidential Palace is waging a behind-the-scenes campaign to twist public opinion towards a NO. I hear a rumour that Papadopoulos said he would rather cut his arm off than sign such an agreement. A number of top personalities complain about what they call a deliberate attempt from certain circles to mislead public opinion and spread misinformation. According to reports in the press, the Presidential Palace has intervened to scupper a television interview with members of the UN team who were going to be replying to questions from viewers regarding the plan. Moreover, a request to publicise and endorse the free booklet and a UN website containing the plan in Greek, Turkish and English, has fallen on deaf ears. What's more, the state radio and TV station CyBC publishes an 'independent' opinion poll from a totally unknown company saying that most citizens do not want a solution and will not change their minds, even if their parties tell them to vote YES, as if sending a message to the mainstream political parties that the people won't follow you this time.

Firmly in the 'YES' camp, my friend Calliope and I take it upon ourselves to sway public opinion single-handedly. A powerhouse of a businesswoman, Calliope's dynamism is hard to resist. Convincing one person a day is our strategy, and we each follow our own tactics in order to achieve this. Sometimes we do so stridently, sometimes calmly, sometimes insistently. We keep our eyes and ears open, and, as soon as we spot a likely candidate, we zero in on him or her. Often we don't even bother with niceties, wagging a finger at them and cutting straight to the chase: "Are you a YES or a NO?". We then proceed to argue our case until the other person runs out of arguments or gives up, and move on, smug in the knowledge that we have managed to convince yet another person to come to their senses and see that there really is only one possible choice.

To our horror and surprise, however, we begin coming across individuals who we had ticked off as being in the 'YES' camp, but who we find have switched back to the 'NO'. Suddenly, our efforts feel like a Sisyphean task.

When this happens to two of my best friends, who even have property on the other side, which they would regain, I'm suddenly reminded of Eugene Ionesco's play, *Rhinoceros*. Written as an allegory on the rise of fascism in Germany, the play touches on how easily people can be swayed by whatever their leaders tell them. It doesn't even have to make sense. "All cats die," argues one character, "Socrates is dead. Therefore, Socrates is a cat". The solution will cost £16 billion. We can't afford £16 billion. Therefore we don't want a solution. It's all utterly absurd.

I can barely believe my ears when I first hear this kind of syllogism from yet another of my friends, someone who owned a beautiful house on the beach in Varosha, which is to be given back in its entirety, according to the plan. Instead of being delighted at the prospect of getting it back, she looks totally downcast, complaining that it was probably derelict and would require fixing, something she can't afford. Not only that, but she wouldn't be getting it straight away. "But, you've waited thirty years," I tell her stunned. "What are a few months more? And if you don't want it, you can sell it." What's the matter with people?

None of their arguments hold water. Take the one against the Turkish settlers. The Annan plan allows for a certain number of mainland Turks who had settled in the north years ago, to remain on the island after a solution and become citizens. Greek Cypriots want all the settlers to go back to Turkey, therefore we should vote 'NO' to the plan, despite the fact that the plan safeguards against the arrival of any more settlers whereas with a 'NO' vote, settlers will continue to come to the north unhindered forever.

Rhinoceritis is contagious. It's an epidemic, like influenza. As the play progresses, more and more people start to turn into rhinoceroses. A woman recognises her husband has turned into one, so dutifully joins him, and one by one all the characters follow suit, until by the end of it, only Berenger, the main character, is left. When I ask a friend why she is a 'NO', she says because everyone else is. "You're the only one I know who is a YES," she adds, looking at me as if *I* were the pachyderm.

Momentarily, I too, in a moment of weakness, feel myself turning. "We shall be ruined financially," warns my doctor one day when I go for a checkup, and proceeds to outline all the reasons why doom and destruction are inevitable if we go down the road towards reunification. I can almost feel myself growing a thick skin and a horn, only managing to shake it off when Stelios reminds me of the extra land we would be getting back, the fact that we would all be operating in a larger market, one that could also open up to a population of seventy million in Turkey, and that in the long term it can only be to everyone's advantage. Whenever I speak out, I'm flabbergasted to find I'm accused of being a fanatic, of selling out. Me, selling out? Can't they see that by saying NO, *they* are selling out? And like Berenger, I end up waving my fist at all the rhinoceroses out there, shouting "I'll never join up with you! Never! Not me!"

As the first phase of talks between the two leaders in Cyprus comes to an end, the UN Secretary-General, Kofi Annan, sends invitations to the Greek Cypriot and Turkish Cypriot sides, as well as Greece and Turkey, to attend enlarged Cyprus negotiations at Burgenstock, a hotel complex on the outskirts of Lucerne, Switzerland, that will be United Nations premises for the duration. He asks that all concerned "be in a position to make final commitments" and says that he will be personally involved in the effort as it draws to an end. Greece's Prime Minister Costas Karamanlis accepts the invitation and so does Turkish Prime Minister Erdogan. Denktash, however, perhaps seeing the writing on the wall, refuses to go. He authorises Turkish Cypriot prime minister Mehmet Ali Talat and his son, Serdar Denktash, to represent the Turkish Cypriots. Papadopoulos agrees to go reluctantly, warning before leaving that "I will not sacrifice the rights, security and fate of Cypriot Hellenism on the altar of deadlines or pressure." Alvaro de Soto wishes that more progress had already been made here in Cyprus, but is hopeful about the phase ahead. "Pray for me!" he says as he leaves.

I'm filled with excitement and anticipation as the participants and their entourage arrive in Burgenstock. It's cold and snowing but looks chocolate-box picturesque on my television screen. Also present are special envoys from the US and Britain, while powerful EU countries are also watching developments closely. Enlargement Commissioner Mr Gunter Verheugen comes and goes, while US Secretary of State, Colin Powell and President

George W. Bush are also expected to intervene actively. Idyllic scenes of the snow clad Swiss resort lead some journalists to wonder if Annan chose the place on purpose, to calm the participants' souls.

However, the reports we get from Switzerland are confusing. It's hard to get at the facts. The press are staying in town and don't come into contact with the participants who are holed up at the luxury resort. We hear that Serdar Denktash is complaining that all cell-phone reception has been deliberately blocked and he can't even get in touch with his father. Only photographers are allowed in for a photo shoot on the first day. Surfing the channels gives different versions of what's happening. They all quote "sources". Nothing is clear.

The UN Secretary General Kofi Annan arrives in Burgenstock and officially hands over the new version of the plan, dubbed Annan 4, to the two sides, calling on them to show political will and be ready to negotiate. Having heard the reactions of all concerned, he will then make an evaluation and see whether it is possible and necessary to work out further adjustments in close consultation with the parties, with a view to coming to conclusions on the 31st of March, which is the last day of the meetings.

Erdogan is due to arrive in Burgenstock later this afternoon. The Greek Cypriot press say that on the basis of his statements, they don't hold out much hope for the talks. Curious to see what he actually said to make them so gloomy, I look for his statements online and find nothing to merit any pessimism. Anatolia News Agency reports that he said: "*Inshallah*, our attendance will give an impetus to negotiations. We're going to Switzerland with good will." Erdogan also said he would call U.S. President George W. Bush, German Chancellor Gerhard Schroeder and French President Jacques Chirac to discuss Cyprus before he flies to Switzerland. "I'm going to ask for support so that the negotiations continue more positively," he said. "We want to solve this problem, which has not been addressed for years."

The next morning, Stelios comes down to breakfast holding his radio looking pale. "They're saying the Turks got everything and we got nothing!" he tells me. I briefly listen to the newscaster and roll my eyes at him. "Have you gone mad?" I say, having ceased believing a word the media says. "Have you forgotten who is doing the reporting? It's just more misinformation."

But Stelios is not the only one to have been taken in. Everyone is depressed. The general impression is that if Annan 3 was bad, Annan 4 is worse. Everyone believes the Turks got everything they asked for. Even ardent YES voters are crestfallen. A sense of gloom and doom descends on the TV talk shows. The two big parties, DISY and AKEL, are desperately saying let's wait and see, while Papadopoulos' party is screaming that we shouldn't believe anyone who tries to present the plan as logical and a good deal. An opinion poll puts the NO voters at 95%.

There's a feeling that Erdogan worked the phones and got what he wanted and our side didn't. Some people are blaming Papadopoulos for not negotiating. An article appears claiming that Erdogan has gone to Burgenstock with a map in his pocket giving the whole of the Karpas peninsula back to the Greek side, but that Papadopoulos had not put in a demand for more territory. It has become blatantly obvious that Papadopoulos doesn't want to make the plan more attractive. He wants Greek Cypriots to vote NO in the referendum and is only paying lip service to wanting a settlement. Instead he allows the NO campaign to cleverly manipulate public opinion, whipping up hysteria against the plan, while the few people who dare to speak out in favour are attacked and discredited.

Finally, Annan hands over the last version of the plan, Annan 5, to the two Cypriot sides, Greece and Turkey. Speaking at a press conference before leaving Switzerland, he says the process of negotiation is not a football match.

"It is not a question of keeping score of goals and own goals, of winners and losers. Rather, we have tried to accommodate the expressed concerns of both sides, so as to create a win-win situation. I believe that we have succeeded."

He calls on the people of Cyprus to accept his plan, which he describes as a compromise, "the best and fairest chance for peace, prosperity and stability that is ever likely to be on offer" and one that is fair and designed to work. He urges us not to make the mistake of missing yet another opportunity to solve the Cyprus problem.

"The choice is not between this settlement plan and some other magical or mythical solution," he says. "The choice is between this settlement and no settlement."

Next it's the turn of the prime ministers of Greece and Turkey to speak. Erdogan goes first. He speaks in Turkish with an English translator at his side. He's impeccable. He stands tall, self assured, and speaks quickly, calmly and eloquently. He says no one has come out from the talks as a loser and that Turkey's efforts had concentrated on securing a result from which everyone would be a winner. Turkey's priorities had been to make sure that the settlement would become part of EU primary law, to reinforce bizonality, to secure political equality for the Turkish Cypriots, to strengthen the guarantees and the economy of the Turkish Cypriot community and to protect the rights of the Turkish settlers. He says "a new road map for Cyprus has been drawn in Burgenstock," and that "now we are ready to bring about our responsibilities regarding this plan." He calls on Greek Cypriots and Greeks to walk with him along the path of peace started in Burgenstock. "We are taking the necessary steps together, let us continue taking those steps."

When the Greek prime minister takes the podium he looks around furtively with what seems to me to be a false smile, or pursed lips. He speaks in Greek and doesn't even have a translator. He says that it has not been possible to reach an agreed settlement on the question of Cyprus during the talks and expresses the hope that the people of Cyprus and the political leadership would decide with prudence, a sense of responsibility and foresightedness. His statement is half the length of Erdogan's. On the whole he looks as if he wants to get out of there as quickly as possible and does so as soon as he can.

Alvaro de Soto then takes the podium saying that the final plan is now in the hands of the people, but that the leaders have an important responsibility to explain the plan to the people. Asked if this was the last effort by the UN to solve the problem if one side in Cyprus rejects the proposed plan in the forthcoming referendum, he replies, "Pretty much."

As our political leaders come back home, everyone starts speculating about what Papadopoulos will tell the people. Can he really urge us to vote NO? Can he shoulder such a large responsibility? Some people believe he won't have the guts to do so but will tell us to vote what our heart tells us to, while letting his henchmen do the dirty work—just as he has been doing all along. The TV talk shows are not so hostile and people are beginning to realise the picture may not be as bleak as the president and his men are trying to make out.

Meanwhile on the other side of the divide, a spokesman for Denktash says that far from being a victory, as the Turkish press is trying to make out, the Annan plan is a terrifying fiasco. Turkey has managed to abolish a state that it has recognized, one that, if they vote YES, the Turkish Cypriot people will be destroying with their own hands. Denktash himself says the Annan Plan has not given us what we wanted. It has weakened the guarantees in the 1960 Agreements, weakened bizonality because "many Greek Cypriots will return to live among us," and as regards the property issue, the plan contains everything required for the disruption of peace. He describes the plan as a time bomb.

I meet an Irishman who has come to Cyprus to advise us on how to run the YES campaign. He tells me he was involved in the Irish referendum and since then has been going round the world whenever there are referendums giving campaign advice and assistance. He tells me he doesn't think the YES campaign has much chance unless AKEL withdraws its support for Papadopoulos, sacrificing its position in government, and takes the risk of coming out in support of the plan.

"You need someone in authority to back the plan, otherwise it's a lost cause," he says.

A week after Burgenstock, Papadopoulos finally addresses the people in a live televised speech that lasts over half an hour. He urges Greek Cypriots to reject the plan with a resounding NO. He says the plan does not satisfy the minimum aims set by the Greek Cypriot side, and instead meets the main demands of the Turkish Cypriot side. It does not lead to the reunification of the island but makes the division permanent. He lists all the possible pitfalls of the plan playing on people's fears, in a speech that echoes all the arguments of the NO campaign—doubts about whether the federal state would function, the weakness of the central government, the long delays between the implementation of each stage of the plan, doubts that Turkey would honour its promises. He hints that it would bring about a collapse of the economy, as it would lower people's standard of living, that it would bring about insecurity and an unpredictable future. Turkey would keep its army here, albeit a smaller one, the Turkish settlers would stay, only a few refugees would be able to return to their homes, and those who did wouldn't have any schools for their children. He even doubts that we will continue to live in a state governed by the rule of law, democracy and consensus, or that human rights would be respected. He throws out hope for a better solution down the road by claiming efforts to solve the Cyprus problem will not end here. All things considered, he says, he cannot endorse the form of solution proposed by the Annan plan.

He ends by saying, "I took over an internationally recognised state, I am not going to deliver a community without a say internationally and in search of a guardian, and all this with empty, deceptive promises that Turkey will honour its commitments."

As he reads, his voice starts to tremble, once at the beginning, and then again at the end. I watch dumbfounded as he deliberately removes his glasses so we can all see he has tears in his eyes, astounded that anyone can be taken in by such theatrics.

The speech is followed by studio discussions on all channels. At one point they interrupt the programme to go live to the Presidential Palace where a small crowd of people has gathered in a supposedly spontaneous demonstration. They are waving Greek and Cyprus flags, as well as large NO banners, and chanting, "We are by your side" and "Tasso fight on, we give you our blood." A few minutes later, Papadopoulos himself appears and beams at the crowd. He makes a short statement saying that whatever he said tonight was both from the heart and from the head. "Trust me," he says. "I will not change my mind." He leaves to chants of the Greek national anthem. I feel like throwing up.

Former president George Vassiliou is a guest on one of the panels I'm watching. Undoubtedly the best president we ever had, well respected amongst world leaders and a successful businessman, he is always a pleasure to listen to, because he is sensible and cuts to the chase. He has gone bright red in the face watching the footage and says it looks suspiciously as if the whole thing has been staged. As for Papadopoulos' speech, he says it saddens him because it has made him realise that the president doesn't really want a federal solution even though he says he does.

"He said it clearly—'I wasn't elected in order to deliver a community'— but that's what a federal solution means!"

We are all waiting with baited breath to hear what the two big parties will do. AKEL's political office convenes a meeting which lasts two whole days and ends on Good Friday with a call to the UN and the international community to postpone the referendums for a few months so that they can present the plan objectively to the Cypriot people and to continue the negotiations in order to fill in the gaps, thereby ensuring that it gets approved. In other words, they're voting NO. Christofias, the party leader, tells a press conference that their NO is not the same as that of others who oppose the Annan plan. They're voting NO in order to cement the YES, he says, whatever that means. More rumours are saying that US president Bush personally called Christofias and asked him what he needed in order to support the plan. Christofias replied he wanted postponement of the referendum and guarantees that it would be implemented in conditions of security. But the UN says postponing the referendum is not an option.

Speculation is rife as to what happened inside that meeting. The party had been leaning in favour of YES. What happened to make them go overnight from supporting the plan to opposing it? Some people are saying that Christofias received the results of an opinion poll of the party's grass roots and felt he could not turn the tide. Others that Papadopoulos had threatened to kick him out of the coalition government if they chose to support the YES. Whatever the reason, in my eyes, Christofias didn't have the guts to try and fight it.

DISY convenes a special conference on the plan at which Anastasiades gives a powerful speech with sound rational arguments and positive passion. No tears, no tissues and no stage-managed sentimentality. He is followed by old Clerides, the president before Papadopoulos who had been the mastermind behind the plan. He is helped hobbling onto the stage. Loud shouts of NO come from the back of the auditorium and huge NO banners are raised, as the party contains a number of extreme right wing nationalists within it many of whom had played a major role in the EOKA campaign for *enosis*. Clerides' speech has many people in tears. He says in over fifty years in politics he has been proven right in many of his warnings and lists several powerful examples. He says a NO vote means we can forget our ancestral lands. He concludes by saying that at eighty five years old he would rather go and meet his maker than live to see the outcome of a NO. The party votes overwhelmingly in support of YES.

The war in the streets is raging. YES and NO banners are competing for space, alternately being pulled down by the opposition. For a while things start to look up. The YES campaign gathers momentum. I spot YES stencilled on the pavement all the way down the main shopping streets where the ladies who shop are bound to see them. I watch as the driver of a car in front of me, on seeing a whole lot of NO stickers in the window of a bookshop, leans out of his car and yells, "Illiterate! Read the plan!"

AKEL's constitutional expert Toumazos Tsielepis, who has been on the negotiating committees from day one, appears on TV. He calmly and patiently explains exactly why certain controversial provisions in the plan are the way they are. He explains what the Turkish point of view was, what their fears are and how we had sought to meet them. When a viewer calls in to say 'better them (the Turks) over there and us (the Greeks) over here', he calmly replies that as far as he is concerned, such backward attitudes have no place in the future we are trying to build. For a brief evening hearts and minds begin to sway towards the YES. It dawns on people that maybe this is a fair compromise after all, as they see the other point of view. In fact the interview makes such an impact that people call for it to be shown again. The government, realising the danger, quickly squashes it.

Then Vassiliou accuses the state radio and television channel CyBC of blocking EU Commissioner Verheugen from addressing the people and the UN from broadcasting information programs. Verheugen himself launches a blistering attack on the government, effectively accusing Cyprus of cheating its way into the European Union. Addressing the European Parliament, which was debating a Cyprus resolution, a clearly angry Verheugen lashes out at Papadopoulos and the Greek Cypriot side for failing to keep a promise not to oppose a settlement. Verheugen recalls that in 1999, the then Greek Cypriot government had promised to do everything possible to secure a settlement in return for which the EU would not make a Cyprus solution a prerequisite for accession.

"I am going to be very undiplomatic now," he says. "I feel cheated by the Greek Cypriot government. We had a clear agreement on this point. Mr Papadopoulos must respect his part of the deal. Under no circumstances was a solution of the conflict going to fail as a result of opposition from the Greek Cypriot authorities."

Now the government is reeling. They are facing attacks on Papadopoulos' negotiating tactics, as well as attacks on trying to control the news. In addition, a couple of ministers have resigned from the government and joined the YES camp. Verheugen eventually gets his interview but with the English-language CyBC Radio 2, a station that hardly anyone listens to. Nobody pays the slightest attention.

With the referendums a few days away, it's the turn of the UN Secretary-general Kofi Annan to address the Cypriot people. He says this Saturday, each one of us has a difficult decision to make—one that will determine the destiny of our country. We will be asked whether we wish to make this plan the basis for our common future.

"I know you call it 'the Annan Plan'," he says. "Indeed, parts of the plan were put together by the United Nations. But all of its key concepts emerged out of four years of negotiation among your leaders. And most of its 9,000 pages were drafted by hundreds of Greek Cypriots and Turkish Cypriots. Their extraordinary efforts produced one of the most comprehensive peace plans in the history of the United Nations."

He acknowledges that this plan does not meet the full demands of either side. In fact it is a compromise, as is inevitable in any negotiation. It is also the only foreseeable route to the reunification of Cyprus.

"There is no other plan out there. There is no magic way of accommodating the maximum demands of one side while at the same time accommodating the maximum demands of the other. This is it."

He says, "After forty years of conflict, and thirty years of division, the choice before you this Saturday is one of truly historic importance. The vision of the plan is simple: reunification and reconciliation, in safety and security, in the European Union. The world is ready to help you turn that vision of the future into reality. But we cannot take that fateful decision for you. We await your call. *Efharisto! Çok teşekkür ederim*! Thank you very much."

Annan's statement hardly gets any publicity. It is completely ignored. No one raises it in any of the TV discussion shows. Only one paper covers both Annan's message and Verheugen's statement. Its headline reads: "Is anybody listening?"

The tension in the streets is palpable. It's no longer safe to display a YES sticker on your car or anywhere else. When I put some on a skip near my house, the police ring my doorbell and threaten me. I take my nine-year-old daughter downtown to the central square where opposing kiosks have gone up. The YES kiosk is invitingly green, gentle and happy; the NO kiosk is ominously black, threatening and mean. Seeing the NOs with their black T-shirts, shouting at us aggressively from across the road, my daughter senses danger and doesn't want to stay. Later I hear the NOs attacked our kiosk, trashing it completely. When one girl said she was from Kyrenia and wanted to go back, she was accused of being a traitor and a "Turk lover". A friend of mine tells me that she was chased by a group of NOs who spotted the YES sticker on her car. She narrowly escaped by parking in someone's garage and quickly removing the sticker. I particularly abhor the bumper stickers of NO voters that righteously proclaim "Kyrenia is not for sale." Can't they see that with a NO they're just giving it away? NO graffiti has been painted on the walls of the English School. It reads, "A good Turk is a dead Turk." And this in a school that has Turkish Cypriot pupils. I'm ashamed of my old school. Canon Frank Newham, the school's founder, must be turning in his grave.

The YES campaign has died down almost completely. There is hardly any money to do anything with. The TV spot we had planned never materialises. We are reduced to tearing up bed sheets and painting giant YESes on them to use as banners. The NO campaign in contrast is raging. They have paid for TV spots with angry people saying "Annan plan? No thanks!"

Papadopoulos deftly manages never to appear on any of the talk shows. Only once do I briefly catch him being interviewed on one of the mainland Greek channels, Mega Ellas. The interviewer is good and keeps pressing him trying to get past his vague inanities. Finally he asks, "But what *do* you want, Mr President?" I watch delighted as Papadopoulos visibly squirms in his seat. The only answer he can come up with is, "Well, I definitely can see that to go back to the pre-1974 situation is not realistic." He wants a solution that is "viable" and "workable", is all he can say.

I hear that the government, in an effort to terrorise them into voting NO, has sent a letter to civil servants, police, and national guard officers saying it cannot guarantee their positions or benefits in a federal government. Anastasiades reports this to European institutions, as well as the manner in which the media were handling the campaign. As a result the President of the European Parliament has asked the Committee of Civil Liberties to examine the situation in Cyprus. All the NOs are up in arms and brand him a traitor to the country for having snitched on them. No one cares to discuss whether there is any truth in his allegations.

The YES campaign holds one last mass rally in the square. We go to it, of course, even though we know it's a lost cause. I sit with my sister and friends on top of the old Venetian wall looking down as the crowd gathers in the moat below us. There's a general air of dejection and futility. The square fills up, but not enough. Saddest of all is when the extreme left wing group EDON arrives with their green banners, green being the colour of the left. Everyone applauds them, hoping against hope that the rest of the left, namely AKEL, would somehow see fit to join us too.

All campaigning is banned by law twenty-four hours before the vote so there are no interviews or discussions on television. An item on the evening news claims that "Attila is arming himself". The newsreader says that the Turkish army is bringing in more arms to Cyprus, while behind her, footage of tanks and armaments rolling off some nondescript military vessels is shown. It's clearly archive footage. I feel incensed at this brazen bit of propaganda and attempt to spread fear. And it succeeds. "Did you hear?" my paediatrician tells me. "The Turks are arming themselves more!" I scold him for allowing himself to be fooled. "And you, an educated man!"

Since there's nothing in the news regarding the referendum, we're all suffering from withdrawal symptoms. Some people who have satellite TV, watch the Greek mainland stations which continue to show interviews with our party leaders. They also cover a mass rally held in the north. There, fifteen thousand Turkish Cypriots sing songs in favour of EVET (YES), unity and peace, as well as Greek songs. Greek Cypriot stations barely gave it a mention. Everyone's main concern is the polls. The Greek stations shows a poll which put the NO vote at 65%. Another puts it at 71%. While yet another says 54%. Any way you look at it, YES is doomed.

On the day of the referendum Stelios, Celia and I cast our vote and immediately cross over to the other side. We can't bear to be on our side listening to the NOs celebrating the lack of a solution. The final results of the referendum are that just under 76% of Greek Cypriots have voted NO, while almost 65% of Turkish Cypriots voted YES.

The UN Secretary General Kofi Annan issues another statement: "A unique and historic chance to resolve the Cyprus problem had been missed," adding that Cyprus will remain divided and militarised and the benefits of a settlement will not be realised.

He hopes that ways will be found to ease the plight of the Turkish Cypriots and stresses that he remains convinced that his proposal was fair, viable and a carefully balanced compromise. He also hopes that the Greek Cypriots will have second thoughts and may arrive at a different view in the fullness of time, after a profound and sober assessment of today's decision.

Alvaro de Soto, who reads out Annan's statement, says that he and his team will be leaving the island this week. "You're on your own now," he tells us ominously.

Later, speaking at a conference on federalism in Brussels, de Soto puts things in a nutshell. He says Greek Cypriots have to decide if they are "specifically prepared to embrace the political equality of the Turkish Cypriots and share power with them." He says the answer to this question "will make it possible to ascertain whether a viable, sustainable reunification is possible." It's a question we do indeed need to ask ourselves, but one we would much rather sweep under the carpet.

One by one I hear the various officials from the YES camp being interviewed. They all say, through gritted teeth, that they respect the outcome of the vote. Well, I don't. How can I respect a vote that was not won fairly, through laying out of the pros and cons, and genuine arguments and discussions? This vote was won through manipulation, lies and subterfuge. Like Verheugen, I feel cheated. As I see it, Papadopoulos did not want to share power with the Turkish Cypriots, did not want a bizonal, bicommunal federation. What he really hoped for was that Cyprus would become a unitary state once more with the majority running the country and the minority simply enjoying legitimate rights, even though he knew it was unrealistic. Failing that, he was quite happy to forget the north, just as long as Greek Cypriots can be masters of their own little patch. The wounds of the people of this island had only half-healed when along he came, like some evil witch, with his beady eyes and raspy voice, ready to scratch them open and make them bleed again. Instead of healing those wounds, by helping us come to terms with our loss, accept the illegality that had happened, because life just isn't fair, and atone for past mistakes, he made things worse so that he could justify the resounding NO he was asking for. He tricked the people. His campaign was one big con.

The outcome is we get to keep the border, this line that shows we need to be kept apart artificially, with barbed wire, sandbags, sentry posts, soldiers with guns, minefields and UN in between. We are not mature enough, not human enough to respect the other, embrace the other's differences and accept them. We are not ready to get rid of the wall of hatred and mistrust that has been fortified over the years and build a common future. We are like children who haven't yet learned how to share the gift of our island. Since we can't share it as a whole, we will continue to each rule our tiny little realms separately, until perhaps one day we will see ourselves as Cypriots, or perhaps even, citizens of the world, human beings, with little to separate us.

As I lie in bed mulling things over on the morning after the referendum, listening to the hodja's cry wafting over from the other side, I notice to my surprise that my pillow is wet.

14 DRAGON TERRITORY

It is customary amongst Cypriots to decorate their homes and offices with framed sepia-coloured prints of medieval maps of our island. You can usually tell how old the maps are by the island's shape, the older ones resembling amorphous blobs, the newer ones having more intricate and accurate renditions that include every bay and promontory. What always amuses me about these maps is the habit of the medieval cartographers to adorn the blank areas with pictures of dragons, sea monsters or other mythological creatures. Of course, there weren't actually dragons there. The warning simply reflects a fear of the unknown. These were areas about which little or nothing was known and were therefore considered dangerous. Don't go here! Here be dragons!

In the debate about how we should solve the Cyprus problem, similar fears have long prevented us from pursuing a logical strategy outside the accepted dogma. Saying NO is easy, what's hard is saying YES, because it means living up to the responsibility of your decision. Yet NO is not necessarily safer. It too carries responsibilities and perhaps even greater dangers. Choosing the status quo does not necessarily mean staying as we are. It could just as easily set forth a chain of events not of our choosing or liking. What we really needed on the Greek Cypriot side was a leader brave enough to cut through dragon territory. Unfortunately, our political minions shook in their boots at the mythical dangers of the solution dragons, while blithely ignoring the very real dragons hiding in plain sight along the 'safe' path of conventional wisdom. We failed to slay those dragons. Now here we are staring partition in the face.

My feelings of loss double with the result of the referendum. It's as if we've lost Kyrenia a second time. A friend of mine, who I meet for coffee one day, feels the same way. Before the referendum, he tells me, he used to go across regularly, happily cycling into northern Nicosia, meeting Turkish

Cypriots, having coffee in the Büyük Han, wandering round the local market, filled with a sense of optimism at our joint future. "Now, after the NO, I refuse to go," he says sadly. "What for? It only makes me feel bad because I feel that now it's lost forever."

The NO is a huge disappointment for the Turkish Cypriots as well, who take it as yet another rejection from the Greek Cypriots. They feel ostracised and left behind, as the south joins the EU and they don't, and bitter as even promised EU funds fail to materialise because Papadopoulos vetoes them.

In the early days after the referendum, many in the YES camp on both sides desperately try to find ways to push for a solution. The Turkish Cypriots are the most organised. They set up a Civil Initiative Movement and try to get Greek Cypriot NGOs to join them. A meeting is arranged at which we are urged to attend.

As I don't know how to get to the Turkish Cypriot Chamber of Commerce where the meeting is being held, I hitch a ride with Andreas who is also taking three other people. We drive through the Ayios Dometios/Metehan checkpoint, past the Greek Cypriot policeman who just counts people crossing and jots down licence plate numbers, supposedly for statistical reasons, and line up at the Turkish checkpoint for passport checks and to purchase car insurance. Andreas jumps out to present his papers, while the rest of us wait in the car. I just have to laugh when one of the guys in the car tells me that he just can't bring himself to take out annual car insurance for the north preferring to renew it every three months "just in case the Cyprus problem is solved in the meantime!"

At the Chamber of Commerce we all gather in the auditorium. Mustafa and a guy called Andros chair the meeting. Mustafa starts off doing a roundup of where we stand. Andros briefs us about what they've been doing, namely setting up an umbrella organisation for all NGOs in the south. Then he opens the floor to discussion. One woman asks what the Turkish Cypriot experience has been in changing public opinion in the north. Mustafa describes how in the space of two years they managed to go from most people not wanting to have anything to do with the Greek Cypriots to a 63% call for reunification. They first drafted a common position paper, which they then presented individually to each NGO.

"We started with one, then got four on board, then sixteen, forty and so on. In the end we managed to hold a rally in the streets with two thousand people, the next time with ten. At the last rally we were twenty thousand people," he says.

"But it was different on your side," says another Greek Cypriot. "You had a very strong incentive to get out of isolation and join the European Union. You won't believe how difficult it is on our side. The opposition has been practically beaten into submission. Everyone is afraid to express an opinion because it is misconstrued or blown out of all proportion by the media."

Another woman agrees, saying it's all pointless, that nothing can be done. She says she was at a party the other night where nine out of ten people were NOs.

"They were all saying that Papadopoulos and his camp are now openly saying that we must go for partition," she tells us. "When I said, 'but what about my property?' they said 'sorry, you'll have to sacrifice your interests for the good of the country. They will never change. It's too late."

Others echo her sentiments. The Turkish Cypriots patiently hear everyone out. Then Ali, Hasip's brother and head of the Turkish Cypriot Chamber of Commerce, stands up. He tells us that actually it was all far worse for them. Not only did they have to face equally negative and nationalistic sentiments from both their leadership, as well as ordinary people, but they also had the Turkish army to contend with. For them it was not simply a question of being in danger of losing their livelihoods by going out on a limb and expressing a desire for reunification, but also their lives. He tells us if we are really serious about fighting this fight, we will have to accept that it will be difficult.

"No one said it will be easy," he says in a calm, compassionate voice. "You will go through times when you will argue with your best friends, you will argue with each other, but still you must endure. You will be attacked from all quarters. You will be called a traitor. They will harass you. They will go through your accounts to try and find something they can get you on. You will be accused of being on the payroll of the Americans, the British, anyone they can think of. Hardly a week goes by without a picture of a cheque appearing in the papers with my name on it as having received money from some foreign interests. These things will happen. You will have to grow a very thick skin and persevere. Just know that you can do it. We did it against worse odds."

There is silence after he sits down. Then a Greek Cypriot says, "but you had the incentive of the EU, the plan was good for you."

Ali gets up again. "Let me tell you something, the plan was not good for Turkish Cypriots either. Hundreds of people would have had to leave their homes, some for a third time, in order to allow the Greek Cypriot owners to go back, like in Morphou, for example. But we were able to sell it to them, to convince them of the benefits of reunification. You can too. It's a question of vision, of persuading them that the good parts outweigh the bad."

The meeting finishes with heart-warming words from Mustafa.

"Remember that you are in the right. They are in the wrong. The world is moving away from racism, nationalism, and separation and towards acceptance, integration and mutual respect. These attitudes of theirs will not last long. It's just a question of time."

Despite the pain of the referendum result, I go across more frequently now. Stelios and I explore Kyrenia. We find little bays where we go swimming, as close to the house as possible, as well as places we used to frequent in the past. We swim at what used to be Five Mile Beach, where the invasion took place and visit a friend's house on the top of the cliff there that has now been turned into a museum in honour of the Turkish colonel, Karaoglanoglu, who died there, his uniforms displayed in his father's cupboard. Every time we go something interesting and even touching happens. Once, as we were getting out of our car near Eight and a Half Mile Beach, we were approached by a man proudly showing us his *Teach Yourself Greek* book eager to practice what he had learned. "I'm going to London to find work," he tells us. "I will come back when there is peace." Turkish Cypriots talk in terms of peace; Greek Cypriots talk in terms of a problem needing a solution. Another time I meet a Turkish Cypriot friend's mother-in-law, who, despite having her brother killed in the sixties troubles in Paphos, greets me without an ounce of bitterness, hugging me as if *I* were her long lost relative. With the coffee club we visit the Karpas and stay in Yialousa where we meet a Greek Cypriot couple, who originally came from the area and now live in Larnaca. They told us they come back here every weekend just to be close to their former home.

Meeting and talking with Turkish Cypriots, listening to their concerns, changes me. I learn to see things from their point of view. I hear the anguish and incomprehension in their voices when they ask "Why are the Greeks trying to punish us by keeping us in isolation? We said YES." And I contrast it with the arrogance of a Greek Cypriot radio presenter, who, when asked one morning if isolating them was fair, replied: "That's *their* problem."

The reason why it proved virtually impossible to get a NO supporter to change his/her mind, despite the fact that none of the NO arguments stood up to logical scrutiny, puzzles me. Equally, why was it that the YES camp were so unperturbed by the NO fears? Why didn't we mistrust Turkey, worry that the system would bring about a stalemate, or balk at the possibility of economic collapse? Why were we so blithely willing to take these risks?

Was it fear of change? Change was at the heart of the 2004 referendum. Here we were, peacefully getting on with our lives, more or less having coming to terms with the past, when suddenly we were asked to take a decision, one that could change everything, one that would have a profound effect on our existence, our careers, our livelihoods, our safety, one that would alter the course of our history. Any change is hard, even the most trivial. We worry that we will regret it, that we may be making a mistake. The more comfortable our current state the more difficult change is. It's all very well when life forces us to change, but what happens when we need to force change of our own free will, as we were asked to do? Two things make us want change—one, suffering where we are, and two, a hunger for something better. We Greek Cypriots weren't suffering where we were and allowed ourselves to be lulled into a false sense of security that it's OK to stay as we are. They preferred to be stuck in the safety of the past, railing against the wrong that was the Turkish invasion, than to face up to the fact that the Republic of Cyprus was a comfort zone that was not really comfortable. In order to achieve change and get past the electric fence of fear, you need to have a vision. You need to see clearly where you want to go in order to have the impetus to get out of your current state. Perhaps the difference between the YESes and the NOs was that the YESes could see that there was something we wanted on the other side. The NOs on the other hand came up against their fears, fears perhaps born from the experience of the intercommunal troubles in the sixties and the war a decade later, and stopped short. These were the fears the NO campaign exploited. So was the failure of the YES campaign, as Ali had said, that we hadn't managed to convey our vision?

On the other hand, referendums, like elections, are emotional things. Logic has very little to do with how people vote. Ultimately, people are hard-wired to conform. Following the group is an essential characteristic for our survival as a species. Group beliefs, like nationalism or religion, is how humanity has been able to control larger and larger groups, as populations grow and societies are amalgamated. In the final analysis, it made very little difference whether the people had read the plan or not, they just followed the leader. The leader on the Greek side didn't want change and made sure it didn't happen with a fear campaign. If a government had been in charge that supported reunification, or if the two big parties, AKEL and DISY, had come out in support of the Annan plan, waging a campaign promoting the vision of a united Cyprus and isolating Papadopoulos, the majority may well have voted YES.

Or was it simply prejudice, the result of centuries of bad blood between Greeks and Turks? Greek Cypriots didn't trust Turkey and by extension the Turkish Cypriots, saw themselves as superior to them and had no desire to share power with them. That would explain why they were so resistant to all rational arguments in the referendum. If that is the case, how to reduce prejudice? One way to do so, social psychologists have long suggested, is through inter-group contact. Contact enhances knowledge about the other side, reduces anxiety and increases empathy by enabling one to see the other's point of view. But when I try to persuade Greek Cypriots to cross to the north, I find I am no more successful in doing so than I could get them to vote YES to the Annan plan.

Then I read about a landmark experiment on intergroup conflict and reconciliation carried out by social psychologist Muzafer Sherif known as *The Robbers Cave Experiment*. Sherif himself was touched by conflict, having grown up in Smyrna around the same time as my grandmother, barely escaping massacre at the hands of Greek soldiers in 1919, three years before the Turks paid back the injury and burned the place down.

In the summer of 1954 Sherif brought twenty-two twelve-year old boys to a camp in Oklahoma and divided them into two social groups, the Eagles and the Rattlers. During the first phase, the boys developed an attachment to their groups by doing various activities together, like hiking, swimming, building a diving board and a rope bridge together, preparing group meals etc. They also stencilled their group names onto shirts and flags, further increasing their common identity and their strong feeling of cohesiveness. In the second phase, the researchers set the stage for conflict, with competitive games and awarding prizes to the winners. Hostility and ill will broke out, initially expressed verbally through taunting or name calling, becoming more and more aggressive until the researchers had to separate the boys physically. Fourteen days after arriving as strangers, these boys who more or less looked alike, were the same age and came from similar backgrounds, turned into two disdainful and opposing tribes throwing insults and punches at each other, believing their own group to be superior than the other, and characterising the opposite group in extremely unfavourable terms.

In the third phase the researchers tried to reduce the animosity and low-level violence between the groups. They stopped the competitions and introduced greater social contact. However, they found that once hostility had been aroused it was very hard to get rid of. In fact it continued and escalated even when the two groups were engaged in benign activities, such as sitting around and watching movies. Simply by increasing the contact of the two groups, only made the situation worse. The solution they eventually found was to force the groups to work together on common goals. They created a series of situations in which competition between the groups would have harmed everyone's interests, in which co-operation was necessary for mutual benefit. For example, on a day long outing they arranged for the only truck available to go into town for food to get stuck. The boys had to get together and push and pull in order to get the vehicle moving again. In another instance the researchers interrupted the camp's water supply, whereupon the boys organised themselves harmoniously and fixed the problem. When the boys were told that they couldn't rent a movie because the camp couldn't afford it, they pooled their money and rented it themselves and sat happily enjoying it together. Gradually the boys began to view each other as allies instead of opponents. By having common goals that required co-operation to achieve them, they experienced the rival group members as reasonable fellows, valued helpers, and friends. They began to like each other more and when their mutual efforts resulted in success, it became even more difficult to maintain feelings of hostility towards each other.

In Cyprus we've been stuck in phase two of the Robbers Cave Experiment long enough. We need to get into phase three. But how?

Nelson Mandela, undoubtedly a great leader, saw how to do this when he came to power in South Africa. Following the dismantling of apartheid, he faced enormous challenges in the mistrust that still existed between black and white South Africans, which could easily have led to violence. When South Africa was due to host the 1995 Rugby World Cup, Mandela realised how sport could unite the country and put all his efforts behind achieving support for the mostly-white Springboks team, which had hitherto been a symbol of prejudice and apartheid. The event was wonderfully dramatised by Clint Eastwood in his movie *Invictus*, a must see for all Cypriots. Mandela succeeded. Could we?

One Saturday I enter Ledra Street, on my way to the Büyük Han and come across a demonstration. I remember reading in the papers that it was in support of a rally held in the north against Ankara's spending cuts. A previous rally in the north a few weeks ago had provoked Erdogan's ire and sparked angry exchanges between Turkish Cypriots and motherland Turkey. Furious by what he saw as the ingratitude of the Turkish Cypriots, Erdogan branded them 'freeloaders'. He hinted that it was only a question of time before the north becomes a province of Turkey and Turkish Cypriots lost their political say. This latest rally was an act of defiance by the thirty unions and opposition parties which refused to be intimidated by Erdogan's bullying. Demonstrators again held flags of the Cyprus Republic in an act calculated to infuriate Erdogan who had taken great offence at the appearance of the flags at the previous rally. Placards declared "This is our country, let's run it ourselves" and warned "Hands off the Turkish Cypriots". Other slogans highlighted Turkish Cypriot fears that the north was being overrun by Turks, declaring: "No, to our extinction". Some demonstrators even demanded the immediate re-unification of the island. All in all, about twenty five thousand Turkish Cypriots had gathered in Inonu Square.

Meanwhile, on our side, there are no masses milling, no loudspeakers blaring in support of the Turkish Cypriots. Just a small group of people gathered round a stage at the bottom of the street, next to the sandbags. A few individuals with long grey hair are strumming on guitars and singing protest songs. I pause and listen as the announcer presents the next speaker, a pretty young girl called Xenia, who I recognise from the YES campaign. Her words are clear, simple and refreshing. I stop to listen, riveted.

"Fellow citizens of Nicosia," she says eyes blazing as she pans round the handful of onlookers. "Just a few hours ago, in this very city, the same city we are standing in now, one of the largest demonstrations that has ever been held in Cyprus took place. I'd like you to think long and hard about that. Because sometimes I feel like an alien from outer space in this country. I call on you to consider that while half this city is making history, the other half continues its day to day existence oblivious." She pauses a moment for emphasis. "Nothing seems to move us."

She says she belongs to the post-invasion generation, growing up in the eighties, the period of the economic miracle, with the slogan 'I don't forget' written on her school exercise books. "I was raised with hatred for the evil Turks," she says, "as if there were no Turkish Cypriots. Whatever existed just a few metres from our doorstep was all hushed up. I grew up with half a history, with no memories of lost homes and lands. With politicians calling for 'all the refugees to return home'. I grew up with suffering, anger, injustice and slogans."

"Today I'm angry," she says, and it's as if she's speaking for me. "Because, while all the myths have collapsed, nothing has changed. Even though the checkpoints have opened, we are still living as if they are closed. Even though we have got to know one another, we are pretending that we haven't seen anything! I am angry because our president, who supposedly wants a solution by Cypriots for Cypriots, has still not found the strength to invite half the Cypriots living on this island to unite with the other half. I can no longer stand hearing about events held to commemorate the occupation, nor about anti-occupation rallies supposedly against Turkey, not even about bicommunal excursions to the mountains!"

She concludes by urging us to take a leaf out of the Turkish Cypriots' book and fight for change, to take to the streets outside the Presidential Palace, or outside the House of Representatives, outside the party leaders' homes, or wherever our politicians will emerge to pay lip service to a solution. Apart from a handful of people, her appeal falls on deaf ears.

As I walk away from the stage towards the checkpoint, thinking about the state of affairs on the island, I realise that I'm marching furiously. I slow down and take a few deep breaths before going through the gates at the entrance of the Han.

When I sit down, I express my frustration to Mikis who happens to be sitting next to me. "How can we get rid of all this prejudice and pave the way for reunification?" I ask. "Verbal persuasion and logical arguments don't seem to work. I can't get anyone who voted NO to even cross to the north."

"Tell them not to cross, not even when the Cyprus problem is solved," Andreas snorts. "We don't want them to come."

"They're afraid to come to the north, in case they change," Kokos says.

"They're afraid that if they come it'll harm their Greekness," Mikis says in his usual calm objective way. "In psychology it's called cognitive dissonance. Whereby the idea you have of yourself clashes with reality and you can't accept it. So therefore you avoid reality in order to protect yourself. For example, you might hate a particular race and decide that you don't want to talk to them in case you start to like them. These things are like warts on the brain."

"Or donkey-headedness," Kokos says.

Ahmet is called over for more drinks and Andreas catches Hasip asking for "*ena megalo lemonada.*"

"*Mia, re, mia,*" he yells, his patience finally running out. "Lemonade is female. How many times do I have to tell you?"

Hasip rolls his eyes.

"Ahmet *dayı,*" Suleyman says turning to the coffeeshop owner with a serious expression on his face. I notice he has a devilish gleam in his eyes. Ahmet stands obediently to attention and Suleyman quietly asks him something in Turkish in his slow deliberate tone. Then he folds his arms across his chest, leans back in his chair and smugly waits for the answer. For a moment there's a pause. Then Ahmet suddenly becomes animated, gesticulating wildly at Suleyman and arguing loudly. At the same time Hasan also explodes at poor old Ahmet. I cannot imagine what is going on, but whatever it is, it's intriguing. Even Andreas stops chatting and looks at them bemused.

"What on earth did you ask him?" I ask Suleyman when there's a lull in the tirade.

Suleyman grins mischievously. "I asked him… how come Fenerbahçe has agreed to come and play in this … *unrecognised* and … *illegal* state of south Cyprus? Besiktas, I told him, would *never* have agreed to come. Then I sat back and waited for the fireworks to start!" He throws his head back and laughs delighted with himself.

They inform me that Fenerbahçe has been drawn to play a Greek Cypriot team, AEL of Limassol, in the Europa League and the match is being held in southern Nicosia.

"Ahmet is a bit of a nationalist," Hasan explains.

"Is he going to go to the match?" I ask.

"Ah!" Suleyman says with relish. "Let's ask him!" He turns to Ahmet and asks innocently, "Ahmet *dayı,* Marina wants to know if you're going to the match."

At that Ahmet blasts a torrent of words in my direction, which even though they are Greek, tumble out of him at such a rate as to be completely incomprehensible. All the while Hasan stokes the fire in Turkish from the sidelines, which Ahmet makes a point of ignoring, as one would ignore a dog yapping at one's ankles.

"Don't listen to them, Ahmet," Andreas tells him in Greek taking pity on him. "Fenerbahçe will do well in the match. These guys are all *sierokoutales*. Do you know what that is?"

"Of course," Ahmet replies indignantly. "Soup ladles for stirring things up. But you know there are *sierokoutales* with one handle, and there are *sierokoutales* that have legs that can stir things up even more. That's what these two are like." With that he shuffles off in a huff.

Just then Suleyman's son and daughter-in-law arrive with their new baby. Suleyman proudly takes his grandson out of his pram and shows him around. Everyone fusses over it, while its mother, Ayla, a doe-eyed beauty, sits down at the table opposite me, evidently glad for a bit of rest. We chat and she tells me she's half-Irish half Turkish Cypriot, born and raised in the UK and a professional singer, songwriter, actress and one-time model. She worked with a number of top Turkish performers both in Turkey and the UK.

"Oh," I say, as an idea occurs to me, "why don't you try and represent Cyprus at the Eurovision Song Contest?"

"I've already tried that," she says. "I took part in the CyBC selection performance a couple of years ago." I brace myself for what I think is coming, namely that the selection board blocked her. To my surprise, she tells me they loved her and gave her thirty-nine points out of forty, which counted for sixty per cent of the final vote. "I didn't win because I didn't get enough votes from the public," she says. My heart sinks, realising what a lot of prejudice we have to overcome. Later I listen to her on YouTube and hear a rich, resonant voice, a professional performance and a lost opportunity to bring our communities together.

After we leave, I'm a little concerned about the football match, because I hear that some Greek Cypriot football hooligans have threatened to 'kill the infidels', but fortunately it all goes smoothly, as Andreas informs us the following week.

"Some idiots did try to unfurl a Greek flag but they were immediately stopped, not by the police, but by other Greek Cypriots in the crowd. Then somebody else tried to unfurl a TRNC flag but they were stopped too. There was just one massive banner that read: 'Football is peace and friendship'. So it all went quite well."

"In fact we were treated like first-class citizens," Hasan adds. "When we arrived the traffic police immediately said, 'oh, you are Turkish Cypriots, come this way,' and they showed us where to park. They even escorted us to our seats!"

I think how wonderful it would be if this were the norm, the Greek Cypriots bending over backwards for the Turkish Cypriots and the Turkish Cypriots doing the same for us!

15 HOME

One evening we're watching TV with Stelios and chance upon a discussion between a couple of lawyers on the issue of Greek Cypriot properties in the north. Since 1974 owners have been suing Turkey for compensation for their properties and there has been a backlog of cases before the European Commission of Human Rights (ECHR). The ECHR has recently ruled that we must first exhaust "domestic remedies" to our property issues before resorting to the court and as a result Turkey has set up an Immovable Properties Commission (IPC) in the north to which we will have to apply if we want compensation. Some Greek Cypriots are already beginning to do so, despite accusations of being traitors for indirectly recognising the pseudostate.

We have no choice but to apply, says the first lawyer and advises us at least to apply for 'loss of use'. The other lawyer is adamant, saying on no account should we apply to the IPC. It is our duty not to sell off our country and not to recognise the government in the north. The first lawyer replies that recognition doesn't come into it, as the ECHR's decision clarifies that the IPC constitutes a domestic remedy of the government of Turkey and not of the Turkish Cypriot state, meaning that Turkey continues to be responsible for the violation of human rights in the Turkish occupied areas of Cyprus. The IPC, he says, accepts the title deeds of the Republic of Cyprus, since Turkey accepts that Greek Cypriots are the legal owners of their land in the Turkish occupied areas.

When next I visit the Büyük Han, Hasip informs me that over five hundred cases have already been submitted.

"They will probably give a lot of money to the first ones who apply in order to encourage more people to do so, but afterwards they will give much less," he says. "You should hurry up and get in line."

It's a clever move on the part of Turkey. The more people apply for compensation, the more they can legalise the land they hold. And if ever there's a prospect for a settlement, it would strengthen their negotiating hand. However, I'm torn. If everyone with property in the north were to apply to the IPC would it mean that it's over for the Cyprus problem? Problem solved? Would it mean that Greek Cypriots would have less of an incentive to reach a compromise with the Turkish Cypriots and reunite the island? By applying for compensation, would we be bringing on partition ourselves? The Cyprus government should be very concerned. They should be taking this very seriously, if only as an indication that the people have little faith in the talks getting anywhere concrete. They should be feeling pressure to solve the Cyprus problem before the Cyprus problem is solved de facto on the ground. Hopefully they can see the bigger picture and are aware of the danger we are facing. In that case, maybe applying to the IPC is our way of forcing them to come to an agreement as soon as possible. Doubtful. If I felt that there was the slightest chance they were negotiating in good faith and that they felt even the slightest sense of urgency to make a deal, I would wait. As usual, the government hasn't got a clue. Nor does it seem to care. Our president is still harping on that he will never accept any "asphyxiating time frames". What's wrong with having a deadline? Deadlines are good. Especially when it comes to negotiating. It concentrates minds and gets the job done. Otherwise, as we very well know, things can go on forever. We don't have forever.

My sister and I decide to apply to the IPC.

First I need to get recent title deeds. I head off to the Kyrenia Land Registry Department in the southern part of Nicosia and put in an application. Thinking I may need it on the other side, I ask the woman behind the desk if I can have the document in Turkish as well.

"Turkish?" she says looking at me aghast.

"Yes, it's an official language of the Republic." Doesn't she know that, or has she forgotten?

The woman can't believe her ears. "Turkish?" she says again. "An official language? Now I've heard everything!" She looks at me as if I'm the scum of the earth. I know for sure that Greek and Turkish have both been Cyprus' official languages since 1960 and am amazed that there are people who don't, but for a moment I begin to have doubts. Perhaps the law has been changed and I haven't heard about it, as I haven't been reading the papers or watching television since the referendum.

I don't feel like arguing, so I tell her English will do, and two days later return to pick up the two documents, one for Celia and one for me, certifying we are each half owners of one acre of land in Kyrenia with a house. They are not strictly speaking title deeds, just certificates of ownership. The Turkish Cypriots have the real title deeds in the archives of the real Kyrenia Land Registry Department in the north.

Next we need a lawyer. A number of Greek Cypriot lawyers have jumped on this bandwagon, but all have to co-operate with a Turkish Cypriot lawyer as well. We decide to skip the Greek Cypriot lawyer and go directly to a Turkish Cypriot one. We approach someone who has successfully represented one of the first Greek Cypriots to have received compensation from the IPC for their property in the north. I tell him I haven't quite decided whether to proceed and he reassures me that I can withdraw at any stage. He also says he doesn't expect payment until the very end and if we don't settle he doesn't expect to be paid at all. I ask him what happens if the Cyprus problem gets solved in the meantime? He says he doesn't expect to be paid then either. He calls me a few weeks later and we arrange to meet at the Hilton hotel. I arrive at the appointed time and find he has booked a meeting room especially, having scheduled meetings with a number of other potential applicants like me. His son is also there, young, polite, and quietly spoken, with perfect English. I take to him immediately. He himself is not a lawyer but calls himself a management consultant.

They explain to me that there are three possible outcomes—restitution, exchange (with property in the north, or with property in the south), or compensation. My eyes light up at the prospect of getting our house back, but they quickly put a damper on that, saying that is the least likely outcome in view of who is living in it and that it is situated in a military zone. I briefly contemplate the possibility of exchange with other land nearby and they marvel at my willingness to live in the north. Restitution in the south could also be an option, except the Cyprus government blocks such deals from happening by refusing to issue legal title deeds. However, that is already being challenged in the courts and it is only a matter of time before the government will no longer be able to do so, although it could take years. Which leaves compensation.

"How much do you expect to get from this?" the son asks me tentatively.

I have no idea. I hum and haw and stammer and stutter, while he waits patiently. I finally throw out a number that I believe reflects the value of the house.

He nods approvingly. "I believe we can get you that," he says quietly. He says he will get a valuation in the north and will get back to me.

Before I leave I ask for one small favour. "Most other Cypriots who wanted to were able to go back to visit their houses," I tell them. "Except us. We'd like to see our house at least one more time before we settle. Can you arrange it for us?"

They smile and say they'll see what they can do.

A few days later, they send me an email with a valuation by a Turkish Cypriot surveyor. He values the house at a little less than half of my asking price, calculates the loss of use on top of that and, surprise, surprise, arrives at my asking price.

"We'll ask for double so as to get your price," the lawyer says. "As for your request," he adds, "we passed it on and were told that it might indeed be possible."

Ultimately the committee can offer us whatever price they like and we have no real recourse to question their judgement. Theoretically, if we aren't satisfied, we can then appeal to the ECHR, but they have no way of valuing real prices so tend to put their trust in the Turkish Cypriot authorities' valuation. The court in the north is in essence a kangaroo court.

Nevertheless we also decide to get the property valued in the south so I call up a few professional surveyors. The first one I talk to has no idea how to go about it in the north or how much to charge for the valuation, as nobody has asked him to do such a thing before. I ring up a few more and settle on another father and son establishment that sound the most experienced. The father knows our family and the house having worked in the area before 1974. We decide to hire them even though they're expensive, reasoning that we're going to need a valuation if in the future we end up having to go to the ECHR.

Their valuation is ready in a matter of days. The son calls me in and we go over the numbers. It's all logical and based on precedent. His father even drove to Kyrenia specially to have a look at the area around the house to see how it has developed over the intervening years and how that would have affected the value. He also unearthed past transactions in his own archives dating back to before 1974 so as to have comparables from which to start to calculate the value. They tell me that the house, being fifty years old, isn't worth much as such, but what is valuable is its location. The surrounding area has been built up, although the immediate vicinity is still green land, as the house is currently in a military zone. He also unearthed an old zoning law allowing buildings up to four storeys high to be built in the area. Therefore the value lies in the house being pulled down and replaced with a block of flats. He also explains that, based on a past ruling by the ECHR, we can calculate the loss of use as increasing at a rate of 10% per annum. The total figure they come to sounds over the top, but they seem confident in what they are saying.

When I take this new valuation back to the Turkish Cypriots they dismiss it outright. They feel the sum is so unrealistic they cannot possibly argue it in court. I tell them that, since the Commission is bound to lowball us, what's wrong with us highballing them? The middle ground will be that much higher. But I am unable to persuade them. Our surveyors are adamant too and refuse to lower their valuation. Frustrated at finding myself going back and forth between the two, I arrange for a conference call for them to speak to each other directly.

Celia and I arrive at the surveyors' office at the appointed hour to find the conference call is already underway. We sense immediately that things are not going well. The surveyor son is on the phone, while his father is pacing back and forth, barking instructions and throwing lines of argument at his son. The tension in the air is palpable. I can't tell if it's because the surveyors' patriotic feelings have been aroused, or because their professional judgement is being questioned. Probably both.

The Turkish Cypriots are quietly insisting that the valuation is unrealistic and dispute their zoning argument.

"Ask him about the Majestic hotel!" bellows surveyor senior, who is as aggressive and belligerent as the lawyer son is calm and polite. "Ask him, how many floors does it have?" He holds up five fingers and answers the question himself. "Five," he says, hopping up and down. "Five!"

The Turkish Cypriot quietly explains that legally the present building zone only allows for three floors but that the owners of the Majestic had added the other two floors illegally.

The argument risks getting out of hand and, as I don't want to quarrel with any of them, we agree to think things over and talk again soon.

After we hang up we chat a bit more with the surveyors, who are adamant about their valuation and passionately object to us allowing our property to be sold cheaply. We appreciate that and wonder whether perhaps our best option would be to ask for restitution. We leave disappointed. We need lawyers who will believe in our valuation and fight it with us. If our lawyers aren't willing to do so, then we can't do business with them. Then who can we do business with? We decide to shop around.

We arrange to meet Turkish Cypriot lawyer number two, in northern Nicosia. He meets us at the Ledra Palace checkpoint and takes us to a nearby cafe. He is young and serious having graduated from college only two years ago. He says he came back to Cyprus because his father wanted him to. He proudly informs us that his father was a Supreme Court judge, who passed a landmark ruling whereby ECHR decisions form part of the Turkish Cypriot legal system ensuring that Turkish Cypriot courts take international principles into account in interpreting domestic law. As for our case, he says we should not base ourselves on current market value but on ECHR criteria. When we tell him who represented us when we applied to the ECHR many years ago, he stops short. He thinks for a minute then says that in the interests of full disclosure he already has an arrangement with the lawyer in question and that if we want his services we would have to go through him.

Turkish Cypriot lawyer number three, is the wife of a politician who for a while was ostracised from Turkish Cypriot politics for fighting for reconciliation. Her office is in the old part of town near the law courts, down a narrow side street with signs of '*avocat*' on practically every doorway. When she tells us she cannot get more than a ridiculously low figure for the house, we bid her farewell.

Turkish Cypriot lawyer number four, is delighted to hear who is living in our house, relishing the opportunity to represent us. Rubbing his hands together gleefully he tells us about the time he took Denktash on and won. He asks to see our title deeds, takes one look and promptly shuts his files with a bang. "Can't be done!" he announces as we stare at him with open mouths.

He explains that the IPC law clearly states that only the legal owners in 1974 or their heirs can apply. As our house was in the name of the family company when the invasion took place, only the company can apply to the IPC. Unfortunately in 1996 in an effort to tidy up his affairs before he died, my father decided to transfer the house out of the company and put it in our individual names. The IPC doesn't recognise this transaction. It doesn't consider us heirs of the company since individuals cannot inherit a company's assets, only its shares, irrespective that we were also company shareholders in 1974.

"Fine," I say, "let the company apply, since we still have the company and we are both shareholders of the company. Let them compensate the company."

"Can you provide a recent title deed proving that the company owns the property?" he asks.

"We only have photocopies of the old pre-1974 title deeds."

"That's no good," he says. "The IPC needs recent title deeds no more than six months old."

"The Land Registry Department will only give us title deeds that show us as owners, not the company," I tell him.

"Can't be done, can't be done!" he repeats, hands back our papers and shoos us away. It seems we have a problem.

My sister emails our original Greek Cypriot lawyer for a meeting and also asks him about his fees. Just as we suspected, we would be paying extra for both him and the Turkish Cypriot lawyer. What's more, if we don't settle with the IPC and end up going back to the ECHR, his fees would rise. This doesn't sound promising, as surely it gives him an incentive to encourage us to go to the ECHR. That could take years. We want to settle at the IPC level, now. Nevertheless, we arrange to meet.

We're a little late for our meeting, but he's running late too. He bursts out of his office to ask his secretary something and stops short on seeing us in the waiting room.

"Oh, I'm sorry," he says. "This is my last day in the office as I'm going away on holiday tomorrow and I've got a million things to do." He sits down anyway, since we had an appointment. "Now tell me ladies, what can I do for you?"

We tell him we're thinking of proceeding with the case and also that we have seen his Turkish Cypriot lawyer.

"Ah yes, he did mention it," he says, quickly adding, "and of course you're entitled to see whoever you wish." He proceeds to give us a rundown of our options, which we are already aware of. I raise the issue of his fees, preparing to negotiate, but he quickly silences me.

"That's my price, take it or leave it," he says. "I'm not going to start haggling with you or anyone else and then have to remember who I gave what discount to and when." So much for my negotiating tactics, I think, but fair enough.

Celia asks what happens if we get restitution? He says in that case he would expect ten per cent of what we asked for as loss of use. The same would apply if in the meantime the Cyprus problem were solved.

Later we think over what he said. If we get our house back because of a solution and therefore no money for loss of use, we'd have to come up with a small fortune because of our high asking price based on the surveyors' valuation, meaning we'd have to sell the house in order to pay the lawyer. It's all so ridiculous.

At the Büyük Han a week later, I ask my friends if they know any other Turkish Cypriot lawyers.

"The Greek Cypriots are getting screwed," sighs Hasip.

"It's not just the Greek Cypriots who are getting screwed," Hasan says. "The Turkish Cypriots, who are having to sue the Cyprus government and the so-called Guardian of Turkish Cypriot properties, which is holding their land in the south, are also getting screwed. Seriously, all these lawyers are crooks. We should do it ourselves. In fact we should set up something like a citizens' advisory committee."

That sounds like a good idea to me and I encourage Hasan to find out as much as he can about the official procedure that is required.

"Leave it to me," Hasan says. "I will find out whether we actually need a lawyer or not. Give me a couple of weeks or so."

"A couple of weeks?" I say. "Why so long?"

"Well, it is the summer holidays, you know…"

A few weeks later an uncle of ours says he knows a Turkish Cypriot who might be just what we are looking for and invites me to his office to meet him. Bulent is not a lawyer, but a businessman, educated at Dartmouth College in the US. He worked at the World Bank until he was recruited by the Turkish president Turgut Ozal to prepare Turkey's application to join the EU. After Ozal died, some say murdered, Bulent moved to Cyprus, where he set up a bank.

"He was one of Ozal's princes," Hasan informs me.

"But he is no longer a prince," adds Hasip. "Not since Ozal died."

Bulent has a typical American can-do attitude that I like. He gives me the impression that he thinks outside the box, and may find solutions and compromises. He seems unperturbed by the problem with the property not being in the name of the company, and has no qualms about using our valuations. It seems we have found our man.

One day I join him for lunch at Hamur, a restaurant in a beautiful neo-classical house across from his office near the Ledra Palace checkpoint. We sit in the garden in the dappled shade of an old rubber tree and discuss the property issue.

"The reason why the Cyprus problem can never be solved," he says, "is because of the property issue."

"Oh? Why is that?"

"Because there are about a thousand people with a vested interest in the property, who are blocking the solution."

"What do you mean?"

"These people were given this property—stolen property, I grant you, though through no fault of their own— and some sold it and bought other property with it, paying good money for it. Why should they agree to give it away? They have a lot to lose from a solution."

"Can't they be bought off?"

"Who would pay?"

Ahmet, the restaurant owner, comes to take our order. He's an affable fellow with a ready smile eager to chat. He tells me that he too went to the English School and, like all Turkish Cypriots, had to leave when the troubles started midway through 1964. We order a selection of *börek*, the restaurant's speciality.

Bulent continues. "In any case, for me a solution means ending the hatred. It should have three components. First, all the people who committed crimes in the past, the murders and killings, must be encouraged to come forward and confess. They should come before a tribunal and the people would have to pardon them. Secondly those who don't come and confess should be persecuted. And thirdly they should pass laws, strict laws, whereby anyone who says anything racist or anything against the other community, is severely punished. For me that's what a solution would look like."

A waiter brings the *börek* and puts them in the middle of the table from where we help ourselves. Some are filled with *halloumi*, others with minced meat and still others with spinach.

"Cyprus is small," Bulent says. "Everyone knows who did what. A guy I know told me how they used to go to the top of minarets and shoot at people walking by below. The whole point was to create terror. To scare the population. Both sides did it. In '58, '64, and '74 you could kill somebody and get away with it. You could go manhunting in this country. Some of these guys still brag about it. But they were never prosecuted. Well they should be punished. You can't have faith in any new country if these people aren't prosecuted."

Just then a man walks up the old stone steps of the restaurant and stands at the entrance. Bulent recognises him and calls him over. They greet each other warmly. He introduces me and asks him to join us. Alecko is grey-haired, smokes heavily and has a raspy voice that is almost a whisper. He looks familiar and he too feels he knows me. After a few questions we discover that we were both at the English School at more or less the same time; he was a year older, in Hasan's year. He knows a lot about property matters and he and Bulent seem to have had dealings in the past. He tells me that Bulent helped his cousin, Mike Tymvios, an Olympic athlete in shooting, win substantial compensation from the IPC for his property in the north, one of the first Greek Cypriots to do so. He himself had recently agreed to exchange part of his property with Turkish Cypriot land in the south and was now suing the Cyprus government for refusing to sign it over to him.

"Do you know who lives in her house in Kyrenia?" Bulent says grinning. "Denktash!"

Alecko lets out a wheeze in what is meant to be a laugh and asks if I have submitted to the IPC. I tell him that I'm about to and explain the problem we have encountered.

"So this property according to Turkish Cypriot records belongs to the company but according to Greek Cypriot records belongs to you?"

"Exactly," I say.

Alecko takes a long slow drag on his cigarette, then declares, "You should transfer the house back to the company."

I tell him I can't do that because now there are huge transfer fees to be paid. He doesn't think it will cost that much and urges me to go back to the Kyrenia Land Registry to find out exactly how much they value the house and what the transfer tax would be.

Alecko himself had a large tract of land in Karakoumi, near Lapithos, that ran all the way down to the sea. The IPC compensated him for the part that had been built upon and gave him the rest back. He's one of the few people who got restitution. I ask him what he's going to do with it. He says he doesn't know, he's still thinking. He doesn't want to sell it, but would prefer to develop it.

"Perhaps I'll build myself a house there and live in it," he says wistfully.

The restaurant owner comes back to see if we want a sweet or some coffee. When I decline both, he asks half offended, "But why, dear girl, won't you have anything?"

"We don't give money to the Turks!" Alecko says and wheezes with laughter, making fun of Greek Cypriot clichés and propaganda.

Alecko tells me that after the ECHR ruling, he was one of the first to apply to the IPC. After he won and was given his official title deed from the Turks for his property, he was driving back home through the Agios Dometios checkpoint in Nicosia when the Greek Cypriot policeman spotted the documents bearing the official TRNC stamp lying prominently on the seat next to him. "What's that?" he asked. "It's the title deeds to my property," Alecko replied matter-of-factly and sat back waiting to see what would happen. The policeman wouldn't believe him and made him step out of the car while he made a few phone calls to his superior. Nobody knew what to do about this man so brazenly parading Turkish Cypriot title deeds. "Why don't you call the Attorney General?" Alecko suggested mischievously egging him on, knowing full well that the Attorney General was aware of the case and the Strasbourg ruling. The policeman did so, and duly got told off. Alecko giggles with pleasure at the memory. His delight at teasing the authorities for the mess they have made of our country reminds me of Suleyman.

"Our authorities are clueless," Alecko says. He takes a bite of his *börek*. "And you needn't worry about capital gains tax either because if they were to acknowledge that we got compensation for our property, they would have to recognise the pseudostate, which they are never going to do." He cackles again at the bind the authorities are in.

"What will you do with the money?" Bulent suddenly asks me. They both lean forward curious to see what I will say, a glint in their eyes. I get the impression that this is a game the two of them like to play at the expense of every potential compensee, to check out what their dreams are, their values, or what stuff they're made of.

"I don't really know," I stutter, unable to imagine even winning my case. "Invest it, I suppose. Let's get it first and we'll see."

Bulent laughs and I wonder if I've passed the test. He says, "The other day I asked one of my clients what he was going to do with the money and he replied 'I'm going to change my wife'. Most people say things like, I'll pay off my loan, or I'll buy a house for my daughter, or something like that. This guy wanted to change his wife! I just had to laugh."

Bulent also tells me the story of two brothers who owned a beachside restaurant in Kyrenia. They hadn't been back since 1974. That fateful morning they opened their windows and, like us, saw the Turkish gunboats in the sea. The boys were in the army so they immediately headed back to their camp. The rest of the family headed towards Kyrenia but were killed when a bomb fell on their car as they were fleeing. The two brothers went back to their home for the first time with Bulent to check the place out in order to submit a case for compensation. When they saw it they broke down and cried, but quickly composed themselves to finish what they had come to do. Bulent said he watched as one of them walked up and down the beach looking intently at the loungers in the sand. 'What are you doing,'

I asked him," Bulent says. "'Are you flirting with the beautiful girls sunning themselves?' 'No,' he told me. 'I'm counting the sun beds, so that I can work out the loss of use!'"

After my chat with Alecko, I go back to the Kyrenia Land Registry department and ask the department head how much he values the property for transfer tax purposes. He says they have a special formula they use to work these things out. He asks me to wait and goes off to consult someone in another office.

The valuation he comes back with, however, is so high it would make the transfer tax we would have to pay unfeasible. I ask for it in writing, thinking it might help our case before the IPC. But for some reason he refuses.

When I walk up to our table at the Büyük Han the following Saturday, Hasan greets me somewhat more enthusiastically than normal. I watch suspiciously as he uncharacteristically gets up to find me a chair, which he even dusts down for me. A man I don't recognise is sitting next to where he places the chair. Hasan is looking from me to the man and back at me again, a mischievous smile on his face, his eyebrows jumping up and down expectantly. I nod hello to the man and sit down ignoring Hasan, who seems to be up to something.

"Do you know who this is?" Hasan says eventually.

"No," I reply looking at the man more closely. He's our age, has a hangdog expression and designer stubble, yet looks vaguely familiar.

With a flourish of his hands Hasan announces: "This is... Serdar..."

"Pleased to meet you," I say.

"... Denktash," he finishes.

"Oh!" I say as it sinks in. "OH! I've been wanting to meet you!" I get straight to the point. "I was told it was okay for us to visit the house!"

"Yes, I know," Serdar says pleasantly. "My father said it was okay. We can arrange it next week if you like."

I tell him that next week is too soon, as my sister would also like to come with her family and explain that she doesn't live in the country any more, although she visits regularly. "Can I let you know next time she is here?"

He agrees and we exchange phone numbers.

"I don't believe you didn't recognise him," Hasan says after he leaves, his shoulders heaving with laughter. "After all, *everyone* knows who Serdar is. I'm sure *he* isn't used to people not recognising him!"

"Well, how should I know?" I say crossly. "It's not like I see him all day on television. I don't even watch television any more."

Andreas remembers the time he accidentally visited our house just after the borders opened. He had been having dinner in Kyrenia harbour with some Turkish Cypriot friends, when they suddenly got a phone call inviting them to come to a party to celebrate the engagement of their daughter with Serdar's son. They asked Andreas to join them. Not knowing whose house it was, Andreas went. Only after he walked in and went down to the pool where Serdar was playing the guitar and entertaining the youngsters and their friends did he put two and two together and realise this was our house.

"I felt very uncomfortable, what with them laughing and singing in that place," he says. "So much so that they noticed. I didn't stay very long."

When Celia and her family are all on the island for their summer holidays, I contact Serdar. With the recent comments of a friend railing against the ignominy of Greek Cypriots going to visit their old homes ringing in my ears ("Do they realise what they're doing, asking for permission to visit their own house?"), we arrange to visit the house the following Wednesday. Denktash senior himself will not be there, as he is ill in hospital. I tell Stelios and Koulla of our plans and ask if they want to come too.

Stelios says, "I can't make it on Wednesday, can you make it on Friday?" Koulla says she too has something else on and can we make it Tuesday. I look at them both dumbfounded.

"Celia and I are going on Wednesday," I tell them. "If you want to come, come, if not, don't. I didn't wait for forty years in order to risk them changing their minds." Needless to say both Stelios and Koulla adjust their schedules.

When the day comes Stelios and I and our two children are in one car with Koulla, while Celia and her family are in another. I can barely believe we're going home after all these years. And yet as soon as I say that word, I stop myself. Does it really count as home any more? If the definition of home is "the place where one lives permanently, as a member of a family or household," a place where one feels comfortable in, a feeling, something that defines us, gives us our identity, makes us a part of a social environment, then that is no longer the case. And yet, home, as the tired old cliché goes, is also where the heart is.

We are to meet Serdar at the Chinese restaurant on the main road near the turning to our house. We have been instructed to park our cars there because cars with Greek licence plates are not allowed into the military zone. Serdar is already there waiting for us when we arrive, together with a friend of his in a double cabin pick-up truck with wide wheels and smoked glass windows. We get out of our cars and straight into theirs and set off down the road. The sentry at the gate salutes us as we go by. We travel along what used to be a dirt road but is now asphalted, past a group of small empty houses.

"It's Sakkas' houses," whispers Koulla excitedly. "And Kokkinos'."

She used to come here and sit with the members of these two families shelling peas and chatting in the summer evenings. We're being swept past at what feels like breakneck speed. I want to tell the driver to slow down to give us time to take it all in, but I don't. In a few minutes, seconds—it's too fast, slow down—we're outside our house. It's as if it's the most normal thing in the world. As if we've just come back from lunch at Zephyros or Theos. Except my parents aren't here any more and our kids are the age we were when we left. I feel nothing. The only thing I'm thinking of as we step out of the cars onto what used to be a rocky field behind the house but which is now an asphalted car park, is I wonder where his aviary is. We go down four small steps through our back wall, steps that didn't exist in our day, and onto what used to be our back lawn. There's no sign of the caged birds I had read in newspaper reports that Denktash senior kept. I look up at my mother's trees. They've grown so high they're unrecognisable.

Celia, Koulla and I stop at the front door on the eastern side of the house. There's shiny black granite on the floor and the wooden door looks old and worn. Was this our door? It doesn't look at all like our door. Did they change it? We must look very strange to the others peering closely at the texture of the wooden door, touching the stone walls and spending an inordinate amount of time there. We don't want anything to escape our attention.

Serdar who has gone up ahead notices that we have stopped and doubles back.

"When we came here the front door had been destroyed and we fixed it," he says by way of explanation. That would make sense. The house may have been attacked after we left. A hand grenade to the front door would have done the damage.

We move on. The bougainvillea is still there, leaning over the railing in purple profusion, its long triffid-like branches reaching out to grab us as we walk past just as it used to. The others have already turned the corner onto the front verandah. I register my children's smiling faces and gasps of pleasure, calling me to come and see, and isn't it wonderful. As if I had never seen what they are seeing before, as if it wasn't etched indelibly in my memory. Even when memory fails me in old age, this image will undoubtedly still remain, will be the cause of my grandchildren's amazement that I have forgotten what I had for lunch, but still remember Kyrenia. Just like my own grandmother would sigh about Smyrna. I hold back a little longer, savouring the moment, then turn the corner too, into the familiar blue light, the dark blue of the water, the turquoise of the pool, the pale wash of the sky, while the steady breeze caresses my skin, welcoming me back. My children feel the awe of this mythical place, I feel the contentment of familiarity, of coming home.

Something's different. I look around and notice the greenery. A fig tree is growing out of what used to be my mother's rock garden. The terraces are no longer neat and manicured. Instead it's a jumble of bougainvilleas, bignonias, shrubs planted higgledy piggledy, in such a way as if it didn't matter what went where, did not take into account the overall scheme of things. We need a bougainvillea, where shall we plant it? There's some space here, let's put it there. A lemon tree would be nice. Let's put it in that corner.

A part of me had hoped that the house had been altered beyond recognition. But the only thing changed about it is the patches of wall and the overhang of the veranda that have been painted pink. Our house is now a pink villa. I feel the urge to touch the mottled grey stone wall of the house, this place that holds my past, my history, my youth, embrace it and tell it that I missed it, but control myself. That would be silly. If it hadn't been wrenched from us and had we sold it in the normal course of things, would I still feel the same about coming back?

Serdar's sister comes to meet us. She is short and plump and wrapped in a summery pareo, the kind one wears when one is relaxing at one's beach house. She tells us she lives in the house next door and points to the steps they've cut through the dividing wall, now connecting the two houses. She offers us something to drink and then invites us to have a look inside our house.

The living room is brighter than I remember it. They have all the windows open and light streams in from all three sides. In our day, we only ever bothered to open the front windows onto the veranda. Gone are my mother's heavy curtains, behind which we used to hide. They've been replaced by roller blinds that roll all the way up leaving the whole window free to let the light and air in. They've blocked off the fireplace and placed a sofa in front of it and they've changed all the floors. None of the furniture is ours and, of course, the painting of my mother that the British painter Corbridge had done that used to hang above the fireplace is long gone.

With slight feelings of discomfort at prying into someone else's privacy, we troop upstairs. And yet this isn't someone else's home. It's ours. I wonder briefly what it must feel like for the Turkish Cypriots to know that they're in someone else's house, a house that shouldn't have been theirs, that they have taken it, claimed it, and that the legal owners are back, and appreciate their willingness to let us wander around freely. But then I remember, it wasn't just any Turkish Cypriot who had taken our house, but the man himself whose unwavering belief in the centuries-old enmity between Greeks and Turks and that the two communities could never live together peacefully, whose vision of partitioning the island and setting up an ethnically pure Turkish part controlled by Turkey, blocked all re-unification attempts and resulted in the political situation remaining for years the way it was. I wonder how much being so comfortably ensconced in our house may have contributed to his position or his sense that he was the lord of his little fiefdom. I'm not surprised he didn't want to give it up for the sake of a solution. Neither would I! And yet, I don't hate him. On the contrary, I try to put myself in his shoes and wonder what experiences led him to his beliefs, how he felt he best served his group. It can't all have been self-serving.

As if we needed to be shown the way, Serdar's sister leads us upstairs. A stairlift has been fitted on the banisters and the natural stone wall at the top of the landing has been given an artificially shiny veneer. The bedroom Celia and I used to share, is her father's now. A strange toy with pedals sits on the floor, whose purpose is not immediately apparent. Not a toy at all, but some kind of exercise bike for an overweight, diabetic old man. Where there were two twin beds, there is now a double bed with white lacquered head and footboards and white lacquered bedside tables. We walk through our bedroom remembering. The wooden panelling behind the bedroom door is still there, but gone are the hooks on which we used to hang our bathing suits. In my mind's eye I still see the white crocheted tunic I wore over my bathing suit—all the rage—hanging there. I turn to look at the windows. The old wooden roller shutters are gone, replaced by smoother newer versions. If you leave them cracked a bit open do they still reflect the outside? Doubtful. I turn to Serdar's sister and try to tell her about the window and the *camera obscura* effect.

"I know, I know," she says. Her English isn't very good. Does she know? How can she possibly know?

The veranda where we used to hang our towels when we came up from the pool has now been turned into a conservatory, with armchairs and a few bookshelves for his books. The middle bedroom is his wife's and the master bedroom, his study. That too is now flooded with light as they have opened all the windows, including the one looking east towards Kyrenia that our parents always kept shut. The azure blue sea that can be seen through every window is so beautiful it's painful.

Down we go to the pool, slowly descending those three long flights of steps we flew down as kids, but which seemed like a mountain to climb at the end of the day. Koulla, Celia and I lean against the pool railing staring out to sea, the sea that had once teemed with activity, but which, since those gunboats arrived and this became a military area, has been silent. We turn and look back up at the house, taking it all in, the blue waters of the pool, the greenery of the garden and the welcoming openness of our beloved house.

"Not a penny less than ten million," Celia mutters under her breath. We are silent.

The pool no longer gurgles, nor is it lined with mosaic tiles. But the water is just as inviting. I could so easily dive in. I could. I'd just walk up to the edge and jump, clothes and all. What's to stop me? I would feel the cool water enclose me, shutting out the world, the past, the present, the future. I would allow myself to float suspended in the cool, silent, blueness, just as I used to, the sun drawing figures of eight above and below me, holding my breath in that position for as long as I could, until eventually I would burst through the surface again. It could easily be then—the silent pool, my sister playing in the shallows, my mother watering the geraniums, perched atop the rectangular pots along the garden edge. Similar pots are still there, I see.

When we cannot drag our stay out any longer, we go back up. A tray full of glasses of lemonade has been brought for us on the veranda. We sip slowly. We make small talk.

It's Serdar who makes the first move. "Shall we go?"

I rack my brain for an excuse to stay longer, but can't think of anything. "Let's," I say. Can we come back again? Can we have it back? Can we go back in time? Pretend it never happened? Can we at least come and swim in the sea here? Having left in such a hurry last time we were here, this visit feels like goodbye. The house does not belong to us any more. I can no longer envisage a scenario in which we could ever live in it again.

A few weeks later Bulent calls as I'm driving back from Limassol. He's just had a meeting with Turkey's Permanent Representative in Strasbourg whose idea the IPC was. He says not only will they accept our case, despite the complication with the company, but they will "take it out of the pile" and give it special treatment.

"The Commission called me *three* times about your case," he says. "Three times! They want to close it by the end of the year. I told them I'm not discussing anything until they give me a figure. They promised to do so by tomorrow."

A figure by tomorrow. Closed by the end of the year. "Never sell it," my father's words ring in my ears.

"Oh," I say.

Bulent is surprised. "You don't sound very pleased. I thought I was giving you good news."

The truth is I'm of two minds. I can't let go. Yes, money in the bank would be good. After all, the house—any house—is a store of value. But I would so like our house back. Our life in Kyrenia back. The country whole again. And what if they solve the Cyprus problem and we've sold the house? I shake my head and come back to reality.

"No, I am pleased," I say. "Very pleased."

16 GAME CHANGER?

One warm September Saturday I am lazily sipping my coffee in the cool of the archway, half watching the comings and goings in the Han, half listening to the conversation at the table around me, when I notice Mikis approaching across the cobbled courtyard.

"We're going to be rich! Rich, I tell you!" he says when he reaches the table beaming broadly and brandishing his newspaper.

We all know what he's referring to. Deposits of natural gas have been discovered in the southern territorial waters of Cyprus and the government has just signed a contract with an American company, Noble Energy, to start exploratory drilling. The reserves are in what's called the Leviathan basin, part of which is in Israeli waters. Noble has signed a similar contract with Israel.

Andreas gives Mikis one of his looks and turns to the table. "We stupid Greek Cypriots are very pleased with the Americans. We are feeling very proud because they have decided to give ancient Greek names to their well." In preparation for the drilling, Noble have christened the well Aphrodite and the rig they've set up Homer. "Except it turns out it's not Homer, the ancient Greek poet, who is being honoured," Andreas says, laughing. "It's actually an American called Homer Farrington who used to work for the company and retired a few years ago!"

"Homer is now drilling Aphrodite," Suleyman says in his usual cynical tone.

"Yes, and everyone is very excited," Andreas adds.

Everyone, that is, except Turkey, which, as we all well know, has been issuing a number of bellicose threats, claiming that the gas does not belong to the Greek Cypriots alone but that part of it belongs to the Turkish Cypriots. "It is illegal to explore waters that do not belong to them," Erdogan says. He tells us that if we continue exploring, "you will see a

Turkey you never saw before." As Noble Energy prepares to start drilling, he sends naval vessels to circle the drilling area.

Turkey has long claimed that islands like Cyprus and the Dodecanese do not have their own Exclusive Economic Zones (EEZ). It believes that, as a large country with a long coastline, Turkey is entitled to divide the Eastern Mediterranean basin with Egypt and the countries on the Eastern shores of the Middle East. Besides, it does not recognise the Republic of Cyprus as a legitimate state, only as two national communities with equal status.

"I don't understand why Turkey doesn't look for its own gas," I say grumpily.

"Turkey is only interested in other people's gas," Suleyman says. "It's always been like that."

"It's easier," Hasan adds.

"In the end they will find a way to get the whole island and then they will have all the gas," Hasip says chewing on a toothpick and leaning his chair back against the sandstone wall.

"Ahmet *bey, gunaydin*," Andreas says, as the old man shuffles up to take our order. "*Bir Kıbrıslı çay, lutfen. Çifte. Büyük.*" One Cypriot tea, please. A double. A big one.

"*Ena sketto*," says Hasan. One without sugar.

Mikis laughs. "Whoever comes here will be confused. The Greeks are speaking Turkish and the Turks Greek."

"Aren't we going to call *Köylu*?" Andreas says. *Köylu* is the coffee club's nickname for a *börekçi* we have discovered who not only makes the best *börek*, but is willing to deliver them to us here at the Büyük Han. He and his wife have a little shop in the old part of town from which he delivers his *börek* on his bicycle. Andreas tells us that he has property in the south and that his wife has often urged him to give it to the TRNC government in exchange for Greek Cypriot property in the north, as everyone else did, but he refuses. He'd rather stay where he is, renting somewhere than take over somebody else's house.

"Why doesn't he sell his property in the south then?" I ask.

"He can't," Andreas says. "The Cyprus government won't give him a title deed unless he is resident in the south for six months."

"If I were in his place," says Hasip, "I would move to the south for six months, get residency and then claim the land back from the Guardian of Turkish Cypriot properties. Then he can sell it or do whatever he wants with it. If my Greek was as good as his, that's what I would do."

"Me, I would build myself a house in the Kyrenia mountains and retire there," Andreas says taking a sip of lemonade. Then he laughs. "What's the matter with us—you want to move to the south, while I want to move to the north!"

"It's true," says Hasip laughing too. "The other day I was having an argument with my son about the Cyprus problem. He got angry with me and accused me of sounding more and more like a Greek Cypriot. 'It's all the company you keep with this Andreas,' he told me."

"That's funny," Andreas says, "my son said the same thing to me. He said you are sounding more and more like the Turkish Cypriots."

"We're turning into each other!" laughs Hasan.

The *börekçi* eventually arrives on his bicycle and the boxes of food are distributed down the table. We eat hungrily, watching the comings and goings in the Han. I squeeze some lemon juice on my *bulgur köfte* and take a bite, savouring the dry crunchiness of the exterior against the soft juicy minced meat stuffing. The *börek* with the halloumi filling are divine, thin and crispy and not at all greasy, as they are cooked directly on a hot plate.

A group of young twenty somethings in trendy athletic outfits go by speaking Greek and we catch the words 'the other side'. Mikis leans his chair towards them and, like the Caterpillar in Alice in Wonderland, tells them playfully, "This is the other side. When you're over here, this is the right side and the other side is the wrong side!" He laughs seeing the confused expression on their faces.

"Here, have some Turkish *börek*," Andreas tells them offering them the box. As usual, the *börekçi* has taken so long to bring the order that most people round the table have gone, meaning there's more *börek* left than even Hasip can eat. The Greek Cypriots eye the *börek* suspiciously.

"Are they ... guaranteed?" one of the girls asks hesitating. She takes off her sunglasses to take a closer look, pushing her long silky black hair out of the way.

Andreas laughs. "Are the *bourekia* you eat in the south guaranteed? Come on, have some, we've ordered too many."

The girl tentatively takes one. "Mmmm!" she exclaims turning to her friends with a look of surprise. "Try them, they're good!" With that seal of approval, her friends all reach in and take one before moving on. Everything gets gobbled up until only one *börek* is left, which nobody seems to want to touch.

"That one is for the *antropi*," Andreas says.

"What is this *antropi*?" Hasan wants to know.

"It's the polite last bite, the one everyone's too embarrassed to take," Andreas explains, stroking his chin to indicate shame.

"I'm not," Hasip says and polishes it off.

Just as we're about to leave, my mobile rings. It's my friend Calliope, sounding breathless. "A solution is coming! A solution is coming! I have it from inside information!"

"Says who?" I say wearily, always wanting to know the source before believing anything on this island of rumours.

"My husband has a friend who is a friend of a very good friend of someone whose friend is involved in the talks," she says barely able to contain herself. "He says that they are preparing a new plan and what's more, we will accept it. They will give back Morphou and Famagusta and the plan will be based on a seventy-five to twenty-five ratio, both as regards property and population. If the settlers make up more than twenty-five per cent, they will have to go back to Turkey."

When I inform the members of the coffee club of this new development, they are all unimpressed.

"We shall believe it when we see it," Andreas scoffs. "We have been disappointed far too many times."

"Actually, she may be right," Hasan says. "I, too, heard talk of the seventy-five to twenty-five ratio."

"You realise, of course," Andreas says after a bit, "that if there are actually one million settlers in the north, we are not going to give you any natural gas at all. We are not *that* stupid. We are going to partition the island forever rather than give *you* lot any of *our* natural gas."

"But you *are* giving us natural gas all the time, Andrea," Hasan says. "Real gas."

Six months go by after our visit to the house and nothing happens, either about the house, or about the talks. One cold blustery winter's day in January when even the four walls surrounding the courtyard of the Han are not enough to keep the gusts of wind from pushing me quickly along as I walk across the cobbles, I find the group huddled together in a corner of the archway where it is slightly more sheltered. They are all wearing thick coats and jackets. Hasan is wrapped in an enormous scarf, while Hasip is wearing a beanie and gloves and is cradling a steaming cup of rose-coloured apple tea. Suleyman has kept his Panama hat on, and Andreas has turned up the collar of his coat in an attempt to keep warm, while still looking suave.

"Your tenant is no longer your tenant," Hasip informs me, taking a sip of his tea as I pull up a chair.

Of course, I already know that Rauf Denktash has died. It's been on all the news channels in the south, his whole life summed up in two lines, "a hardliner who fought all his life for a separate Turkish Cypriot state and strongly opposed all the efforts for reunification of the divided island."

"Will you be going to the funeral?" Hasan jokes.

"Why not?" I say. "I could hold up a banner saying 'Now give me my house back!'"

Mikis leans forward and asks, "Is it true that just before he died Denktash's last words were Greek? This was the main thing the Greek Cypriot media was interested in." He points at the headlines of his newspaper.

"Well, some of his last words, yes," admits Hasan.

"Really?" says Mikis, eyes bulging. "Greek?" He can't believe there might be some truth in the rumour, after all.

"Yes, apparently just before he died he spoke a few words to his daughter in Greek," Andreas says, who already knows everything. "She asked him, 'why are you speaking to me in Greek? I don't speak Greek.' Denktash then told her in Turkish to tell the Greeks that we are an independent nation and don't let them forget it, before closing his eyes forever. Like in some Hollywood movie."

"I can just see Andreas in fifty years time on his deathbed speaking to us in Turkish," Hasan says.

"By which time I will be fluent, of course."

"Apparently Denktash's grandmother was a Greek Cypriot," Hasip says. "But for some reason he developed this complex against the Greeks."

"He felt victimised," says Mikis, nodding wisely. "People are always trying to deny what they really are."

"Actually in the north they say that Makarios' grandmother was a Turkish Cypriot," Hasip says.

"Why does it matter?" Suleyman interrupts crossly. "We are all Cypriots."

"It is ridiculous in this day and age," Mikis agrees.

There's very few people milling around the inn today and our little company for once has only taken over a single table. We lean in towards each other, as if to keep the cold out.

"Denktash always felt 'you can't trust the Greeks'," Mikis continues. "He used to say you can't force two people to marry if they didn't want to."

Andreas takes a sip of coffee and says, "For as long as he was the leader of the Turkish Cypriots and blocked all re-unification attempts, we Greek Cypriots could live under the illusion we were willing partners in such a marriage. Only when Ankara dumped him and opened the way for the marriage, did we realise that he was right—we were unwilling partners as well." He laughs at the irony of it.

Unfortunately, I realise, this unwillingness is still very much in evidence in our leaders today. The current Turkish Cypriot leader, Dervis Eroglu, is a hardline nationalist opposed to reunification, while the Greek Cypriot president, Demetris Christofias, despite paying lip service to reunification, has proven to be indecisive. Talks are going on, but how can you get anywhere with reluctant participants? Then they grind to a halt completely.

"Nothing can save us," Kokos says gloomily one day as we discuss the situation yet again. "Nothing. On either side. We have a liar over there, and another liar over here. They're fooling the people. And all we, the people, are doing is saying bravo to them for fooling us."

"Why do you want to spoil the good mood of the day?" Andreas says suddenly turning on him. "We come here on Saturdays to laugh and to relax and forget about these idiots."

"Yes, mambo!" Suleyman says.

Christofias' presidency, which followed Papadopoulos', has been an unmitigated disaster. For one thing he was deemed responsible for an explosion at an army base that killed thirteen people and almost destroyed the island's main power station. For another, the country is now also facing bankruptcy, the result of overspending on benefits and unproductive expenditure by his communist government as well as our banks' exposure to Greece's bankruptcy.

Presidential elections are coming up and while Nicos Anastasiades seems to be the best bet for anyone wanting reunification, we are no longer under any illusions that he will prove to be any different from all previous presidents. Something invariably happens to them as soon as they get to sit in the seat of power.

"He was a YES before," says Hasan. "Will he be a YES now?"

"Now that's the big question," says Andreas.

"How is it possible that almost all our presidents have failed us so badly?" Kokos asks.

"Every nation gets the government, or leader, it deserves," Mikis says, matter-of-factly.

Suleyman puts up his hand as if to halt the conversation. "Don't worry," he says in his slow deliberate tone. "It makes absolutely no difference who gets elected president. Turkey will make you an offer you can't refuse."

Mikis shakes his head unconvinced. "Even if the best offer were made, you never know what these stupids will do." He stops to take a sip of his coffee, making a grimace as he reaches the grainy dregs. "Einstein said two things are infinite, the universe and human stupidity. And he wasn't sure about the universe."

"Don't worry," I tell them, trying to inject a little optimism into the conversation. "The wheel will turn."

But the truth is that even I am having doubts these days. I feel more and more that we, the people, should be doing something to force the politicians' hand, instead of always just criticising from the sidelines. I think of the women in Liberia, who put an end to their country's twenty-year civil war by surrounding the five-star hotel where the warring parties were meeting, refusing to let them out until they reached an agreement. Or in the thirteenth century, when it took three years for the cardinals to elect a pope, the people walled them in, passing them food through a hole in the roof. And when that didn't work, they removed the roof to expose them to the rain. We should do the same. At the very least, we should be out on the streets protesting, but whenever I make that suggestion I'm told that it's always the same fifty people who turn up and we will look ridiculous.

"We missed our chance with the Annan plan," Hasan insists gloomily. "As long as those cheats are there, we're never going to have a solution."

"We need more traitors on this island," says Mikis. "We have too many leaders, and too many heroes. We need a few traitors."

Suleyman dismisses all this pessimistic talk with a wave of his hand. "You stupid Greek Cypriots," he says crossly. "You just don't get it, do you…. I keep telling you … Turkey is ready to make a deal. All you have to do is name your price."

"It's too late," Mikis says gloomily.

"They are ready, I tell you!"

I look at him to see if he's joking as usual, but he looks quite serious. Something tells me Suleyman knows more than he's letting on.

Nicos Anastasiades wins the February 2013 presidential elections by a landslide. Stelios and I watch his victory speech on television. The stadium is filled with a sea of blue and white Greek flags and you can barely hear him over the sound of football horns. My heart sinks, afraid this means a resurgence of nationalism. Towards the end of his speech he addresses "our Turkish Cypriot compatriots" with a message of peace and friendship. No sooner do the words 'Turkish Cypriot' leave his mouth, the crowd starts to boo and whistle. He stops and scowls at the audience menacingly. "Please, please!" he says, like a teacher trying to regain control of a rowdy classroom. "You must all realise that unless we behave in a nationally responsible manner, we will lead the country to partition. And that is something I WILL NOT ACCEPT," he thunders, wagging his finger at them crossly. It sends a shiver of optimism down my spine.

The new president focuses on saving the economy and heads off to Europe to ask for a bailout. At the Eurogroup meeting he is effectively ambushed and told either bank depositors are given a haircut or the European Central Bank cuts off liquidity and shuts down the economy.

The next morning we wake up reeling to the news that we've been bailed in. The government will receive a bailout for its deficits, but savers across the board at all banks will have to pay up to ten per cent of their deposits to recapitalise the banks. Even supposedly insured depositors are to be taxed at almost seven per cent. Cyprus hits the world's front pages.

A very subdued president comes back from Brussels and addresses the people. He urges parliament to approve the levy, saying it is essential to save the country from bankruptcy. In the streets, a crowd has gathered shouting slogans against the Europeans and urging the House to vote NO. The House, in a fit of irresponsibility, promptly does so. As a result the ECB cuts off liquidity, one of the country's major banks promptly collapses and depositors in the largest bank, the Bank of Cyprus, are forced to accept a haircut of almost fifty percent. The 'heroic' NO from our parliamentarians has resulted in an even worse catastrophe for the people. The population feels battered by this new disaster. Many people have lost their life's savings. It's as if 1974 has happened all over again,

The bankers' union boss declares that he will not allow a single bank job to be lost. "Yeah, and all refugees will return to their homes," I hear a cynical bank employee telling his colleague as I stand in line waiting to be served. That's interesting, I think. Have people finally realised the consequences of 'heroic' NOs?

Hasan, meanwhile, has his own theory about what happened. "You know, they planned all this after the referendum," he says nodding meaningfully one Saturday.

"Who planned it?" Andreas says, whirling round abruptly at the whiff of a conspiracy theory. "Who are 'they'?"

"Our own stupidity planned it," Kokos mutters.

"The Americans planned it," Hasan insists. "They wanted to bring both communities to their knees."

Andreas has no time for this sort of nonsense. "*Re*, do you seriously think the Americans planned for some idiots running our banks to go and buy Greek bonds in order to bankrupt the country and force us to solve the Cyprus problem? Do you think they have nothing better to do?" He wags his finger at him, as if at a naughty child.

"Because they want our natural gas!" Hasan insists meekly.

"Look at the bright side," I tell them. "Next time there's a plan it will be easier to reunite because we will both be equally poor!"

"From now on we will only be able to afford to eat *koutchia*, beans!" Andreas says. "Like in the olden days."

"*Makaroni poulli* used to be a posh dish," Hasip says. "Talking of which, let's go and have lunch at Sevtap."

We walk towards the restaurant, accompanied by Mikis' son and his Croatian girlfriend, who are visiting from Berlin.

"Tell us, Petra," Andreas asks the girl, "what Greek words have you learned?"

"*Ne*," Petra says, the word for yes.

"In this country it's much safer to say *ohi*, no," Mikis says sighing.

The days get longer and the fields start to flower as winter turns to spring. I watch the swallows back from their winter migrations playfully swooping over the cobbles, rediscovering their old haunts. We too migrate from the centre of the courtyard back to the shade under the arches. What with all our attention on the economy, for once the Cyprus problem seems to have been forgotten.

"Don't worry," Kokos tells me, smiling to himself as if privy to a secret. "The talks have already started behind the scenes."

"But they haven't even sat down at the table and they have already started the *bazarlik*?" Andreas says.

"This is the pre-*bazarlik bazarlik*," Hasan says. "Unfortunately this is the Middle East."

Soon it emerges the two sides are indeed talking. Talking about talking. They're arguing about the wording for a 'joint communiqué' that will launch the talks officially. However, this pre-bargaining bargaining, as usual, lasts several months, as a document goes back and forth between the two sides. Statements that this is the final document, no, this is the final document, take it or leave it, these are our last proposals, we won't accept any more changes, emerge from both camps.

Then Turkey starts falling apart. Erdogan is in the middle of a power struggle and there are riots in the streets. The whole question of resuming talks in Cyprus is up in the air again.

"Should we stop being optimistic, Suleyman?" I ask him the following Saturday, as he seems to know what's going on behind the scenes.

"No," he says calmly. "We shall continue to observe what is happening in Turkey and wait and see."

"We're always waiting for something to happen," I say despondently. "And nothing ever does."

In February 2014, a year after Anastasiades' election, the joint declaration is finally released. As I read the long detailed text consisting of eight paragraphs, the realisation hits me. This isn't just an opening statement. What I'm looking at is the outline of the solution itself!

An editorial in one of the papers explains the bigger picture. It says the game-changer has been the discovery of natural gas, the exploitation of which requires regional stability and regional co-operation. A settlement of the Cyprus problem would pave the way for joint ventures in which Turkey, Israel and Cyprus would participate. It would be part of grander designs aimed at bringing America's two closest allies in the region into a strategic, mutually beneficial partnership that might also act as a counter to Russia's growing influence.

"Thanks to the basil plant, the pot also gets watered," Andreas says, quoting an old Cypriot saying.

Even the Archbishop comes out in support.

"I think a pot must have fallen on his head," Mikis says.

"Now even Mikis will go to church!" Hasip laughs.

Every day Calliope calls to tell me of some friend who has suddenly turned from an ardent NO into an ardent YES. And there isn't even a plan in sight! "People have had enough," she says.

Facebook becomes the place to hang out to hear what people are saying about the Cyprus problem. The members of the Famagusta group are ecstatic. Every day people post pictures of the town, some with images of barbed wire, broken windows and weeds, others of pre '74 days, of turquoise waters, a busy beach and a line of high rise hotels and apartment blocks. Someone takes it upon himself to populate the pictures by superimposing the photoshopped faces of some of the group members, making it seem as if they are already there—on the beach, at a café, in a supermarket, in cars, in trucks, eating ice cream, riding bicycles, like those pictures you take at a funfair of your head in a preset background. Each time he posts one, the other group members coo with delight, joking and poking fun at each other, wishing, hoping, dreaming. "We're having coffee and relaxing on the beach at last," says someone. "Forty years the politicians have been tricking us; no more. We're going home," says another. "Time we took our fate into our own hands." "We're not saying NO again!"

"I want to know how many people are in the Optimists Association today!" I announce gleefully when I arrive at the table the following Saturday.

"It's true, a lot of people are joining it now," Andreas reluctantly acknowledges. I can see he's one of them.

"I've been a member for ten days," Hasan announces cheerfully.

"You have not," Andreas says turning on him. "You've always been down in the dumps."

"Yes, but in the last ten days, I've changed," Hasan protests.

"It's all very exciting!" Hasip says.

"Isn't it just!" I say, doing a little jig before sitting down.

"Don't get too enthusiastic," Andreas warns me. "We've been burned too many times."

"*Re* ignorant Cypriots," Suleyman scolds us. "How long have I been telling you—the sale is on!"

"Anastasiades will sell Cyprus to Turkey and Turkey will sell the Turkish Cypriots to the Greeks," Kokos says.

Someone suggests we move the tables out from under the arches and into the glorious winter sunshine. Everyone gets up and carries bags, chairs and drinks. Andreas takes charge, shouting orders to Hasan to stop being lazy and to help lift the table. The table is placed in the middle of the courtyard and we're just about to sit down when someone decides it would be better if the table were moved a few feet to the left so that it would be partly in the shade for those who might not like the full sun. Hardly is this done, when someone else decides it should be a little further towards the centre of the courtyard to allow room for more tables to be added in case more people arrive.

"No more changes," declares Andreas exasperated after the tables have been moved back and forth several times.

"But here are negotiations, we have to compromise!" cries Hasan.

"This is the end of the negotiations," Hasip says panting, as he sits down heavily on the nearest chair.

"Before we sit down, I want a joint communiqué," Hasan says.

"You can tell we're Cypriots," Andreas says, when everyone finally settles down.

Hasip shields his eyes from the sun and looks round the table. "Even football is looking up," he says. He has a point. The Greek and Turkish Cypriot football associations have signed an agreement paving the way for the reunification of football on the island under the umbrella of the Cyprus Football Association.

"This must have Turkey's backing," Hasip continues. "They're preparing the ground for a solution. Like they did when they opened the checkpoints in 2004." He pauses a moment and adds, "You know, we all suffer as a result of this non-recognition. As a businessman, when I write a letter to somebody in the world, for example China, to import some products, they say we already have an agent in Cyprus. Then I have to explain that we are in the north, we are Turkish Northern Cyprus. Then they say, oh we have an agent in Turkey. Then I have to explain that it's a different market and that we have to go through customs again... We're fed up.... Now pass us a *koullouri*," he says, reaching for the bag of Cypriot pretzels in the middle of the table.

"To *çözüm!*" the toast goes up.

"What's *çözüm?*" I ask.

"Solution!" Hasip says and we all clink glasses.

Hardly eight months later, the talks suddenly stall. The reason is because Turkey has sent a seismic vessel, the *Barbaros*, supposedly to carry out oil explorations of its own within Cyprus' exclusive economic zone. The Cyprus government has interpreted this as a major insult and Anastasiades has withdrawn from the talks saying he won't return until the *Barbaros* leaves. We don't know what's really going on behind the scenes, but it sounds as if Turkey wants to make natural gas part of the deal and the Greek Cypriot side doesn't. Sending in the *Barbaros* may be their way of flexing their negotiating muscles. A gloom settles on our table.

"Why does he have to leave the negotiations?" Andreas says his head in his hands. "Why couldn't he just ignore the Turks?"

"The *Barbaros* is not even breaking any international laws by being there," Mikis adds his face flushed with suppressed anger and frustration. "As long as they don't start drilling, they can sail anywhere they like. After all, they're in international waters."

It reminds me of a ridiculous event in our history that occurred in the fourteenth century during the crowning of Peter II when a quarrel broke out between the Genoese and the Venetian merchants of Famagusta over who should take the right-hand rein of the king's horse when he came from the cathedral. That quarrel escalated with disastrous consequences for the island. Fortunately this one is just a standoff, with each side stubbornly digging in.

The new UN Special Advisor for Cyprus, former Norwegian foreign minister Espen Barth Eide, who has replaced Downer, has arrived on the island in order to defuse the situation. He suggests a twin-track process in which the natural gas would be discussed in parallel to the settlement talks. Both sides reject this. They're back to their old games.

Eide throws in the towel, saying it's up to both sides to find a way back to the negotiating table on their own. Before leaving the island, he gives several interviews. Recalling that statistically, any country that discovers hydrocarbons can go one of two ways—the road to mismanagement and/or political conflict, or the right way—he says, "Cyprus is now exactly at the point where you have to choose between these two destinies. There is no middle ground. It will either take you into much more trouble and a little bit of income, or it will take you to a balanced politically viable solution or any other agreed solution, and more wealth." He urges us to think about how smart it would be to perpetuate the conflict just as we're moving into an oil and gas economy. Ominously he warns, that "this thing will either get better soon or significantly worse because that's what history tells us." I wonder if anyone is listening.

The stalemate continues until the following spring 2015 when almost beyond all hope, things take a sudden turn for the better. Turkey docks the Barbaros and the Turkish Cypriots vote their old nationalist hardline president out of office replacing him, against all expectations, with a leftist moderate promising to press for a peace deal.

Mustafa Akinci, the new Turkish Cypriot president, is a true Cypriot. He already has a track record as mayor of the Turkish part of Nicosia in the 1970s and 1980s during which time he got on so well with his Greek Cypriot counterpart that together they were able to overcome all obstacles and create a united sewerage system for the capital. Akinci clearly wants a solution, knows how to compromise, and shows a positive attitude that seems to be rubbing off onto our lot. Could this be the politician who can see a win-win outcome for Cyprus and is willing to work towards it over and above his own interests of staying in power? He could be our best and perhaps last opportunity to reunite the island.

"This country has no more time to lose," he says addressing his supporters in northern Nicosia after the election results are announced. He also acknowledges the suffering that Greek Cypriots have experienced, rare from a Turkish Cypriot leader: "There has been much pain in the past. But we were not the only ones who felt it; the community in the south also experienced pain. It is time to heal our wounds."

He and Anastasiades are itching to meet but protocol dictates that he visits Ankara first. Before doing so, though, he does another unthinkable thing, which gains the admiration of Cypriots on both sides of the divide. He asks Turkey to stop treating Turkish Cyprus like a child and calls for more mature relations based on mutual respect. He says from now on there will no longer be a "baby country", as the north has so far been called. The traditional "mother-daughter relationship" between them would be replaced by a 'new sisterly relationship'.

Erdogan is none too pleased. "Do Mr Akinci's ears hear what his mouth is saying?" he thunders, reminding him that mother Turkey was giving them a billion dollars a year pocket money. "For Turkey, northern Cyprus is our baby. We will continue to look at it the way a mother looks at her baby," he adds, through, I imagine, gritted teeth. Undaunted Akinci stands by what he said, calmly adding his words were heard not only by his ears, but uttered by his conscience, heart and brain. "Must we remain a baby country forever? Never grow up and stand on our own feet? Doesn't Turkey want to see its baby grow up?"

Akinci flies to Turkey where he meets with Erdogan and their spat gets papered over. "Get ready for the solution," Akinci says when he comes back. "Everyone is tired of the Cyprus problem, not just the Turkish Cypriots, but Turkey as well."

To kick things off, Eide hosts a dinner with the two leaders at the old Ledra Palace hotel. My friends and I gather outside to express our support. We wear T-shirts saying 'Cypriot' on them and wave banners calling for 'Solution Now' and 'Enough is Enough'. After the dinner Eide announces that the talks will resume in a few days time.

As a goodwill gesture, Akinci announces that we will no longer be required to fill in a 'visa' form when crossing into the north. Greek Cypriots are delighted, even though we recognise it's symbolic, as these visas have no international standing, and we still have to stand in line to present ID cards. At the very least it may result in a few more Greek Cypriots crossing, who for 'patriotic' reasons refused to do so.

"We passed without visas!" Litsa announces triumphantly from half way across the courtyard as she and Eleni approach our table the following Saturday.

"Kyriacos and I crossed by car and we got special treatment," Andreas says. "We were like pashas! We didn't even have to get out of the car as we normally do! The Turkish Cypriot officials came to us!"

Andreas, Kyriacos and Mikis had gone to Famagusta to attend the Good Friday Epitaphios ceremony at the church of Ayios Giorgios Exorinos in Famagusta. This is the second year that mass has been held there since 1957 when the troubles had forced the priest at the time to flee. Four thousand people attended last year's event, a moving ceremony during which the Turkish mufti stood side by side with the Greek Cypriot bishop, the result of a grassroots initiative between Greek and Turkish Cypriots.

"Mikis, you went to *church*?" I ask surprised.

"Only outside," he clarifies, then adds, laughing, "I will even side with the devil for the sake of a solution."

"The only reason I don't attend these things is because they're related to religion." Hasip says frowning.

"I agree," Eleni snorts and runs her fingers through her curly hair. "The church should bloody well stay out of things."

"Well, I completely disagree. Events such as these bring people together," Andreas says, echoing Durkheim's view of religion as a system of social cohesion and a source of camaraderie.

"We should find other ways of bringing people together," Eleni says.

"We went there, we met a lot of our friends, we discussed politics," Andreas continues. "Who cares if God exists or not."

"The church divides people the world over," Eleni says. "In our case, it has exacerbated the difference between Greeks and Turks."

"Well, in this instance it brought us together," Andreas insists.

As this is one argument unlikely to be resolved, the conversation soon turns to the big news of the day, which is that the two leaders will be visiting the Büyük Han next Saturday for coffee. Needless to say, everyone is very excited about it. I imagine them sitting down with us at our table, Andreas asking them to guess who is a Greek-speaking or a Turkish-speaking Cypriot, before calling Ahmet over and ordering coffee in both our languages.

On the prescribed day everyone arrives early. There are three times as many of us as usual under the arches, with a double row of chairs on the side of the table facing the courtyard. It seems that anyone who has ever known about the coffee club over the years has suddenly turned up. The courtyard is teeming with people, some chanting slogans and waving flags, others carrying huge banners calling for *çözüm*, presumably leftovers from Akinci's election campaign, all of which add to the festive atmosphere. There is also a large number of journalists come to cover the event. Television crews are busy setting up their equipment in choice spots, occasionally holding impromptu interviews with passers-by. Andreas stars in a large number of them. He is also busy greeting friends and acquaintances and shaking everyone's hands, almost like a politician himself. Hasip watches him with a wry smile on his face and shakes his head. A journalist stops to ask Eleni if there's anything she would like to say. "Yes, this!" she says and proudly displays her T-shirt with the word 'Cypriot' emblazoned on it.

Suddenly there's a commotion in the entrance just behind us. Almost immediately a frenzy of photographers appears walking backwards through the entrance, almost tripping over the cobbles, while crew-cut men in suits and dark glasses push people aside urging them to make way. In the middle of this melée are Anastasiades and Akinci, like some newly married couple, smiling and shaking hands, while we onlookers clap and shout "bravo, bravo", cell phones held aloft pointing at them as they stumble by. If we had confetti, we would have thrown it at them. Of course, they don't sit down at our table, but are ushered together with their entourage to a corner table where, word quickly gets round, they order coffee and *ekmek kateif*. Their bodyguards surround them, keeping the crowd of journalists and ordinary citizens back. People mill around trying to get as close as possible, standing on chairs to catch a glimpse of what they're doing. Forty-five minutes later the two leaders and their entourage get up and continue their walk, crossing together to the south for a second cup of coffee and some *zivania*, Cyprus' firewater, at a cafe near the church of Phaneromeni. Ecstatic crowds surround them as they go, congratulating, applauding and encouraging them.

After they leave Mikis, Eleni, Litsa and I pose for a selfie in front of a banner proclaiming "Solution Now". Mikis gives me a spontaneous hug. "This has been a very special day," he says beaming.

It's true, never before have Greek and Turkish Cypriot leaders walked together on both sides of the divide. Never before has a Greek Cypriot president taken a stroll in the Turkish-occupied part of town. Today has been a step towards cooperation, towards viewing each other not as adversaries, but as future partners. All around me I see smiling faces.

17 NASH EQUILIBRIUM

But now it's yet another year later, and we're still no closer to a deal. What's happening? What's holding things up? Is it the same old story—talks starting, giving us hope, dragging on indefinitely, only to collapse in the end with no result? Like Einstein's definition of insanity we have been doing the same thing over and over again for fifty years and expecting different results. Meanwhile most of us alive on the island today have been living with the frustration of the Cyprus problem practically all of our lives. Can it ever be solved, I wonder?

"Not if the beliefs and attitudes of the two communities stay as they are," a friend of mine called Zenon tells me when I put the question to him one day, as we drink our coffee in the shade of the Büyük Han arches. Bearded, bespectacled, and professorial, he is on a brief visit to the homeland from the University of Leeds where he teaches philosophy.

He explains that the two sides are playing a complicated negotiations game in which they each have opposing views as to what constitutes a 'just solution' and try to maximize the gains they would be willing to settle for.

"It's hard to see how the gap between the sides can be bridged," he says stroking his beard.

Andreas, despite participating in a conversation with Hasip and Hasan further down the table, chimes in, "On the other hand there are serious tangible benefits from a solution for both sides."

"Unfortunately neither side trusts, or can communicate with the other, so they choose their own self interest above their common interest," Mikis says. "As a result they both lose." He wipes away the little beads of sweat that have formed on his forehead as his side of the table has caught the sun.

I lean back in my chair thinking about a research article I recently read, according to which, contrary to expectations, selfishness declines as society becomes more diverse. Even though we have evolved to think of people as divided into 'us' and 'them', people who share our language, culture and beliefs, and those who don't, eventually we will evolve to a point where we will stop fighting each other, and cooperate instead, so that there will no longer be a 'them' and everyone will be 'us'. It's already happening. Nationalism and racism have been vilified as causing hatred, oppression, genocide and war. War itself is already on the wane, with the toll dropping from about four million a year in the first half of the twentieth century to fewer than a million in the second half, a period when the world's population more than doubled. Hostile aggressive competition is the nature of a young species, while cooperation, collaboration and compromise is a sign of maturity. We are moving from many and small cultures to fewer and larger civilisations, as we head towards Orwell's vision of three states, and even past it, towards global unity. In the current world of terrorism, nuclear and biological weapons, cooperation may have even greater survival value than aggression. Conflict and competition may get us there so that the most robust individuals and groups survive, but our ultimate destination will require us all to get along. It occurs to me that we are far from that future in Cyprus at the moment.

"The problem is," Zenon says, "that each side feels that if they give something up, the other side wins. They're playing a zero-sum game. We've reached a kind of static equilibrium, which we have come to accept, if only silently, as the state of peaceful non-solution of the Cyprus problem. In game theory it's called the Nash Equilibrium. This is when each player in the game is assumed to know the strategies of the other players, and no player has anything to gain by changing only their own strategy."

"So we're stuck," I say, suddenly finding it more and more difficult to see how, despite the current optimism, negotiations can ever lead to an agreed settlement. "If the two sides are not willing to give anything up, what are the alternatives?"

Zenon makes a steeple with his fingers and drums the tips against each other as he thinks. "Well, since none of the parties are willing to go to war, nor are they willing to go to arbitration, and since we, the people, aren't willing to go out into the streets in mass demonstrations to demand our leaders make more concessions for the sake of a settlement, that leaves only one possible outcome." He pauses a moment for emphasis. "We should develop an indifference to the present situation. Maybe even like it." He laughs and looks at me closely to see how I will receive this option.

My initial reaction is, no way. The current situation is untenable. It's a cease fire, that needs to be resolved.

Kokos leaning back against the sandstone column recalls that the *Economist* had an article the other day that said the Cyprus problem was insoluble and we should go for a two-state solution.

"It's a delusion to think that if we choose the two-state option we'll be safer," Mikis says. "We would be overrun by Turks. We will be finished."

"Unfortunately in a few years time, the Turks from the mainland would become the largest ethnic group on the island," Andreas says. "Cyprus would become Turkish."

"Definitely," Hasip agrees. "After the Turkish Cypriots are gone, Greek Cypriots, too, will cease to exist in Cyprus."

I think about forgotten peoples like the Phoenicians, the Philistines and the Aramaeans who disappeared after the Roman conquest. Are we Cypriots destined for a similar fate?

Just then Sarper ambles into the courtyard, smiling happily at everyone as he always does, his blue eyes twinkling.

"There you are!" Andreas says. "Everyone is asking about the *lale*." We're planning our annual spring trip to the tulips. "Are they flowering? When are we going to go?"

Almost simultaneously Kokos chimes in. "Did you make any telephone calls to be informed about the current situation?"

Taken aback by the bombardment of questions and the sea of faces looking expectantly up at him, Sarper hesitates before answering. At length he comes up with, "Well, the current situation is that the Cyprus problem will get solved."

Hasan groans. "He thinks we're talking about politics."

"What politics, *re*?" Andreas scolds Sarper. "We're talking about the *lale*. The *tulipa Cypria*. That's more important than politics." Then, as what Sarper has just said sinks in, he adds, "Wait a minute, have you officially joined the Cyprus Optimists Society?"

"Oh no, I'm with the Realists Society," Sarper says sitting down. "It's like this. When you cut yourself, you either attend to the wound by administering medicine, or you leave it to heal by itself. That's how the Cyprus problem is getting solved, all by itself."

"Hm, this is a dangerous approach," Andreas says rubbing his chin. "Or philosophical, depending on how you look at it."

"*Çözümsüzlük çözümdür*," Sarper continues. "No solution is the solution. We're too late."

This sort of talk goes against the grain for Andreas. He shakes his head. "I don't agree with you, Sarper," he says. "For me, what's important is Cyprus and—"

"—And living together," Kokos and Hasip say in unison.

"—Yes, living together, and demilitarisation, getting rid of the bloody armies," Andreas continues.

"—And starting to think of ourselves as Cypriots," Kokos says.

"We're too late," Sarper says softly. "After all, what does a solution mean? This is a solution." With a sweep of his arm he indicates the courtyard before us with all the people milling around, getting on with their business. "Life continues. People like us, who knew Cyprus the way it used to be, think it will be like that again. But it won't."

I think about what Sarper has just said. No solution is the solution. Isn't that what the nationalists say? And the racists? Yet acceptance is key in so many things in life. Instead of constantly having my hopes dashed, perhaps I should be resigning myself to the fact that the Cyprus problem will never be solved, that I will never get my house back, Kyrenia will never be my home again, and the north will always be like a foreign country. Life isn't fair, stuff happens, we lose things we cherish and there are few fairy-tale endings in real life.

There's something liberating about that approach. I feel a bit like someone I read about who broke his neck coming off a horse and put his life on hold after his injury waiting for the time he would be better. Until finally he realised that whatever he was doing right then *was* his life. Getting better would happen anyway, or not, and so he stopped looking into the future, and put his all into every experience, every unsteady step. That, he said, keeps him "joyful on this journey without end". Waiting for the Cyprus problem to get solved is like that, I realise. Like keeping your life on hold.

"Right guys, I'm off," Suleyman says.

"Where are you going?" Andreas says, "it's still early."

Suleyman laughs as he collects his hat and camera. "I have invented what I call 'the pigeon operation'." He laughs again, pleased with himself.

"Go on then, tell us," Andreas groans. "What is this pigeon operation?"

Suleyman sits back down to tell his story. "Two people were drinking wine and this pigeon comes to their table and starts drinking wine from their glass. They started joking and saying this pigeon can't be a Moslem because he's drinking wine. Then the pigeon flew away and went towards a church and pooped over it. The two men said this pigeon can't be a Christian either. They concluded the pigeon had to be a Cypriot. So what I do now is I cross the checkpoint and go towards the church of Phaneromeni where I sit down at one of the restaurants there and have a drink. Then I come back and have a drink at the restaurant next to the mosque." He throws his head back and guffaws heartily.

"A true Cypriot," Hasan acknowledges.

Kokos says, "In this country there are far too many Greeks, far too many Turks, but far too few Cypriots."

"The only true Cypriots are donkeys, as Denktash used to say," Hasip says.

"Actually," Suleyman says, "there is confusion who said that, whether it was Denktash or Makarios."

"*Ate re*, somebody ask for the bill," Andreas says and waves to Ahmet.

As we all stand up to go, a small group of young friends enters the Büyük Han. They stand in the entrance behind us taking in the courtyard and the people. "Wow, what a nice place!" we hear one of them say in Greek.

Andreas rolls his eyes and turns his back on them. "The Cypriots are discovering Cyprus!" he mutters scornfully under his breath.

"You know," Hasip muses, looking up at one of the sandstone arches, "I don't blame the pasha who chopped off the head of the architect who built this place. I mean look at it…"

"*Re*, don't criticise our favourite building," Andreas says crossly.

"What pasha was that?" I ask.

"Muzaffer Pasha," Hasip says. "Don't you know the story behind this building? When Muzaffer Pasha, who had ordered this place to be built, came to inspect the finished product, he noticed that the arches weren't the same." He points to the right of the courtyard at the row of arches. "Look, you can see for yourself, that one is wider than the other one."

We all look in the direction he is pointing. To my surprise I see that he's right. Not only is the distance between the pillars not equal but the top half of the pillars on the upper floor is not properly aligned with the bottom half.

"The pillars aren't straight," Hasan agrees.

"But was it the architect's fault, or the contractor's?" Mikis asks.

"They're all over the place," Andreas says. "The pasha was right. The man was useless."

"So he cut off his head," Hasip says. "Now he's buried over there, in the square just outside the Han, enjoying the beauty of the building for ever more, while the pasha is long forgotten."

We stand around a bit, taking in the old building and the courtyard, thinking about what it must have been like here at different times in the past, when different rulers held the fate of the people in their hands.

"*Ate re*," Sarper says at length, "now that we've solved the Cyprus problem we can have a good weekend."

"Actually we should be patient," Andreas says. "Give it a couple more months. We're rushing it a little bit."

"Rushing it?" Hasan says eyes bulging. "It's been fifty years…"

We say our goodbyes and I set off across the courtyard back towards the checkpoint, while Andreas, Hasip and Hasan head over to Hasan's shop to play the football pools, their continuing chatter drifting back towards me over the cobblestones before fading away.

"Re, *mousoubet*, did you bet on this team?" Andreas asks Hasan, meaning jinx, a word in the Cypriot dialect which we both use.

"What?" Hasip says. "You got a *mousoubet* to do the betting?"

"Yes, because we come from a country called *Mousoubetistan*," Andreas says.

ABOUT THE AUTHOR

Marina Christofides lives in Nicosia with her husband and cat, hard at work on her next book. Meanwhile, she still harbours the hope that her country will one day be reunited so that she can add another chapter to give this book the happy end it deserves.

If you would like an automatic email when this happens or when Marina's next book is released, visit www.marinachristofides.com and sign up.

If you enjoyed the book, please consider leaving a review on Amazon. Even if it's only a line or two, reviews are a *huge* help for independent authors.

ALSO BY THE AUTHOR

The Island Everyone Wanted: an illustrated history of Cyprus

An award-winning book, beautifully illustrated and full of fun facts about the history of Cyprus that both children and adults will want to treasure   for   ever.

Made in the USA
Coppell, TX
16 February 2020